Henry Morgan

Ned Nevins

The News Boy

Henry Morgan

Ned Nevins
The News Boy

ISBN/EAN: 9783337054885

Printed in Europe, USA, Canada, Australia, Japan

Cover: Foto ©ninafisch / pixelio.de

More available books at **www.hansebooks.com**

NED NEVINS,

The News Boy;

OR,

STREET LIFE IN BOSTON.

BY
HENRY MORGAN, P.M.P.
(POOR MAN'S PREACHER.)

Illustrated.

FOURTH EDITION.

BOSTON:
LEE AND SHEPARD.
1867.

PREFACE.

The reader asks, "Is this story true?" I answer that nearly all the characters are taken from real life; but names, dates, and places are necessarily changed to avoid recognition, and to prevent embarrassment to parties now living. Nearly eight years of missionary experience among the poor of Boston have furnished me with the undeniable facts of which I write.

I thought at first to publish only a string of incidents taken from my note-book; but I soon discovered that an unbroken sameness of dry detail would never be read. If, by publishing the book in its present form, I add an impetus to any of the benevolent enterprises for elevating the lowly, the act is its own reward. It has been my desire to labor for the down-trodden and oppressed, the neglected, forsaken, and forgotten. For this purpose, I have threaded the lanes of poverty, tuned my ear to the voice of mourning; I have fathomed the depths of sorrow, and taken dimensions of the habitations of woe. From the street have I learned lessons of humanity, and among the lowly have I found disciples of Jesus.

Oh, it is noble, it is Christ-like to battle for the honest poor! It is the true way to lay up treasures in heaven. *The millionnaire* may say, "I have made myself rich and powerful; my coffers are filled with gold." *The poet* may say, "I have touched my harp, and a world has stood silent and entranced; I have sung of love, and a world has melted to tears; I have sung of war, and nations have rushed to arms." *The Artist* may say, "I have transferred the living features to canvas;

I have erected the pillar, and formed the architrave; I have made the bronze to speak, and the marble to breathe; I have reared the monumental shaft to heroic deeds, and perpetuated the memory of the heroic dead." *The Inventor* may say, "I have invented the telegraph, chained the lightning, constructed the telescope, weighed the planets, and measured the distances of the fixed stars." *The Warrior* may say, "I have changed the face of the earth, brought order out of chaos, crushed mighty rebellions, established governments, scattered dynasties, created monarchies." But the humble *Philanthropist* may outweigh them all. Following the footsteps of Him that cometh with a crown of thorns from the brow of Calvary, he can say, "I have dried the widow's tears, and made the orphan's heart to sing for joy; I have bound up the broken-hearted, and comforted them that mourn; I have reclaimed the wanderer, and led him back to God."

The poor are God's charity-boxes: they are found at the corner of every street: Inasmuch as ye do it unto one of the least of these, ye do it unto me. They are the bank of heaven. We are the depositors. Put in your mite, kind reader; reckoning day is near; verily you shall have your reward.

My first acquaintance with the *Hero* of this story was on Dover-street Bridge, when he picked up the lost pocket-book, as related in chapter second. I also witnessed the court scene, as recorded in the thirteenth chapter.

Having found my "LIFE SKETCHES AND MUSIC-HALL DISCOURSES" to be a success, I now send forth "NED NEVINS THE NEWSBOY," hoping, "If he does no wrong, something good will come to him."

PREFACE TO THE FOURTH EDITION.

ALL hail to thee, kind reader! "Ned Nevins" has become a grand success, surpassing the hopes of the most sanguine. Though but a few months from the press, it has already become a synonyme and a rally-cry for reform. From Maine to Oregon the orders are pouring in for it; and from the Atlantic to the Pacific come congratulations and high encomiums from the pulpit of all denominations; from the press, both secular and religious; from societies for moral reform; from the Sabbath School and the family altar. In the language of "The Boston Journal," "It has enlisted sympathy for the poor, the despised, the wretched, and the outcast, and aroused general interest to the great social requirement of the age."

For a book thought to be merely juvenile, it is making quite a stir in the literary world, and eliciting some sharp criticisms, as well it might. No great evil is to be eradicated without somebody being hurt. The fastidious and the prudish have been fearful of being contaminated by the scenes of North Street; they have thought it awful that Nicholas Nobody should have been so unfortunate as to have had no father, and that he was suffered to confess that "Us fellers be at a discount. There be so many young uns left 'round on the door-steps now-a-days, nobody wants us!" They think it horrible that Tom the Trickster pulled hair and stole jack-knives; that Tim the Tumbler stood on his head instead of his feet; that Dinah the darkey used plantation phrases; that Solomon Levi the Jew exhibited his Jewish propensities in oppressing his tenants and killing poor needlewomen; that old Mag Murphy should have been so demonstrative in her Irish lingo before the Court; that Patrick Murphy should have been deemed by old Mag a saint; that Jacobs the pawnbroker should have his tricks and arts exposed before young readers of the Sabbath School; that the little angel Nellie Nelson should ever have been allowed to *speak* to street-boys, even for the purpose of elevating them; and that Ned Nevins should thrust in everybody's face his motto, "If I do no wrong, something good will come to me."

It has also been objected to, that the book is opposed to reformatory institutions. This is a mistake: it is not opposed to any means for doing good. None can doubt, however, that whole communities aroused to philanthropic action will accomplish more for preventing crime and reforming the fallen than a few paid officials in costly institutions. Go on, then, young lad: victory is thine; "Success is a duty."

HENRY MORGAN,
9 *Groton Street, Boston.*

MARCH 7, 1867.

CONTENTS.

CHAPTER		Page
I.	Introduction of Ned Nevins to Mr. Benedict	9
II.	Ned and the Lost Pocket-book	19
III.	Mary Munroe and the Counterfeit Bill	28
IV.	Mary's Rescue. Tragic Death of her Mother	39
V.	Night School; Character and Condition of the Pupils	48
VI.	Instances of Street-boy Heroism. "Touch not, taste not."	60
VII.	Street-criers, Beggars, Boot-blacks, and Newsboys	72
VIII.	National Characteristics. Out-door Sports. In-door Sufferings	85
IX.	Ned Nevins forced into a Street-fight	94
X.	Introduction to Mrs. Sophia Nevins, Ned's Mother	104
XI.	Ned a Penitent Prisoner. His Companions in the "Black Maria"	114
XII.	Mr. Benedict's Argument with Solomon Levi	122
XIII.	Court Scene. Ned's Trial and Narrow Escape	131
XIV.	Solomon Levi and David Nelson	142
XV.	Death of Ned's Mother in Orange Lane	152
XVI.	Funeral. Ned the only Mourner. Appeal for the Needle-woman	162
XVII.	Ned a night in the Street. Vision of his Mother	171
XVIII.	Ned's first Flogging, by David Nelson, who is incited to Cruelty by Mrs. Nelson	181
XIX.	Ned's Sickness. Angel Watcher. Angel of the Staircase	192
XX.	Mrs. Nelson's Visit to Mrs. Noodle in Chester Park	203
XXI.	Anniversary Meetings. Addresses by the Governor, Mayor, Wendell Phillips, &c	214

CONTENTS.

Chapter		Page
XXII.	Snow ball Riot. Appeal to the Rioters	229
XXIII.	A Lot on the Avenue. Mysterious Epistle	240
XXIV.	Nellie Nelson's Plea to a hard-hearted Mother. The Mother's Conversion	250
XXV.	Mrs. Nelson's Visit to North Street, Black Sea and its Waves. Louisa Lovell	261
XXVI.	Three Vehicles. A Trinity of Woe. Clarrissa Leland	270
XXVII.	Photographic Album of Night-school Teachers. Nicholas Nobody	280
XXVIII.	How Nicholas Nobody was reclaimed	292
XXIX.	Creatures of the Coal-dump. Ned and Dinah in a Coufab	302
XXX.	Ned suspected of Bond Robbery. Perilous State	312
XXXI.	Mr. Nelson's Secret Vow. Unfortunate Occurrence	321
XXXII.	Nellie allows Strange Visitors to her Sick-room	331
XXXIII.	Ned's Last Interview with Nellie	
XXXIV.	Mr. Benedict's Address. School-boy's View of Boston	351
XXXV.	Sealed Vision. The Philanthropist's Reward	365
XXXVI.	Death of Nellie. Its Effect on the Newsboys	375
XXXVII.	Ned in a Fracas with the Pawnbroker	385
XXXVIII.	Ned's Reconciliation to Mr. Nelson. His Adoption	395
XXXIX.	Parting with the Remaining Characters. Conclusion.	409

ILLUSTRATIONS.

Ned Nevins. Frontispiece	
Snowball Riot	48
Ned at the Station-house	102
Effect of Wendell Phillips's Speech	227
View of the Coal-dump	308
The Philanthropist's Reward	374

NED NEVINS THE NEWSBOY;

OR,

Street Life in Boston.

―――⚬⚬⁖⚬⁖⚬―――

CHAPTER I.

INTRODUCTION OF NED NEVINS TO MR. BENEDICT.

"HERE'S th' Heral', Jirnil, Trav'ler, 'Ranscript, five 'clock, last 'dition! — paper, sir?" cried a bright, blue-eyed, delicate-featured boy on Washington Street, thrusting a paper into the face of a gentleman who stood watching him intently. Mr. Benedict, an elderly gentleman, dressed in black, tall, having a high forehead, penetrating eye, benevolent features, a tender heart, and smiles full of love and charity, stood before him. He was struck with the plaintive notes of the newsboy as he cried, "Here's th' Heral', Jirnil, Trav'ler, 'Ranscript, five 'clock, last 'dition!" with a voice that seemed broken by grief, and turned to sorrow as it echoed on the cold winds of evening, unheeded by the surging multitude rolling by, each man intent on his individual interests. He said to the boy, "What troubles you, my lad? are you sick? You look sad."

"No, sir, not 'zactly sick," said the boy, taken all aback by the kind salutation, and wondering that anybody should care for the health or comfort of a poor, ragged newsboy like him. The salutation melted his over-burdened heart: he looked up into the face of Mr. Benedict as though it were the face of an angel; and, with tears streaming down his bronzed cheeks, he repeated, "No, sir, I's not 'zactly sick; but it goes kinder hard with me this cold weather," — then burst into a flood of tears.

"What is your name?" said Mr. Benedict. "Where do you live? and why are you not at school?"

"My name is Edward Nevins, sir. I lives in Orange Lane. I have no father. My mother is sick and poor. I cannot go to school; I wish I could. I has to pick coal on the dump in the mornin', and I sells papers in the evenin'; and some days I gits a little job at a provision-store, to carry out baskets."

"Can't your mother do any work?"

"No, sir, she be too sick to work. She coughs

bad, sir; she can't sleep; she sweats the bedclothes through: yet she be so cold, it takes all the coal I can git to keep her warm."

"Don't she have any help from the city?"

"No, sir. I had no father to pay taxes, and they wouldn't give her any coal."

"Why don't she go to the Poor-house, where she can be kept warm and comfortable? and why don't you go to the Reform School at Westborough, where you can learn something?"

Then the poor boy shuddered as if a dagger had pierced his soul, and tremblingly said, "Ah! sir, that's jist what the city-man said when he came and seed her. He came near killin' my poor mother: she fainted away, and I thought she be a-dyin'. I told her she must not die, for Eddie would have no mother. Then she threw her arms around my neck, and kissed me, and said I must not be parted from her, she would not go to the Poor-house, no! she could never come to that; she would sell her stove, and her bed, and all her things, and die on the floor first. Then she held up my face, and gazed into my eyes, as if she had something to tell me, but said I was not old enough to hear it now, — I shouldn't allus be so poor; I must be good, and say my prayers, and tells the truth, and never drink, nor swears, nor go to the theatres."

"Then you don't go to school at all?"

"No, sir; but I am goin' to the Franklin Night School. I hears they teaches boys to read there, and learns 'em to cipher and write, and gives good boys clothes, and gits places for 'em to work, and speaks kind to 'em, and 'courages 'em, and tells 'em to try again when they gits hard up, and don't let the police have 'em, and take 'em off to the Island when they gits broke, and can't buy no more papers."

"But wouldn't you be better off at the Island, or in the School-ship, where you can be kept warm, and have good books to read?"

"No, sir, there be too many boys there, too many bad boys together. They learns more that's bad than good: the bad uns spiles the good uns. Besides, sir, I wants to be free, — that is, what mother calls *self-reliant*, — and takes care of myself and my poor mother, where I can reads and says my prayers, and nobody will laugh at me and mock me."

"But you hear swearing and rioting every day in Orange Lane?"

"Yis, sir; but, when I sees 'em fightin', I jist shets the door, and turns the key, then I tries to talk to mother, and sings to her, so as to drown the noise."

"Couldn't you do the same in the School-ship?"

"No, sir: the boys be mockin' you, and pinchin' you, and persecutin' you all the time; and you can't git away from 'em. Besides, you know, 'taint 'spectable," said the boy, standing erect, and assuming a more dignified bearing. "Taint 'spectable: it is disgraceful. Mother says if I don't keep 'spectable, she can't tell me any good news before she dies."

"Then wouldn't you go into the country, and live on a farm, where there are no boys to trouble you?"

"Yes, sir, I would choose that; but then my poor, sick mother! Oh! what would she do?" and again he burst into tears. "She would have no Eddie to pick coal for her, and I should have no mother to pray for me. Oh! sir, you can't tell how much she prays! She spends most all her breath in prayin' for me. She says if I do no wrong, somethin' good will come to me."

"Did she always pray so?"

"No, sir, she says she was once gay and lively, but sumthin' came over her, and broke her heart; and she wouldn't tell me what it was: she never would. Sometimes I asked her why I didn't have a father, like other boys; then she hushed me, and turned so pale, and trembled so, I dare not ask her again."

"If I give you some money," said Mr. Benedict, "will you carry it to her, and not spend it?"

"Certainly I will, sir: I never spends nuthin' that's gin to her. I fear God would smite me dead if I should."

"There! take that" (handing him some money), "and meet me at the Night School in Franklin-school Building to-morrow night if you can: I have long desired to witness the workings of that institution."

"Thank you, sir. I will try to be there if my mother aint too sick." Then he went on his way crying his papers, "Here's the Heral', Jirnil, Trav'ler, 'Ranscript, five 'clock, last 'dition!" with a heart filled with conflicting emotions, and in a plaintive strain that drew tears from the eyes of the philanthropist.

"*Self-reliant* and *respectable!*" soliloquized Mr. Benedict, as the newsboy's cry echoed down the street on the cold, unfeeling brow of evening,— "*self-reliant* and *respectable!*" What noble aspirations from a poor, ragged street-boy, working on an ash-heap! Oh, how my heart yearns after that child! I shudder at his prospects. I weep in pity, and tremble at his probable fate. His surroundings of moral degradation are like an avalanche settling on a tender plant, crushing every fibre and bud of hope. God has given him a bright intellect, generous heart, and a holy ambition; yet his fate seems like that of a flower striving to bloom on the frosty bosom of winter, — a lamb among wolves, a frail bark drifting, wind-bound, on a lee-shore. Ten chances, perhaps a hundred chances, to one, that he early becomes a wreck on the reefs of crime. Thrown out on the cold charities of an unfeeling world, without parent or friend to protect him; in a calling the most dangerous, a school for obscenity, profanity, and crime; with his way hedged up, and the suspicious eye of the police ever upon him, — how can he escape? What but a super-human power can shield him from a felon's fate? Weep, O my soul! weep and shudder at his prospects! Yet he is but one of a thousand in this city who need our succor and protection.

Now, Mr. Benedict is a noted philanthropist. His closets are filled with goods for the needy; he is seen almost every day on the public street, or at the auction rooms, gathering in stores, and disbursing them among his various co-laborers; yet he has a strange way of giving. Somehow, he has not the most explicit faith in public reformatory institutions. He believes in individual effort, in every man performing his part. His appeal at the bar of public opinion is *individual effort* versus *public institutions*. He thinks the power and example of missionaries and philanthropists as wholesome before boys as that of aldermen, legislators, and directors; especially if the tone of these men be not particularly pious. He does not donate much for brick and mortar to erect buildings. nor for salaried functionaries. He does not believe that a few salaried officials, with whip and lash, teaching by rote, parrot-like, will accomplish more than a whole community of volunteer, uncompensated laborers, fresh from the fields of benevolence, battling against sin by moral suasion alone. He does not believe that any one master, by rigid force, ma~,ing a hundred boys into a class, would win their sympathies and fire their hearts, like twenty teachers with five or six pupils in each class. These teachers become acquainted with every temperament, every capacity, and appeal to every individual ambition.

Neither has he been converted to the "huddling" system, — a system that congregates culprits together, plague to plague, fire to fire, in order to quench the flames of vice. True philanthropy scatters them; despotism huddles them together. Despotism feeds and clothes them at an enormous cost; philanthropy lends them a helping hand, and makes them reform voluntarily, and almost at their own expense. To place the street-boys of Boston in institutions, and feed them, and clothe them, would cost five hundred dollars a day. To educate and reform them, while on the street, by night-schools and similar means, and allow them to earn their own living at some honest calling during the day, saves the State five hundred dollars a day, or *one hundred and fifty thousand a year.*

Recent developments show that there are as many families wishing to adopt children as there are parentless children to be adopted; while public institutions are overrun, good homes and willing sponsors are left childless. Parental homes are better than public institutions. Reforms, to be genuine, must be voluntary; and, in the midst of temptation, hot-house plants cannot stand the storm. There is no moral grandeur in abstaining from thieving where there is nothing to steal. There is no virtue in fasting where there is nothing to eat. Reformed culprits and reformed Magdalens, at five hundred dollars a head in public institutions, are costly ornaments, and of uncertain tenure. The world has not wealth enough to reform its delinquents at that price. Mr. Benedict had known of one Magdalen institution, which, at a cost of four thousand dollars, had furnished diplomas to six graduates, all of whom fell in less than six months. He had also been acquainted with boys who had graduated from the Reform Schools, who could not sign their names to an indenture, but had to make their mark. One boy, who had been at the Farm School nine years, had progressed in arithmetic only as far as fractions. These boys appeared as bright as ordinary boys; but they had become discouraged, disheartened, saying, "No man cares a copper for me."

Mr. Benedict's plan is to give them homes, or lend them a helping hand in the street, to inspire them with ambition, make them self-reliant, heroic, independent, while battling with the tempter face to face.

But Mr. Benedict had strange notions for this age and the customs of our times. So long as there are men who love to endow institutions, to win a name rather than to scatter their charities unseen among the lowly, just so long there will be congregated Magdalens, culprits, paupers, and even war-worn soldiers, with no family ties, no heavenly ministrations by friends, no hallowed influence of woman, all huddled together in a contaminating mass, only to breed corruption. Besides, institutions have such a knack of showing-off on examination-day! Ah, Mr. Benedict you are behind the age, — altogether behind the times! Never, never, till the advent of the millennium, can your theory be universally adopted!

CHAPTER II.

NED NEVINS AND THE LOST POCKET-BOOK.

"I CAN'T do it! It is wrong! My mother says, 'if I do no wrong, sumthin' good will come to me.' I can't do wrong! It is wrong!" said Ned Nevins the coal-picker, as he was coming over Dover-street Bridge with basket in hand, when he picked up a large pocket-book. Before him was a man walking leisurely along, with an overcoat on his arm, out of which had fallen the pocket-book. Ned saw it fall. Behind him were two wicked boys, living near the bridge, who tried to dissuade Ned from giving up the pocket-book.

"Keep it! Keep it, ye fool ye! Don't give it up!" they said.

But Ned replied, "It aint mine. I can't do it! It is wrong! My mother says, 'if I do no wrong, sumthin' good will come to me.' I can't do wrong!"

Ned was poor; his mother was literally starving in Orange Lane. Ned's earnings in picking coal and selling papers were her only support.

The mother was past work; she was dying. Oh! how acceptable would even a trifle be to her now! What little dainty meats it might purchase! what relief to her dying frame! what comfort to her over-burdened heart! But no! she died as a martyr dies; she died for a principle; she died penniless, without a cent to purchase a coffin even; and was placed in a box, and carried by the city-cart to the potter's field. She would starve rather than have her boy do wrong.

"I can't do wrong!" said Ned. "It would be wrong to keep it!" and quick as thought, without parleying a moment with the tempter, or listening to one argument against his conscience, he flew to the man, and said, "Here, sir, you have lost your pocket-book!"

The man turned round, exasperated with astonishment to think he had so carelessly lost it; and, forgetting even common civility, he snatched the pocket-book from Ned's hand, for it had large sums in it, and said, "Ah, you rascal, you thief, you *stole* it! Get out of my sight!" and he cursed him with an oath. But the noble-hearted boy did not look for reward or favor, he only wished to do right: a good conscience was its own reward. He coveted no money but what he honestly acquired: he wanted to be "*self-reliant and respectable.*" Ah! how the boys laughed and chuckled and crowed over him, when they saw how unkindly Ned was treated by the cruel, ungrateful man.

"Ye had better a gin it to us, ye had: we would have had a bully of a time with it, so we would!" (They did have a good time when they stole twenty-five dollars from a till. They went to Portland, and had a "bully time;" and, when they came back, were arrested, and are now serving out their time on Deer Island.)

Oh, what a motto was that for a boy coming from the purlieus of vice from Orange Lane! What confidence does it imply in the principles of justice and truth! What trust in God! What a shield against temptation! What a charm against the charmer! Noble sentiment! Angels heard it, and rejoiced. Sunbeams photographed the impression from that boy's lips, and bore it on spirit-wings as a balm of comfort to many a praying mother's heart. The waters saw it, and were glad; yea, the waters of Boston Harbor, that have borne on their bosom so many young men to perdition, as they entered this great city from their country homes,—waters that are now wailing requiems over thousands lost, as they roll in with the tide from the Kennebec and Merrimack, dashing against the piers and wharves in dirges that make the heart shudder over the wreck of Maine and New Hampshire's children, — the waters saw it, and were glad, when one child, bursting from the many predestined to a career of vice, had for his shield of defence, "If I do no wrong, something good will come to me." But, alas for Ned! he had held the sentiment more in theory than in practice: he, too, may fall at the very next temptation, and his name be added to the long roll of sons who have gone out with noble sentiments of morality from the nursery, to rush into sensuality and crime.

Ned was sent on an errand to one of the gaming-houses of Boston, where the *beau monde* do congregate. While waiting for the proprietor, he saw what he never witnessed before; sights which, at first view, must deeply shake his faith in the prosperity of the righteous. The whole establishment was conducted on false principles. It was wrong to drink and gamble and cheat and lie; yet by these means were purchased all this costly furniture, and all this glittering show of wealth and pleasure. Here vice revelled in luxury, and science and the gifts of genius pandered to appetite. This was a gala night, and dancing, as well as gaming, was the order of exercises. The hall seemed one bright halo of light and loveliness. Gilded chandeliers looked down on the faces of fair women and voluptuous young men, moving for the dance. Ruby decanters, with silver stopples, stood more inviting to the votaries of Terpsichore and Silenus, after the fatigues of the hour, than the classic fount of Castalia. The tinsel adornments of the saloon shone like silver and gold, and the features of the guests seemed to betoken nothing but pleasure. "Hark to the music!" On with the dance! Choose your partners!" and an array of beauty sweeps over the floor to the centre of the hall. Motionless, and like statues, these magnificent figures stand at each other's side, awaiting the signal that shall send them whirling over the floor like snow-flakes in the winter's breeze. The signal sounds; the dance commences. In a twinkling, those motionless statues breathe and stir with life, and the air is filled with clouds of floating beauty. Forms beautiful as seraphs float like fragrant exhalations of grace and loveliness, through the palpitating ranks of beauty and fashion. Eyes look in loveliness to answering eyes, and cheeks glow with ardor, while ravishing tones of music intoxicate the senses, and seem to breathe oblivion to all human woes. Ned's brain whirled with excitement as he gazed upon the giddy maze, and his soul was stirred with wonder at the apparent pleasures of sin.

This 'was no low dance-hall, no North-street

affair, but one of the most fashionable resorts of Boston. Ned saw and wondered, but wondered more, when he discovered what was going on in other apartments. As he entered another room, there were several fast young men trying their luck at games of chance. Some of them were clerks in the first houses; and some, professional gamblers. Some were playing at faro, some with dice, and some with cards. There was one young man, or lad, whom Ned knew: he had been his companion on the coal-dump. How changed his appearance! Then he was in rags; now he appeared fashionably dressed, and in luck. He bet and won, then bet again, until he had amassed quite a sum. How quickly and how easily was the money obtained! Just by turning over the hand, and the thing is done! This staggered Ned's faith in his motto. "Ah!" thought Ned, "how is it that this boy has suddenly become so changed, so smart, proud, and flush? How is it that I am still in rags, working on the dump, and my mother starving, while he struts about like a prince?" Ned looked on with a heavy heart: he became sad and unhappy. Oh the inequalities of life! Some seem born to luxury and ease, while others are doomed to toil, to drudgery, and to starvation. Why should he be so miserably poor? Why should his mother be left alone to die? Why should she hunger after the smallest crust?

Ned began to doubt God's goodness. The ways of Providence seemed unequal and hard. He was discontented with his lot, when he saw Dick Bowler flourishing in broadcloth and satin, while he was garbed only in rags and tatters.

"Ye haint got nuthin' to bet, have ye?" said Dick, looking in derision upon Ned's rags. "Ye be still pickin' coal, heh? Ye carry all yer money hum to yer mammy, don't ye? Pshaw! why don't ye try your luck at cards?"

"Yes, I do carry the money home; and I only wish I could do something more for my poor sick mother. I would work my flesh off my bones if I could make her well."

"Work! who said any thing about work? We don't have to work. Why, it's jist as easy as nuthin'! Here, look at these shiners (showing a handful of change)! I made them all in less than half an hour, an' so you might."

"Do you think it is right, Dick, to get money so?"

"In course it be. If a feller is lucky, who be to blame, heh?"

"Yes, but is a feller allus lucky?"

"Why, ye must know how to finger the cards. If ye bet high, ye loses a little at first; but ye soon gits the hang of things though. Don't ye want, now, to be dressed up smart, like other folks, and be somebody? Then try your luck. I commenced small; but I tell you what, Dick Bowler is some, now, among 'em (throwing open his fashionably cut coat, and displaying the satin vest, and a frilled shirt-bosom studded with imitation diamonds)!"

Ned was perplexed. The magic spell was creeping over his soul, and the serpentine charmer was weaving its network tighter and tighter around him; yet he would not gamble, no, not even to save his life. But he was dissatisfied, discontented, and unhappy. He went home, repining over his lot, and mourning at his fate. For several nights, he well-nigh forgot his prayers; and he murmured against God. But when he learned the fate of some of those men; that most of the clerks that appeared so gay had been dismissed for want of confidence, and that Dick Bowler had been employed only as a guy, a stool-pigeon, to decoy others into gaming; that all his gains were fictitious, and only for a bait; that soon after, he was arrested, and sentenced to jail for obtaining money under false pretences, — then Ned came to his senses, and thanked God for his escape, and took courage. Now he was content with his lot; he toiled early and late;

he trusted in Providence, every day striving to be more faithful to God, and to his mother, repeating his motto in the face of every temptation, in hunger and cold; by the bedside of his dying mother, and over her grave,—"If I do no wrong, something good will come to me."

CHAPTER III.

MARY MUNROE AND THE COUNTERFEIT BILL.

"OH! don't, mother! you will kill me! Don't beat me, mother! I will go! yes, I will go!" said Mary Munroe to a rum-infuriated woman at the foot of Kneeland Street. Mary was her daughter, a modest tender-hearted child of fourteen. "Don't beat me! I shall die! Oh dear, oh dear! you will kill me!" But, the more she screamed, thicker and faster came the blows, until at last, bruised and bleeding, she fell, exhausted and almost senseless, upon the floor. A policeman, hearing the outcries, rushed into the house, and demanded an explanation. "Plase seer, yer 'onor, I ba a-teachin' my cheeld obagence. I'm after thinkin' ye won't interfere, seer!"

"Well," said the policeman, "what has the girl done?"

"Done? done? yer 'onor! She bees done nuthin! the idle trollop! She won't do nuthin! That's jist what I bate her fur!"

"What did you want her to do?"

"Wan't her to do? did yer say? Why, I told her to do an errand for me, seer."

"What errand?" asked the policeman sternly.

"Why, seer! yer 'onor, I told her to go to the store, and buy somethin'."

"What thing did you send for?"

"Ah, ha! seer! that bees no gintleman in you to be after inquiring into a woman's wants; an'it's yourself that bater be asy, and ask no sich questions entirely."

"Didn't you send for rum? and didn't you send a counterfeit bill?"

"No, seer! I didn't, yer 'onor. Niver a bit of a counterfeit bill did I send: no seer!"

"Then let me look at your money," reaching forth his hand. "Don't cum neer me!" she said with repulsive gestures, "I has got no money. Niver a bit of counterfeit money will ye find on ma at all at all."

"She has got it, cried the prostrate girl, coming a little to her senses, and striving to rise, her face still bleeding. "She has got counterfeit money, and she told me she would whip me to death if I didn't help her to pass it: so I gin two fives to some girls to pass, and they both went to the House of Correction. And 'cause I showed this bill to you, and you said I mustn't pass it, then she almost killed me. Oh, sir! I don't want to stay here: she will murder me! She says I must go with those girls, that come here all dressed up fine, and I must bring her money to pay for my bringin'-up! Oh, sir! take me away from here, and save me from this dreadful place."

Now the policeman was no stranger to these premises: he had often been called here to quell disturbances. The fact is, Mr. Munroe and wife were not equally matched, were not harmonious in living. He was a Protestant, and she a Catholic, in faith. He thought her Catholicism did not tend to harmony in the family; so he resolved to have no more babies christened by the priest. Oh! vain resolve! He ought to have known, that, to pique a woman about her baby, brings war and bloodshed. So when he came home, and found the priest performing ceremonies over the new-comer, he strove to interfere, when a row ensued, and Munroe came out of the *mêlée* second-best, with a broken jaw. This ended his opposition for a time, and his wife only did the jawing; for he was minus an instrument for such performances. But, in their last fight, things became more serious, and his wife got the worst of it, as the sequel will show.

But Mary, the kind-hearted, lovely Mary,

who will take care of her? Who will protect her from the plots of that unnatural and brutal mother?

In sabbath school, she had learned the principles of morality; and she determined to hold to them. But what chance of success has she here? How can a young, delicate girl withstand the temptations of her own heart, and the snares of an artful mother? "Oh, do protect me! Oh, take me!" she said, — "take me away from this dreadful place!"

The policeman took her, and placed her in a neighboring dwelling, for protection, until he could get a home for her; but the enraged mother ran to the dwelling, dashed in the window, and secured the child, and gave her another beating.

At the first opportunity, Mary again fled from home, determined never to enter it again. She sought out the kind policeman on his nightly round, and followed him a little way in the distance, so as to be within hearing in time of danger; and, all the long weary night, she staid in the streets, and sheltered herself from the cold, and from sight, within an unfinished building near by a lumber-yard, trying to escape from the cruelty of that monster mother.

Ned Nevins, at a late hour of night, was returning from an apothecary's shop with medicines for his distressed and dying mother, when he saw Mary in the street. As she told her story, he could but weep for her fate. When he left her, he felt that something ill might befall her that very night; and on his way home, as he saw a man muffled up, looking mysteriously and suspiciously about, and travelling in her direction, the thought occurred with redoubled force to him, that she might be in danger. He hastened home with the medicines, and, finding his mother more quiet, he ventured out to watch Mary's fate.

It is a dark and foggy night; no lamps shine in the streets; a deep and heavy mist hangs over the city. The clock on Castle Street Church has just struck eleven. Washington Street is yet full of pedestrians; but those narrow streets on what is called the "Cove" are comparatively empty. Now and then a single individual is returning to his home; but most of the inhabitants are asleep.

A door is seen to open on Genesee Street, and from it emerges a man wearing a black cloak. His cap is closely drawn over his head; a muffler is tightly bound round his neck; his head is bowed as if in shame; and his face is partly covered with the folds of his cloak. It is not extremely cold, neither is this individual afflicted with cough; then, why this disguise? Ah, reader! he is one of those individuals who would be called a gentleman, yet steeping himself in the fumes of sensuality and debauchery, — one whom mothers teach their daughters to shun as they would a viper. He is so insinuating, that innocence itself might be deceived by him. He has respectable connections, a fine education, superior talents. He has had the best advantages; but he has wasted them all on objects of lust. A night dark, misty, and uncomfortable, is the time for such men to stalk abroad: the elements are in harmony with their dark designs. Thieves and burglars are honest men compared with these fiends incarnate. Thieves steal only gold, and such merchandise as gold will purchase; but these educated ruffians, these saintly villains, steal life, character, reputation, hope, heaven. The pestilential contagion of their infectious breath breathes ruin, anguish, despair, death, and hell. Hell itself is moved from beneath to meet them at their coming.

At this dwelling, the gentleman has been foiled. He has found the one he trusted in to be as false to him as to others; so he saunters out like a roaring lion, seeking whom he may devour.

To avoid the crowds that may be seen on

Washington Street, he turns eastward into Albany Street, and, looking backward and forward, he passes on as if unsettled in his purpose. Soon he hears a piteous cry in an unfinished building near a lumber-yard. He approaches the place; but all is still again. He stops and listens, till, at last, the sound is renewed in doleful cadences, which strike him as the moaning of a child. He speaks; but no answer is returned: he knocks and raps upon the building until the dreaming child awakes.

It was Mary Munroe.

She had taken shelter in that building, waiting for the policeman to come round on his beat, until she had fallen asleep on the shavings. There in her distress, she was dreaming, and crying aloud. At the knocking of the stranger, she awoke, and said, "Oh, Mr. Policeman! have you come so quick?" But she soon discovered her mistake, and started back in alarm.

"Do not be frightened, my pretty girl, my little duck, my darling!" said the stranger. "I am not the policeman; but I will be your friend. What can I do for you?" At his approach, she started back in terror, and shuddered with horror. In fleeing from that mother, she had perhaps fled from the jaws of the lion to fall into the paws of a bear. Oh! how could she escape?

But the stranger was elated at his success. He saw, as the misty clouds gave way and the half-concealed moon appeared, that he had found a beautiful female, of tender years, just the object of his search. Oh! how greedily his ravishing eyes gloated on that pure young maid of innocence and love! "Oh, happy fortune!" thought he; "spirits have favored me! angels have directed my steps!" Angels indeed had guided him; but they were fallen angels, such as minister to the damned.

"Come here, my child. Are you not cold?" said he. "No sir," said the child tremblingly, and looking for a chance of escape. "I am not cold, sir. I am waiting for the policeman to come." — "Policeman! what have you to do with a policeman?" — "Oh, sir! my mother has beat me, and almost killed me. She is so cruel, and threatens me so, that the policeman is going to protect me till I can get a home."

"Capital, glorious!" thought the stranger. "Here, indeed, is the object of my search, the ambition of my life. Poor unfortunate girl; I can adopt her, and make her my own, unbeknown to any living mortal. Oh, favorite of fortune!" And, approaching the terrified girl, he said soothingly, and in most plausible and persuasive tones, "Don't be afraid, my darling. Won't you go along with me? Do not stay here in the cold: I will be a better friend than the policeman to you."—"Oh, no, sir! Do not come near me; do not speak to me. Oh, let me alone, sir! *do!* begone and leave me!"—"But you don't know me: you don't know what I can do for you. I can give you a home, and a carriage, and money, and make you happy. Look at this gold watch, see this chain! here, take this ring! I can make you rich."—"Oh! I don't want the ring! I don't wan't to be rich, sir; No, I don't. Please let me go, and find the policeman,"—starting to go.

"Stop a moment, my child, just a moment," he said, seizing her by the hand, with a grasp that told her but too plainly, that she was at his mercy. "Oh, sir! you are cruel to stop me. You must be a wicked man to hold me here when I wan't to go."—"Where do you wan't to go?"—"I wan't to go to my friend," bursting into tears. "But I am your friend."—"Ah, sir, if you were a friend, you would not hold me here," twitching and jerking her hand to extricate it from his grasp. "Let me go, or I will cry 'Murder!'" she said indignantly. Yet still more tightly did he hold her, and threatened to choke her to death if she uttered a loud word. Oh! how the angels in heaven must have wept at that poor girl's fate! Oh, ye ministering spirits, ye heavenly messengers! is there no protection for the innocent? no succor in heaven for the defenceless? Is justice dead? and doth vengeance sleep? Where is the omnipotent wing, that shelters the pure in heart? where the angels that have charge of the fatherless?

"Let me go, sir," she cried again in piteous tones, "oh, let me go, and may God have mercy on your soul! Let me go, or I will call the policeman."

"Well, what if you do call the policeman? I will call a policeman too, and send you home. You meet this policeman here for no good purpose."

When he spoke of sending her home, and she thought of the blows she had endured, and of the torments she must still more undergo, and the crime she at last must submit to if she returned, she shrieked aloud, she was terrified at her situation. "Oh, sir," she said, "I am not a bad girl, I am an innocent child: this policeman is my friend."

"Friend or not, if you utter another loud word, I will have you arrested, and sent home to your mother."

At the sound of "*Mother*" she shuddered, and cried, "Oh, don't send me back! kill me!

kill me! let me die here, rather than to go back to my mother!" and, throwing her hand to her head, she shrieked and fainted, and fell helpless at his feet.

The victim was now at his mercy.

CHAPTER IV.

MARY'S RESCUE. — TRAGIC DEATH OF HER MOTHER.

"HELP, help! Watch, watch!" said Ned Nevins, when he heard Mary Munroe's shriek near the lumber-yard. "Watch, watch! Help, help!" he cried, as he ran for an officer. Soon the policeman's rattle was heard, and he came to the rescue; but the gentleman in black had fled.

Mary was rescued, and taken to the house of Mrs. K——, at the foot of Asylum Street, on Harrison Avenue. The terrible ordeal to which she had been subjected for the past month was too much for her frail constitution. Her health gave way, and her mind wandered; shadows were flitting about, and images of that cruel and relentless mother haunted her. The constant dread of falling into her power worked upon her mind to such a degree, that, even in her slumbers, she would start up, and, in piteous tones, cry aloud for protection from her imaginary troubles.

Oh, how gladly did that kind protectress love

and cherish the young and innocent girl! with what kindness did she watch over her welfare, and allay her fears, and soothe and comfort her in her sorrows! She appeared to her as a pearl secured from the sea of pollution, a bright, sparkling gem plucked from the gulf of ruin. The child proved not unworthy of her kind attentions: she strove in every way to manifest her gratitude and love. But the fear of being forced away from this refuge depressed her spirits. The least sound startled her; every cry in the street brought alarm; a knock at the gate, or a ring at the door, threw her into spasms for fear her mother had discovered her place of security.

Her fears were not altogether groundless. That mother was hunting her down with the ferocity of a hound upon the track of a hare. She employed street-hawkers and peddlers to assist in accomplishing her object. Finding the child was not placed in any public institution, and supposing she was at service somewhere in the city, the mother determined to ring at every door, in hopes Mary might answer the bell. Equipping herself with a basket of vases and glass-ware, she started on her errand of vengeance and persecution; hesitating not to prostitute that innocent soul on the altars of lust, to gratify her beastly craving for rum. She came fearfully near being successful when she rang the bell at the very house where Mary was concealed. But Mary, having been previously frightened by a tub-mender in the yard, whom she recognized as a visitor at her mother's, could not be prevailed upon after that to answer the bell.

"Any old clothes, mam? any old clothes for vases, mam?"

"No!" said the lady of the house, striving to close the door.

"May be ye will find some, mam?" forcing her way in so as to look around.

"I haven't any, I told you. Now begone!"

"An' is it yourself that comes to the door? Have ye no servants, mam?"

"What is that to you?" said the lady, becoming indignant. "Be off, and let me close the door," giving her a push.

"An' is this the way you treat a poor innocent woman, trying to get an honest living?"

As the lady thrusts her out, she cries, in a rage, "An' its you that's got my child, I bet ye has: ye stole her from her own dear mother, ye did. I'll take the law on ye, so I will!" and, muttering and scolding, she went off in high dudgeon.

As Mary heard the angry tones of her mother, she trembled like a leaf, and hid herself from sight. When the mother had gone, her protectress advised her to go at once to a friend of hers in the country: but Mary objected to leaving the city, for she had an uncle, an officer in the Union army, whose business often called him to Boston; and she desired to be where she could watch the daily papers for his arrival. This uncle had been friendly, and was anxious to adopt her; therefore, for his sake, she was placed in a neighboring dwelling for further security. There she remained until informed by Ned Nevins of the following tragic occurrence.

"Watch, watch! Help, help! Police!" sounded from Munroe's premises, just as the shades of night were coming on. The crowd gathered, the policemen came, the excitement increased; one crying, "There is murder in there!"

"Yis," said another. "They be killin' Pat O'Rielly. What's the use of these ere policemen? Sure an' they'd see a man killed right afore their eyes, the blaguards."

"Move on there, move on!" says an officer. "Don't block up the sidewalk!"

"It's niver a divil of a step will I take, while

my friend Pat Rielly is being killed in there;" and, throwing off his coat, he pitched into the crowd promiscuously. Others soon followed, and O'Rielly's friend got essentially licked.

"Arrah! an' that's good for ye," says one Irishman to another, as he helped to pick up a fallen champion. "Ye better be after going home to the wife an' childers."

Soon the women took part in the affray, and buckets of water flew alike over friend and foe.

"An' who is it that be a-duckin' the water on us?" said Tim Mulloney. "An' I's as wet as a drownded rat, I am;" and, seizing a pail from the hand of Bridget Mahoney, he tore it from her grasp. She clawed at his hair, and it flew by the handfuls in the air.

"An' now will ye come home to the two blessed twins, Tim Mulloney?" said his wife, just making her appearance.

"Sure an' I'll drown the life out of ye!" "Nary a step will I go, till I put my fist through Jim Murphy, the dirty spalpeen who struck me when I was fell down."

But still the cries of "Help! help! watch! murder!" came from the inside of Munroe's dwelling. The officers, bursting open the door, found Mrs. Munroe, and three or four men, engaged in a general fight, — all the worse for liquor; and each showing marks of the others' too close proximity to their eyes and nose. Munroe stood with a billet of wood in his hand, and demanded to know the policemen's business.

"What do you want here? who called you in here?" he said.

"I am come to arrest all of you; put down your stick, and come with me," replied an officer. But Munroe struck at him, and a scuffle ensued, when the rest of the party fled. The policeman soon overpowered Munroe, and he was taken to the Station-house, and from thence to the House of Correction.

Mrs. Munroe, having received a severe blow, tottered, and fell down the cellar-stairs, where she was found next morning by some of the neighbors. Ned Nevins, hearing of the row and its tragic results, hastened to inform Mary, who hurried to the scene. She obtained help, and the body was brought up from the cellar, and laid upon the bed; but the spark of life had fled.

And now Mary felt that she was indeed alone in the wide, wide world, — her father in prison, her mother dead. Cruel as that woman had been, yet she was her mother: the child's tender and affectionate heart was deeply moved to pity. Oh that she could have soothed her mother's pains and agonies in her last dying moments! Oh that she could have alleviated her sufferings, and shown by kindness that her ill-treatment and persecutions were forgiven! But death had claimed its victim. No more could that arm be raised to strike the brutal blow; no more could that voice be heard upbraiding and taunting her; no more should she be forced into peculation and crime.

Still she felt as a child: her sympathies and sense of duty were awakened; she repented of having left that mother. Perhaps, if she had staid, her mother would have been still living, and her father out of prison. Bad as they were, she might have had some influence over them, and restrained them in their mad career to ruin. Oh the thought of that mother's going to judgment, so debased and unprepared! Oh the suddenness of the summons! to be called in a twinkling into the presence of her God, with all her stains of guilt and crime so glaringly apparent. Oh the horror of the thought!

After the coroner's inquest, preparations were made for the funeral. As Mary was waiting for the friends to assemble, her sorrows came over her with redoubled force; and she sobbed and moaned as though her heart would break. At that moment, a kind, affectionate hand was laid upon her head, and she heard the tender, consoling tones of her uncle. He had arrived in the city the day before, and, learning the sad circumstances, had hastened to Munroe's to find Mary. And thus he found her; alone with the dead, the only ministering angel of the household, — she so young, so thoughtful, so self-sacrificing, — she who could forgive her cruel treatment, her persecutions, and forget the brutal blows, and prove herself a noble Christian girl. His sympathies were aroused, his heart went out towards her, and he renewed his offer of adoption. She consented, and, after the funeral, they left together for New York.

Thus was one immortal soul providentially rescued from a life of infamy, — one of the thousands exposed to crime by dissolute and wicked parents, many of whom are descending to early graves of dishonor and shame. Shall this tide of iniquity continue? Shall this multitude of young girls be lost? Shall we stand with folded arms, and look passively on? O Thou who holdest the scales of justice in thy right hand, and weighest our iniquities, let not thy judgments fall upon this city because of its indifference to these thy children! Let thy protecting power be over them, and rouse up thy people to action! Rouse! ye philanthropists, move heaven and earth by your prayers, and labors of love. O ye workers for the public good, ye tender sympathizers of the wronged and oppressed! can nothing be done to stay this mighty caravan in its march to the desert of ignominy and despair? Is there no helping hand to stretch out, and reclaim these fair daughters ere their last hope is fled, and they are driven to poverty and shame? Is there no kind note of warning to sound the alarm? no beacon-light to warn them off the dangerous shores of the burning lake of hell? Are they to go on, rushing madly into the gulf of wickedness, and into the jaws of death, without one effort to save them? Awake, awake! O arm of the Lord! Stretch forth thy hand and pluck them as brands from the burning.

CHAPTER V.

NIGHT SCHOOL. — CHARACTER AND CONDITION OF THE PUPILS.

LET us visit the Union Mission Night School, in Franklin-school Building. We shall find a large gathering this evening, for it is a stormy night: street-prowlers cannot follow their avocations, therefore they will crowd in here. There are four hundred and six pupils in all; but all are not present at one time. There are three rooms; two of them for the older and more respectable classes, and one for the more destitute and vicious. Let us visit the last. Crowded in this small room are a hundred and fifteen boys of various ages and conditions of destitution. Many of them are ragged, filthy, out at the knees and toes and elbows, with slouched caps and hats, and shaven heads; never demanding a peg for their hats, but always keeping them under their arms, or in their jackets, to prevent them from being stolen, or to have them handy.

The weight of an umbrella never cumbered

NIGHT SCHOOL GATHERING. — Snow ball riot. Page 229.

their hands. Many of them have stood a long time in the pelting rain, waiting for the door to open. On entering, their teeth chatter, they quake and shiver, and shake their wet hats, as the water drips, drop by drop, from their tattered garments in little puddles on the floor. Now they instinctively gather up closer towards each other to accumulate warmth, and wait for the slow fire to give out its heat. Now as the heat is felt, and the steam ascends, an odor comes forth not the most refreshing; therefore windows are opened, for ventilation is needed.

At last the soporific tendencies of a warm fire are felt, restless feet become more quiet; and now and then a poor tired street-wanderer, settling down into oblivion, begins to nod with book in hand. He loses thoughts of poverty, weariness, or woe, as the busy hum of voices charms him to sleep. Now a cruel elbow-nudge strikes his side with a cry, "Wake up, Jim, the "beak" be a-lookin'!" Then up he rouses, opens his eyes, stares round a moment, and applies himself to his tedious task.

How shall we classify these boys? What are their motives for coming here? They do not all come to learn; some come for novelty, some for mischief, some to escape the cold, some for food and clothing, and some to learn.

There is an orphan boy on crutches. No mother's prayers bless his slumbers; no father's hand feeds or protects him. Helpless, and almost friendless, he totters along, and hobbles through the world. He has a good heart. Showers of oaths and imprecations fall upon him daily; but they rebound from him like raindrops from a suit of oil-cloth. God, and a good heart, are his shield. He is as gentle as a lamb: who can but pity him?

There is a flaxen-haired, industrious boy, whose mother is a wash and scrub woman. This boy is the oldest of four children: he is compelled to work during the day to help support his little sisters, and to pay the rent. See him pore over his lesson, and dig into the very depths of its contents. That boy appreciates the worth of his time and opportunity.

There is one whose father and brother were both killed in the war: he glories in the memory of their deeds, and appeals to our sympathy for protection. There is one who was a drummer-boy; he has won the hearts of associates both in camp and school. There are a score of boys who have lost either father or brother in the war, and twice that number whose mothers go out washing for a livelihood.

How tender-hearted are many of them! how

susceptible of the kindest feelings! How quickly the tear starts at the sound of a kind word. How their little hearts swell and heave with gratitude at the thought of anybody caring for them! "Thank you, teacher! ye's been so good to us poor boys!" says one of them. "Oh, how kind that lady is to do so much for us!" says another. "By ginger! if I ain't goin' to try to do better now!" says the third. Poor unfortunate boys! they may try; but their chances are small: hard has been their lot, few their advantages. What wonder if they fall into temptation and crime!

The washer-woman's children are to be pitied. She is away all day, and they are left to take care of themselves as best they may; perhaps they are at school, perhaps in the street; or, perchance, they are rioting at home. But, worse than all, these are children of drunken parents, — children compelled to go out, and pick coal and rags, or sell papers or apples or matches or shavings, or beg, or steal. Nearly half of the indigent ones are of this class.

Let us take a step lower, among both the indigent and vicious. There is a coal-picker, a little soot-covered urchin, the ashes still sticking to his person and garments. His tattered rags are stiff with mud and filth; and his straight, wiry hair stands out like "quills upon the fretful porcupine." Poor boy! he has had a hard time of it this wet day; but necessity forced him out, and now he regales himself by the comforts of a warm fire, — a fire that does not consume his own hard-earned coal. There are thirty-six coal-pickers in the school.

There is a boot-black; he too has had ill-luck to-day. The elements are against him; yet the abundance of water has not absolved his hands from the lamp-black of his profession. He is sent out to wash his hands and face before being allowed a book. There are sixteen that obtain an uncertain subsistence by this employment.

There are eighteen boys that drive dirt-carts, — little squalid-looking fellows, scarcely old enough to hold the reins of a hobby-horse. They are forced out by cruel parents upon the cart, instead of being sent to school.

There is a class of newsboys. The school numbers forty-two in all, — lively, boisterous, saucy little imps, full of fun and mischief. Geniuses like these are rarely witnessed; they have been schooled in arts, — perhaps we might say, *black arts*. Some of them might be dubbed A. M.; for they are masters of arts, and graduate in various degrees of strategy from the rogue's college. Their wits have been sharpened on the stone of trial and exposure; they read character in a jiffy; they have learned it by close contact with men; they discern men's thoughts before they are uttered. "Take care there, Mike! the 'beak' be cross to-night," says one. "I guess he has been takin' a wee bit of the crather, he has. Look out there, Jack! or ye'll kitch it this ere night; none of yer foolin'." Thus each warns his fellow, but often forgets his own advice, until a rap from the policeman brings him to his senses.

Ned Nevins moves among them like a light in a dark place: he sells papers only for a livelihood, and not for the pleasure of being on the street. He is too sober-minded to enter into their sports, and too honest-hearted to connive at their deceitful practices. His mother's motto was ever upon his lips: "If I do no wrong, something good will come to me." He was unfortunate on first entering the school, by incurring the displeasure of the bully boys, — a set of blusterers, who browbeat all new-comers. They gave him a handkerchief, which they had stolen from a teacher, to try him. He at once refused it, and gave it to the teacher, without, however, informing against them; but his refusal was enough to awaken their vengeance.

Pat Murphy is one of these bullies, — a coarse

overgrown, green-eyed, straight-haired, short-necked swaggerer. His mother, old Mag Murphy, keeps a gin-shop, and a number of "lady" boarders. She therefore finds it profitable for her son to mix in the crowd, and form acquaintances. Pat ought to be a gentleman, — yes, a tip-top gentleman, that is, if clothes make a gentleman; for he has a gentleman's clothes (but they were bought at a second-hand store, and are seven years old). He wears a long, dove-tailed, blue, brass-buttoned coat; a big striped vest, a flag-colored neckerchief; a great wide shirt-collar, one-half turned down, the other corner turned up, black, capacious pants, with sundry ventilations. There he sits, pretending to cipher, but waiting for something to turn up. Mark that boy : he appears again in our story.

There is a class of "bunkers:" they bunk out in summer-time, on wharves, in lumber-yards, and under steps of warehouses, and sometimes on the outskirts of the city, beyond the eye of the "beak," as they call the police. Little do they care for the dull routine of study : they came to "have a time," and they are bound to make a "stir." The first night of the school, when the policeman was absent for a few moments, three of them were seen standing on their heads in the middle of the room, with their feet clapping in the air; and several were preparing for a game of leap-frog. Back they whirled to their seats when the door opened, and the police appeared; then they looked demure as owls, and perhaps were as wise as that classic bird in Minerva's time.

There is a class of "jacks" and "crackers," or window-smashers. They climb up to a window, and break the panes, and open the way for burglars to enter. They are property destroyers. These are the boys that throw destructive acids on ladies' dresses, while walking the streets.

There is a class of "till-tappers," or petty thieves. They study mischief rather than books. They hire a room, and meet on Sundays and other days to hold council, and drill in the arts of deception. They cover their faces with masks to avoid the "beak," then saunter out on excursions, which sometimes prove quite lucrative. When flush with change, they invite their friends to the theatres, and give them oyster-suppers and liquors and cigars. Soon, however, the fate of all transgressors comes: they are broken up and scattered, and a new club is formed of those who are remaining out of jail.

There is also a class that act as a "signal-corps" for burglars. They watch the police, and give such signs and sounds as will apprise the burglars of danger, yet awaken no suspicion on the streets. They also have rooms for practising the arts of their profession; and all looks, gestures, sounds, names of streets and other objects, have a language known only to the initiated. Hark, hear that whistle! find out, if you can, what it means, and who made it.

Most of the low foreign population are deceitful; their condition is truly lamentable; they are so accustomed to lie, that it is next to impossible for them to tell a straightforward truth. Deceit is bred in their bones, and sucked in their mother's milk: their very prayers are filled with deceit; for many of them *do pray!* Yet, in their devotions, they think to deceive the Almighty, and be *preying* upon your *pockets* at the same time. But there are redeeming qualities in some of them, and palliating circumstances for all. On this tide-wave of immigration, there are beacon-lights of hope to illumine the moral darkness. Under this substratum of oppressed and degraded humanity, there are as bright gems of intellect as ever wielded the pen, or drew the sword, or swayed the sceptre. God scatters his veins of gold in the hidden mountains; he sprinkles his gems of pearl on the unfathomed floor of ocean; and, from this tide of moral obliquity, the philanthropic pearl-diver, searching for spangles beneath the gulf-stream of human pollution, brings to the surface gems fit to deck the brow of science or art or eloquence, and glitter in the starry crown of a glorious immortality.

Here are Nature's noblest heroes. Here to be a saint costs sacrifice and effort. It is easy to be morally good when all your surroundings encourage it, with no uncontrollable circumstances to prevent it. But for a boy crushed to the very earth, and blasted by unavoidable calamities, for him to gather strength by opposition, to shake off the pestiferous load of a false education, as the branches of the willow shake off the winter's snow, or as the lion of the desert, with mighty convulsive effort, shakes from his mane the drenching rain, — that boy is a veritable hero.

He is a hero greater than Alexander or Napoleon or Bacon. Sir Francis Bacon mastered philosophy, became high priest of Nature's mysteries, pioneer in ethical science. He descanted on morals with a sublimity that rendered his name immortal; yet that same Lord Bacon, with all his wisdom, and all the favoritism of his sovereign and of the court, could not keep his own hands from bribes, or save himself from imprisonment in the Tower of London. Napoleon stamped his foot, and continental Europe felt the shock; he commanded armies, ruled empires, distributed thrones like playthings; yet he could not govern his own wanton passions; and the infamy of his unbridled lusts is as revolting to the moral sense as the splendors of his arms are transcendent.

Alexander conquered his way to universal monarchy, became supreme among mortals, and swayed the sceptre of the world's empire; yet he could not govern his own appetite, and died, as the fool dieth, in an hour of debauchery, and in a fit of drunkenness. Lords Chesterfield and Byron mingled genius with titles, blazed like meteors through the sky, blasting the atmosphere of religious purity, and drawing a third part of the stars of heaven with them. These men had no motives for wickedness but the love of wickedness for its own sake; no distress or want nerved them on; no cruel parents forced them out to steal in early life. But for a boy crushed by poverty, surrounded by criminals, where vice itself is popular, for him to stand like a rock against the sea, and stem the tide of vice, and come up out of the sloughs of moral degradation with garments unspotted, and, instead of demoralizing his race, to elevate them, and assimilate them to the image of their God, — that boy is more than a hero; he is a *saint, a saint of the living God!* He *demands* our admiration and protection.

CHAPTER VI.

INSTANCES OF STREET-BOY HEROISM. — "TOUCH NOT, TASTE NOT."

"I DON'T want to go! I don't want to buy any more rum," said Willie Fairfield, as the father repeated the order to go. "I don't want to go! I have signed the pledge to 'touch not, taste not, handle not.' I signed it at the sabbath school."

"Well," said the father, "if sabbath schools teach you to disobey your parents, I want to know it! I tell you to go!"

Then Willie shrieked, and cried, "Oh, I can't, I can't, father! don't make me go!" And for a refuge he flew into the sick-room where his mother lay. "Oh! must I go, mother? Father wants me to go after more rum. I don't want to go, mother! need I go?" Then he fell upon his knees at her bed-side; and, seizing her hand, he kissed it, and wept and sobbed as if his heart would break.

The poor sick woman placed her pale hand upon his head, and, looking to heaven for guidance, said, "Ah, Willie, it is hard to be forced to do wrong. May God shield you! But your father is angry: his turbulence may hasten my death. Soon you may have no mother: let me live a few days longer; go, my child, obey your father for my sake; go, may Heaven protect you!"

The boy rose from his knees, and, receiving a kiss from his mother, went as if ordered of Heaven. But conscience was still at work: he was determined to "touch not, taste not, handle not." He placed his pocket-handkerchief through the handle of the jug, and held it off at arm's-length, as if it had been a viper, whose venom was death. It indeed had been a serpent of death in his home; and he and his mother were the victims. When arriving at the door of the rum-shop, he sat it down, and started back as though it were a gun, just ready to explode. As he started back, the keeper saw him, and said, —

"What's the matter? what's the matter, my boy? What alarms you?"

Then, bursting into tears, Willie cried, "O sir, my mother is dying! I don't want to buy any more rum! I have signed the pledge 'to touch not, taste not, handle not.' Rum has almost killed my poor mother: father scolds her, strikes her, and beats her, until he has most killed her. I don't want to buy rum! no, sir, I don't. I'd rather die than do it. Oh! don't let me carry this jug back; don't let my poor mother suffer any more!"

"Your father!" said the keeper, — "is your father such a brute? Can he crush a child's conscience like this? Come to my arms, noble boy! Such heroic virtue shall be protected. May your mother live forever, brave boy! for your father shall never have another drop of liquor from me." Then he took the jug! and, taking the boy by the hand, he went to the father, and said, "Are you the man, Mr. Fairfield, that could do this? Are you a man? and have you a heart? Can you crush the conscience, and break the heart, of such a child? Does rum do this? Never, never, will you get it of me again! Never will I sell it more! Come, come, Mr. Fairfield, you and I must sign the pledge."

Fairfield at first hesitated; but there was his sick wife, a guilty conscience, and there his boy, — noble hero! — who had already won over the keeper. Could he refuse? No! So they both signed the pledge.

Then Willie went running to his mother, shouting, and clapping his hands, and said, "O mother, mother, father has signed the pledge, he has!"

The mother, awaking from her stupor, gazed thoughtfully, but could not at first believe the tidings: they were too good for her to hope. She stared in astonishment, then wept, then prayed, then hoped, then raised her hands in thanksgiving to God. Tears of joy rolled down her pale and haggard cheek, her despairing countenance lighted up with smiles of joy, the springs of life began to flow, disease stopped, the fever turned, and she recovered, attributing her recovery to the conscientious scruples and noble heroism of her boy.

That was in 1850, when the writer of this article was laboring with Father Streeter and Phineas Stowe in temperance-meetings at the North End. Nearly seventeen years have rolled away; and that boy is now one of the most gallant officers in the American navy, and, I believe, has kept his pledge to this day. Thus much for the conscience of a child.

BITE BIGGER, BILLY.

"Bite bigger, Billy! bite bigger! Take it all, Billy! ye needs it most, ye does," said a hungry little fellow, at the corner of Dover Street, in the spring of 1859. Barney and

Billy had ill-luck that day. All day long they had been looking for work, but found none: no one wanted them, nobody would have them. They were hungry; and cold, night was coming on, and they had no prospect for a morsel of bread. They gazed into the shop-windows, saw the dainty meats and smoking-hot cakes, tempting as the forbidden fruit before the eyes of Tantalus. People came, and purchased, and departed; but there was none to buy food for them. Twenty-four hours since they had tasted a morsel of bread. Once or twice they had ventured into an eating-house; but the fierce look of the waiter scared them from the premises. At last, a gentleman took pity on them, and purchased them a cake. It was a fine round cake, not easily broken. They had no knife for cutting; so they sat down on a door-step, and began to bite it, and nibble it like mice. Oh, what comfort was there in sharing that cake together! what pleasure in vying with each other in generosity!

"Bite bigger, Billy, bite bigger! Take it all, Billy! ye needs it most, ye does," said Barney Bartlett, forgetting his own hunger in seeing Billy eat.

Two years after, when the tocsin of war sounded, that boy heard it, and rushed to the field a drummer-boy. He was wounded, lay in the hospital, recovered, waited on the sick for a time, then enlisted a private soldier, and was shot in the disastrous charge of Burnside against the stone-wall at Fredericksburg. He was in the act of comforting a wounded comrade, was raising up his head, and giving him drink from his canteen, saying, "Take it all, comrade, take it all: I can get more, you know," when a shot struck him, and he fell. Nobly did he fall, showing the generosity of his heart to the last moment. "Bite bigger, Billy, bite bigger! take it all, Billy," was the index of his character, even in his dying. Ah! there are noble, generous souls among street-boys.

THAT'S MY MOTHER.

"Come around agin, come around, and let me git on!" said a drunken woman to a wheelbarrow in Orange Lane. "There, stop there! Come around agin! Stop, I say! Whoa! let me get on! Stop, I say, for a poor tired woman!" So she continued talking to the wheelbarrow, and reeling and staggering around it, until a crowd of urchins gathered round her, delighting in the fun of seeing a woman striving to get on board of a wheelbarrow. Some threw sticks at her, some crowed and laughed, and some said, "See! here is the coach; now get on here!"

Then the boys rolled the wheelbarrow near to her side, and said, "Here it is, here is the coach: now step on board!" thus adding confusion to her bewilderment, until, at last, her son, a boy of fourteen, who was passing the end of the street, saw her, and laid down his market-basket by the side of another boy, and flew into the Lane, and drove the boys back, and said, "Stand back, you! every one of you! THAT IS MY MOTHER!" Then, looking around to see if any policeman was coming to arrest her before he could get her home, he seized her by the arm, and held her up all bleeding in the face as she was, bruised, and filthy, and bore her home.

"*Let her alone!* THAT IS MY MOTHER!" What words from a boy who had experienced nothing from that woman worthy the name of mother! She had beaten him, wished him dead, forced him out to beg and steal, taught him to cheat and lie; called him a burden, a pest, a plague; declared that he had no right to live, ought never to have been born, ought to have been smothered in infancy; that such brats as he didn't pay for their living; he ought to be dead and buried! yet he could call her "MOTHER! MY MOTHER!" Oh what chokings! what deep, guttural chokings, must have filled his throat at that word "*Mother*"! What mortification and chagrin, that would make some tongues black before uttering it. But he was a noble-hearted, heroic boy: he had the big heart of a brave man. In sabbath school, he had learned that first commandment, with promise, "Honor thy father and thy mother, that thy days may be long;" and he kept it; showing, that, with our institutions and privileges, any child may rise, in spite of the blight and curse of beastly parents.

JOHNNY GAFFY.

The steamer "Columbia" was foundering amid the breakers off the treacherous coast of North Carolina. Rebel guns from land were also firing upon her; the poor wrecked mariners saw nothing before them but death. The relief-steamer "Cambridge" was in sight, but could not approach, on account of the quicksands and breakers. Lower and lower was she sinking: every moment foreboded utter destruction. Good heavens! must those brave men go down, without an effort to save them?

See there! On board of the "Cambridge" is Johnny Gaffy, a boy of fifteen, just from the school-ship, in Boston Harbor. See him strip himself for the contest! Off come his blue jacket and his tidy cap; and, with a line fastened round him, he plunges into the deep. He sinks, he rises, and buffets the waves, until he nears the breakers. Now the foaming billows rise up high over him like fleecy clouds, and back he is borne by the receding surges. Again he ascends the snowy crests, battling with the opposing billows; and, taking advantage of an advancing wave, like a duck, he dashes through the breakers, and comes out on the other side.

Oh! how those wrecked mariners cheered and shouted as they saw that brave boy emerge from the foam, with a line for their deliverance! They saw him sink and rise and struggle, often out of sight; but, every time his ear came above the waves, it was saluted with benedictions on his head. "Bravo, bravo! God bless you! Hold on, brave boy! Bully for you! you're worth your weight in gold. Pull away, my lad!" Until at last, exhausted, but undismayed, he approached them, and those brawny arms lifted him out of the waves. Oh, how the brave tars wept and shouted over their deliverer! What tears of unfeigned gratitude burst from eyes unused to weep! They thanked him, and hugged him, and kissed him; for he was their salvation. The small line which he bore drew over a heavier line, upon which thirty men escaped, and were saved. All honor to Johnny Gaffy! Who says there are not heroes among the street-boys of Boston?

See another boy, also from the school-ship, fighting with Grant in the Wilderness! Being wounded, and hobbling home upon one leg, he exulted in the sacrifice, and thanked God that he could do something for his country.

See that charge upon Fort Fisher! The greatest armament the world had ever seen afloat had laid siege to that fort, and had failed. Finally another assault was made, and who but a Boston boy was the first to enter?

See that boy on board the "Cumberland," firing the last gun after she had been struck by the monster "Merrimack." She was sinking; the water was rising to the muzzle of his gun; yet there he stood, pouring forth his balls, which had no more effect upon the turtle-shelled monster than so many foot-balls: they bounded from her sides like rubber. There he stood, facing the foe, and firing his gun, thinking only of duty, until the water rose to his waist; then the vessel gave a heave, and a lurch, and quivered on the wave like an expiring leviathan. She sunk with all her precious freight, her colors at mast-head, still floating in the breeze.

Look at the dashing Philip Henry Sheridan, once a poor street-boy, of Boston, now one of the most renowned major-generals of the age.

Tell us, has Boston not reason to be proud of her street-boys? Yes! She is proud of them; and nothing will make her generous heart more elated than to hear of their success in life, and of their loyalty to the flag. She is not unmindful of their honor; and she follows them with her benedictions wherever they go, by land or sea, on the Western prairies, planting freedom in Kansas, or on the slopes of the Pacific. She is not unmindful of her brave tars that have manned our navy. She is not ungrateful to the noble men of the merchant-service, who have filled her warehouses with the wealth of foreign climes, and spread her commerce over every sea. She is not unmindful of the brave sons who have shouted her patriotic name on the battlefield, shouted the name of Boston in every victory; and she is not neglectful of them in time of need. No boy that sails from her harbor, no son of hers, by land or sea, need suffer. Only let it be known that he is needy and worthy, and the storehouses of the India merchants, the coffers of those men whose vessels he has manned, are open to him, and the wealth of the great city is laid under contribution for his support.

Boston has ever been the beacon-light of liberty. Look at her Sumners, her Phillipses, her Garrisons, and her Andrews! Though presidents may prove treacherous, and cabinets waver, yet Boston, Massachusetts, New England stand as a rock, for free institutions and universal suffrage. Who struck the first blow of the revolution? What city was most obnoxious to the British throne? Who first smote the rebellion? Who first flew to the defence of the capital? What blood was first spilled at Baltimore, but that of Massachusetts? Who established the first railroad, the first printing-press, the first college of America?

Who is not proud to be a citizen of Boston? Who would not be ashamed to tarnish her fair name? When liberty is in danger, let "Boston" be the watchword! For the nobility of the individual citizen, for the success of free institutions, let the world point to Boston. Then let liberty shout for Boston! Let boys of the streets cry "Boston!" Let the seamen's watchword be "Boston!" Let them shout it to the islands of every sea; let them bear it on their pennons, mingled with stars and stripes, round the world!

CHAPTER VII.

STREET-CRIERS, BEGGARS, BOOT-BLACKS, AND NEWS-BOYS, ETC.

BOSTON has the reputation for boasting. It is said to be the "hub of the universe;" therefore feels its consequence. Harvard thinks for Boston, and Boston thinks for the world. Boston leads New England, and New-England ideas rule America. When Boston orators speak, the world listens. "See Naples, then die," was an old adage which may be applied to Boston. She gets up her celebrations on a grand scale. Witness the reception given to the Russians, the ovation to the Prince of Wales, the gratulations to her own Commodore Winslow, and his brave crew of "The Kearsarge," her celebration of Washington's birthday, and her fifty thousand persons on Boston Common Fourth of July. Boasting keeps up the public spirit, and saves many a man from the poor-house. Why not encourage it?

Boasting is a cheap tax-payer; public spirit

is cheaper than pauperism. The street vices and street virtues often catch their inspiration from upper society. Street-criers love to imitate fashionable follies. When the Great Organ was dedicated, nothing else was heard of in Boston, nothing known, but the Great Organ. Women left their bread in the oven, men neglected their work, and boys forgot their play, to talk and read about the Great Organ. And the street-criers caught the sound, and strove to imitate its ten thousand notes, as they cried "*Scissors to grind!*" "*Glass put in!*" "*Umbrellas to mend!*" "*Fresh mackerill, salt herring!*" And captains of charcoal-carts cried " CHARCOAL!" to the *music of the Great Organ!*

BEGGARS.

Beggars are not indigenous to the soil of Boston: they are imported exotics. The native-born Bostonian is ashamed to beg; he would starve first. Better that he starve with his honor bright than lose his manhood, and become a cringing, fawning suppliant. The oppressions of the Old World have sent enough of this class to America. Let it be the boast of America, that no citizen of hers so lowers his dignity as to expose his sores and rags, or puts on a false show, for alms.

Other things he would not do. — How would a native-born Bostonian look, in turning a hand-organ, and twitching the cord of a monkey, for a copper; grinding out, "O Susannah! don't you cry for me"! That business is left for men of other habits and institutions than those of Boston or New England.

FAVOR-CRINGERS.

Neither is asking money for little favors a trait in Boston character. Go to Montreal, or any town of Britain, and ask "Can you tell me what street this is?" — "Yes, sir, 1 can; but please give me two-pence-ha'penny for a mug of beer?" "What building is that?" — "It is the Great Cathedral, sir: jist a ha'penny for a mug of beer, sir?" — "What mansion is that?" — "Why, sir, it's the place where Lord Elgin stopped: jist a ha'penny, only a ha'penny, sir, for a mug of beer? it would strengthen this poor tired body; it would cure my dear throat." Ask a Bostonian to show you round; and he, whether rich or poor, is proud of the honor: he takes pleasure in telling you, "This is Boston, sir, the Capital of Massachusetts, the Old Bay State." Even her adopted citizens partake of her pride; and some of them are christened by the name of Boston. Hence we have a "Boston Corbett," the avenger of President Lincoln's death.

BRIDGET.

Even the servants of Boston are imbued with a spirit of pride and independence, and sometimes, also, of insubordination. Look at modest Bridget. When she first comes over to this country, she appears a pattern of meekness, and saint-like submission. She will wash and scrub, build your fires, black your boots, and carry your water; but let her stay in Boston a while, and breathe the atmosphere of Bunker Hill, and she will tell you, "I don't think I shall like this ere work, I don't." — "Oh, yes, you will, Bridget!" says the mistress. "I want you to do a little of the cooking, — just a little only. I want you to dress this chicken, and cook this sauce, boil these turnips, peel these potatoes (peel them before boiling, you know)." And she will ask, "Dress this ere chicken, did ye till me?" — "Yes, Bridget, I want you to do it well: pick out all the pin-feathers." — "Pick out all the pin-fithers? pick out all the pin-fithers, did ye say? And must I bile these tarnips, and peel these 'taters? — peel 'em afore bilin, heh? By my faith in Saint Bridget! I'll do no sich a thing." — "Why do you insult me?"

says the mistress. "Insult ye? I don't insult ye. I guess ye bitter pick out yer own pin-fithers, ye had; and ye bitter *skin yer own 'taters:* I does parlor-work, I does;" and, slamming the door to, off she goes.

One Boston lady, the wife of a minister, determined to bring her servant into subjection; so she laid violent hands upon her. That little act cost her husband over two thousand dollars. Thus sacred and inviolable is held the personal liberty of even a servant-girl in Boston.

DRUNKARDS.

Even drunkards feel some pride for Boston's reputation, and some self-respect as citizens of Boston. "Thomas Collins," said the Clerk of the Police Court, "you are charged with being drunk: are you guilty, or not guilty?" — "Thrunk, did ye say? thrunk, heh? Hum, who says I was thrunk? Prove it if ye can!"—"Come, say guilty or not guilty," said the clerk, with pen in hand, ready to write the sentence. "Guilty or not guilty? hum, that's what I say."—"But are you guilty or not guilty? Answer at once." Gaping and staring and hesitating, then turning to walk off, he said, with a waggish shrug, "*I am a stranger in these parts! I don't choose to answer that question;*" and down the dock he went.

NEWSBOYS.

The newsboys are a set of independent little fellows, boisterous, wide awake, and full of fun. "Here's the Heral', Jirnil, Trav'ler, 'Ranscrip', five 'clock, last 'dition: paper, sir?"— "How much do you ask?"—"Five cents," was the reply of one of them to a man on Washington Street; so the man took a paper, and, after reading the telegraph news, was about to hand it back, but finally pulled out three cents, and handed to the boy. The boy took it, gazed at it, and held it up, and said, "Three cents, three cents, and hindered me all this time, when I told him five! Papers has riz in war-times: well, never mind, I'll be up with him!" So he seized an old paper, ran up to the pocket of the man, took out the new one, and put in the old one; then he came back to his comrades, one of whom was on crutches, and swapped his coat and hat, and seized a crutch, and ran round the corner to head off the man; and, hobbling before him, he cried, "Here's the Heral', Jirnil, Trav'ler, 'Ranscrip', five 'clock, last 'dition: paper, sir?"— "No, my lad: I have just bought one of a boy back yonder."— "Have you, sir? That boy sells old papers, he does. I bet it is an old one you bought."—"No, it aint: I saw the telegraph, five o'clock."— "I tell you 'taint so, look and see." So the man looked, and cried, "There! *'tis yesterday's paper!* Where is the scamp?"—"There he is," said the boy; "that one with the blue coat on, catch him! catch him!" The man started in pursuit, while the boys set up a yell, clapping their hands, and crying, "*Catch him, catch him! three cents, three cents!*" until the attention of the throng was roused; and the man shrunk away in shame, concluding it best never again to cheat a newsboy.

BOOKS.

Boston is filled with books and book-worms; that is, book-readers. Books make ballots, and ballots rule the continent, except in Mexico, where foreign bayonets rule just at this time, contrary to American ideas. Perhaps no city on the globe, of its size, has so many schools, books, newspapers, printers, teachers, professors, lawyers, doctors, ministers, lecturers, reformers, woman's rights, advocates, female physicians, authors, and artists, as this modern little Athens of America. No audience in the world will perceive a palpable hit, or catch a joke, quicker than a Boston audience. No critics are more acute. Even the common people are native-born critics. Contrast these people with those of the South,—the poor white or the slave.

POOR WHITE.

I saw one of the poor whites of North Carolina. He was a tall, lean, straight-haired, sporting man, with gun in hand. " That's a fine book of yourn," said he, holding the book *wrong end upwards, however.* " I du declar', that are is fine! it is right-smart! It's got picters, it has, heh? What du you ax for it? I du declar', I had 'un most jist like it once, I did! I used it for waddin' to shute squirrels with, I did. It had a picter of old Jackson in it; and I shot old Jackson at the squirrels. A peddler come our way once, and left a boblition paper; and I wadded with that, and I couldn't kill nuthin. But, when I wadded with old Jackson, I killed every time. I said, ' Look a-here, Mr. Squirrel! This ere constitution of mine must and shall be preserved.' Then I jist pinted at him; and down he cum quicker nor you can say Jack Robinson." Such was one's estimate of books, bred under the blight of slavery. *Rise, Freedom!* elevate these groundlings of the Southern race; plant your schoolhouses, colleges, and churches; let Boston notions prevail; let New-England institutions regenerate the South!

SLAVE.

The slave, with the manhood almost crushed out of him, is but a little lower in the grade of civilization than the poor white. He comes fawning, cringing, agitated, with hat off, and thrust under the chair, showing his white teeth, and trying to smile, saying, "Can't I help ye, Massa? Shan't I black ye boots, massa?" Poor thing! a dog could hardly crouch so low.

A Boston boot-black is imbued, perhaps, with a spirit of too much independence. "Hallo, sir! have yer boots blacked?" "How much do you ask, my boy?" "Ten cents, sir!" "Ten cents! that's too much. Won't you take five? I'll give you five!"

The boy looks at him a moment, then putting his thumb to his nose, with his fingers playing, "No, SIR-EE! *I can't ruin the trade ; I can't lower the dignity of the profession.*" And, with a swell-strut, he moves off.

HURRY.

The people of Boston are ever in a hurry. Hinderances are provoking, vexatious. A man came to a street-corner, and said, —

"Boy, can you tell me what house this is?"

"Brick house, sir. Didn't you know that?"

"Well, can't you tell me who lives here? I am in a hurry."

"Well, sir, I'll tell ye if ye *won't be in sich a hurry.* Jennie lives there, and little George lives there, and little Harry and Susie, and the baby and Fido and pussy," —

"Stop, you little simpleton! Tell me who are the old folks."

"Well, sir, they are Jennie's grandpa, and George's grandpa, and Jennie's grandma, and George's grandma, and Harry's grandma," —

"Stop! I say, who is the head of the family?"

"Well, grandpa sits at the head of the table!"

"No, not that! Who owns the house?"

"Oh! that's what ye want to know, heh? Why didn't ye ask that afore? and I'd tell ye. *Aunt Susie's husband owns the house; and he lives at Roxbury.*" So the hurried man left, no wiser in regard to the occupants of the house than when he came.

STAMMERER.

Another man asked a stuttering boy, "How far is it to Bunker Hill?" The boy began to stammer, trying to say two miles, — "t–t–t." But the man kept on walking, the boy still stammering, "t–t–t," till at last he became exasperated, and cried, "G-g-go along! You'll g-g-git there 'afore I can t-t-tell ye."

ELOCUTIONIST.

Boston is noted for its formality of manners. The hearts of the people are moved more by logic than by passion or impulse. Its preachers, its lecturers, and its professors, are formal. One of these professors came to teach the *newsboys* the art of elocution. "Now, boys," said he, "assume this position" (suiting the action to the word), "now that; now perform this gesture, now that. Now we will practise the voice on inflection. This is the rising inflection, this the falling, and this is the circumflex."

"I don't care nuthin' about your 'flexions nor circumflexes nor geneflexes. I want's to speak my piece," said a bold little genius, tired of what he called "this ere humbug and foolin,'" And making his bow, swift as thought, he said, with animated gesticulations, —

"The Turk awoke!
That bright dream was his last:
He woke to hear his sentry's shriek,
To arms! they come! the Greek, the Greek!

Strike, 'till the last armed foe expires,
Strike for your altars and your fires,
Strike for the green graves of your sires,
God, and your native land."

Then clapping his hands, confident of success, he joined in the applause that fairly shook the house. The professor shrunk away into a corner, until the boy had got through; then took his hat, and left.

The truth is, they were native-born orators; while he was merely a theorist, following the profession for a livelihood.

WHISTLER.

Boston is filled with professors; professors of all kinds, from law, science, and theology, down to quack doctors. One of these would-be-professors, travelling South, found himself in want of funds. How to raise the wind was a puzzle; but, as the wind must be raised, he hit upon a plan, and announced himself a professor of whistling, and declared he could teach anybody, man, woman, or child, how to whistle any tune, provided they would *obey orders*. As the announcement was a novel one, his advertisement drew a full house; and, as money was his object, the fees, of course, were obtained in advance. Said he, "Ladies and gentlemen, your success depends upon your implicit obedience to orders. Please sit erect, look straight at me, draw up your lips in this way" (puckering up his mouth in a manner that provoked general laughter).

"Please give me your attention. Those young ladies do nothing but titter, titter! Hush that laughing. You can't whistle while laughing. Attention! Wet your lips; *prepare to pucker!*" (Roars of laughter.) "Ladies and gentlemen, I must have your attention. Are you ready? once more I repeat it, *Prepare to pucker!*" (Continued roars of laughter, and great confusion.)

"Well, ladies and gentlemen, you have paid your money, but have broken the conditions: you will not give that implicit obedience to orders which is necessary to learn the art of whistling. You will not *prepare to pucker;* therefore you can't learn to whistle." Then, soon as possible, he made his exit.

The moral of this is, that one must acquire the rudiments before succeeding in any profession. *Puckering* always precedes *whistling.* "If you won't prepare to pucker, you can't learn to whistle."

CHAPTER VIII.

NATIONAL CHARACTERISTICS. — OUT-DOOR SPORTS. IN-DOOR SUFFERINGS.

THE *Englishman* is said never to be happy but when he is miserable. It is an Englishman's prerogative to growl and grumble. A *Scotchman* is never at home but when he is abroad. An *Irishman* is never at peace except when he is in a fight. A *Yankee* has never got enough until he gets a little more. The *Frenchman* boasts of belonging to *so great a country.* The *Englishman* boasts that *so great a country belongs to him.* The *Yankee* affirms that *he and his country are one.*

A high-bred *Englishman* is surly, sulky, self-important, unapproachable, except by his compeers, with an air of "Stand your distance, sir!"

The *Yankee* is cute, knowing, fraternal, inquisitive, acquisitive, and disquisitive, except in Boston, where he is a little more reticent.

The *Western man* boasts of his extensive prairies and growing cities. Soon he expects to control the nation.

The *Southerner's* boast has been, that "I am a Southern gentleman, sir! No mudsill of toil; my cellars are filled with wine, and my plantation worked by slaves."

The *Bostonian's* boast is not that he is a Northerner, nor an idler, nor a cavalier, but that he is a *cosmopolitan!* his domain is the world.

An *Englishman's* love for roast-beef is proverbial. Johnny Bull's pluck is made *for–mid–a–ble* (bull) by bull-beef.

A *Dutchman* loves his ease, his pipe, and lager. "Te world be too much stirring, te peoples be too much in von big hurry. Be quiet, Mynheer! Tat vas goot!"

The *Frenchman* goes into ecstasies over trifles. His beau ideal is the love of pleasure and female society. With pantomimic gesticulations he says, "*Charmant Mademoiselle!* Go to de Opera? Go to de *Théatre Français? Très Grand!* All de *beau monde* be *présent! magnifique!* capital! capital! *Mademoiselle!*"

The *Bostonian* thinks that frivolous Frenchman too excited, too enthusiastic. Coolly and scrutinizingly, with spectacles on nose, he gazes at his monkey-like performances, as though he were calculating about how much it would take to buy him out.

The solid men of Boston are noted for their coolness as well as smartness. I saw one of them once overwhelmed by a snow-slide from a roof. The ladies in the street were dodging and shrieking, "Oh my! this is ridiculous! We'll be killed!" The bystanders, laughing and enjoying the sport, while he, placing his hands upon his knees, and dropping his head, received the force of the slide, like a true disciple of Zeno. Then looking up, he said, "There, spill your thunder! have you got through?" and shaking himself, he passed on, as if nothing had happened. If the day of judgment were at hand, such a man would be found calculating its effects upon the price of stocks or the rate of gold.

Out-door Sports. — Boston is noted for its love of coasting, sleighing, and skating. Its suburbs are admirably situated for the greatest indulgence in these healthful sports. Many young ladies of fashion indulge in the graceful art of skating. This is a healthful exercise, and seems necessary to those who will not develop their physical frames by hard work. If they will not toil, then let them skate. And I must confess, a young lady looks rather aerial and fairy-like on skates.

Jemima Darling. — But I saw something richer than skating. Six years ago, Ezekiel Tudor, a fresh New-Brunswicker, stood by Williams Hall, waiting for Jemima Darling to come out of singing-school. He addressed her something in this style, —

> "O Jemima, with eyes so bright,
> Here's a big ripe apple meller;
> Let me go home with you to-night?
> Don't let that other feller."

Jemima said, " Yes, Zeke, you may. Give me your arm."

"O Jemima," said Zeke, " I have got something better; I have brought my hand-sled; it is a clipper of a goer, a reg'lar reindeer. Won't you take a ride?" Now it may be fashionable in New Brunswick for a woman to ride on a hand-sled, but not in Boston. She got on the sled, however, and through the streets, and over Dover-street Bridge they went, by the sleighs, phætons, and carryalls, happy as larks. Zeke was never prouder in his life; he now bore " Cæsar and his fortune." He was not quite so swift as a horse; many a steed outstripped him in the race; but never was there a steed of brisker mettle or of prouder spirit. He jumped.

pulled, puffed, and wheezed, while Jemima seemed delighted in putting on the string. *Didn't she give him Jessie, though?* She had the reins in her hand, and, striking with a stick, she said, "*Go faster, Zeke!* DO *go faster! faster!* FASTER! FASTER!

And the poor tired fellow, with renewed spirit, tried his best to go "*faster, faster, faster,*" until at last, almost exhausted, and half dead, he reached her door in South Boston. The best of the story is, Zeke won his bride; but, true to her womanly instinct, she has held the reins, and cracked the whip over him ever since. Still the cry is, "*faster, Zeke! faster, faster!*" and she makes Zeke's trotters step to a tune considerably swifter than Old Hundred.

Bartholomew! or Woman's Rights. — It is amusing to see how some men love to be ordered about by woman. They seem but a shadow of their better halves. This is well; for it is an axiom in mathematics, that the " greater shall comprehend the less." How comforting, to an unambitious mind to be under the guardianship of another. To have no will of your own; to have it completely swallowed up in the will of another. To have your thoughts, like your money, carried in somebody else's purse. You have no need of a purse, for you have nothing to put into it.

I know a man in Boston, who would not have a will of his own for the world; he has no need of it; he lives, breathes, walks, speaks, and acts, under the control of the guardian spirit of his wife. If, by chance, he should break like a comet from the central orb, a word, a look, from his wife when she says, "*Bartholomew!*" brings him all right in a moment. Up go his hands in alarm; he secretes himself in the corner, and yields with lamb-like submission.

One time he determined not to be so henpecked: he would be a man in spite of himself; he would assert his rights. She looked daggers at him. "*Bartholomew!*" she cried; yet he clung to his seat, and braced his feet, and stirred not. Bravo! he had conquered. Again she looked daggers. "BARTHOLOMEW!" Still he clinched his teeth, and held to his chair, and stuck like pitch. "*Bartholomew!* BARTHOLOMEW!! BARTHOLOMEW!!!" My stars! how he jumped! Such is the magnetic power of woman.

One Boston notion is that of woman's rights. From the days of Ann Hutchinson to the present time, there have been teachers, lecturers, ambitious women, refusing to pay taxes without representation, despising the authority of their liege lords. Some claim the right to choose presidents and elect generals. Judging by the valor displayed by some generals and ex-presidents, they must have been chosen by *votes* from the *crinoline persuasion*.

Woman's Wrongs, or Indoor Sufferings. — On the other hand, contrasting with these strong-minded women, what kicks and knocks and bruises some wives will bear from their brutal husbands! God only knows what they suffer! No person will bear or forbear like a drunkard's wife. Being reviled, she reviles not again; persecuted, she threatens not. Such a person was the wife of a man by the name of Perkins, on Kneeland Street.

I visited her soon after she had been beaten: she gazed at me as if I were an angel from heaven. There, upon the stove-hearth, was the blood which she had coughed up, caused by the brutal blow; it was but the precursor of her winding-sheet, yet, without a murmur, she accepted her condition as the decree of fate. Rum formed that decree; rum struck the blow.

Yet the abuse of that man was worse than the blow, more than death itself.

Oh the abuse of a drunken man! Oh the taunts, the threats, the ribaldric jeers!

What wrongs would he not perpetrate? Oh,

how many martyrs are dying by inches in this city's low, back underworld of woe!

Mary Kelley. — "Please buy these shavings, sir. 'Tis gettin' late; I can't sell 'em, sir, my mother wants the money," said a half-clothed little girl at my door. It was after dark, the winds blew, and the snow was falling thick and fast.

"Where does your mother live?" I asked.

"She lives in East Orange Street; she be blind and almost starvin', sir."

So I took the poor little thing by the hand, and through the drifting snow we travelled, until we reached the cellar where the poor woman lived. She raised her head from over the stove where she had been bending, to gather the heat from the last spark of fire. A broken platter with a little tallow, and a burning wick at its side, gave just light enough to show the depths of poverty and misery to which she had been reduced.

There was a pile of filthy rags in the corner of the room, answering for a bed, but scarcely any other furniture except the broken stove.

As I entered, she raised her almost sightless eyeballs towards me, and told her sad story. Her husband was at the House of Correction; she being nearly blind, depended upon her two children for support. They did it by selling shavings, and begging from door to door.

She said, "Sir, I am nearly blind! My husband came home intoxicated, and found nothing on the stove but water, for I could get nothing to eat; and, seizing the kettle of boiling water, he dashed its contents in my face. I threw my hands to my head, and cried, 'O my God! you have murdered me, you have murdered me!' When I took my hands from my head, the skin and hair clung to them, and my skull was nearly bare; and I never saw the light again. People want me to go the poor-house; but how can I go, and leave my poor little children in the hands of strangers? Oh, no! I cannot part with them. I had rather live on a crust of bread than be parted from my dear children."

CHAPTER IX.

NED NEVINS FORCED INTO A STREET FIGHT.

"HILLO there, Yank! whose slid has ye got? Where did ye git that ere slid, and that ere basket of coal? By ginger! if ye hain't stole 'em both," said Patrick Murphy to Ned Nevins, as the latter came trudging along from the coal-dump, dragging his hand-sled with a basket of coal upon it. As Pat had nothing else to do, he took particular delight in crowing over the "young Yank" as he called him, and in tormenting him in every possible manner. His mother kept a liquor-shop near by, and some "female" boarders; and sometimes "gentlemen" lodgers tarried there for the night.

Old Mag Murphy was a noted thief,— a receiver of stolen goods,— and Pat was her chief accomplice in thieving. Only a few days before, a boy was passing that way from market, with a hand-sled and a basket of meat; and, getting into a frolic with his dog, he left his sled and basket on the side-walk for a moment, and, returning, found them missing. Pat's trade was to watch for such accidents. He had seized the prizes, and hustled them into the house. Old Mag Murphy consumed the meat, but thought it dangerous to retain the sled, as search-warrants were often displayed about her premises; so she allowed Pat to cut Ned's name on the sled, and leave it at Mrs. Nevins's door.

Ned, rising in the morning, and seeing the sled with his name marked on it, thought that somebody had left it for a present; so he took it to draw home his coal. Now it was when returning that he met Pat, and received from him the accustomed insults. Nothing riled or daunted by the epithets of "Yank," "thief," and "coal-picker," he passed on as if he heard not, until he saw that Pat was determined to have a fight. "Hillo there, you young Yank! Stop, thief!" he said, crossing his path, and heading him off, and doubling up his fists in an attitude of defiance. "Let me alone; let me go home, for my mother is sick," said Ned. "I hain't stole no sled; it was gin to me, and my name put on't; don't be botherin' me, I want to go along; I told mother I would git home early, and she wants the coal."

"Ha, ha, ha!" cries Pat, with a malicious laugh, knocking off Ned's hat at the same time.

"I'm spilin' for a fight." Then he blustered about, and doubled up his fists, and drew off as if to strike him. "I could knock your eyes out in two minutes. See that ere pile of knuckles! See how I could put 'em between your lookers, heh!" shaking the fist in his face.

"Don't strike me!" says Ned. "Take one of your size; besides, my mother tells me never to fight; it is better to suffer wrong than to do wrong: 'if I do nothin' wrong, somethin' good will come to me.'" So he pressed his way along, determined not to quarrel.

"Stop thief!" says Pat. "Give an account of yourself; ye stole that ere slid," tripping him down.

"Pat Murphy, you must not do that again; big as you are, if my mother hadn't told me not to fight, I would never stand this."

"Your mother!" says Pat; "why don't you say father, heh? Ha, ha, ha! ye hain't got no father! ye niver hed no father. Ye be one of them ere unfortunates that niver knows why they was born. *Your* mother, heh? Ha, ha! she's one of 'em, that's so," bending down, and sneering in Ned's face with a sarcastic grin that made his blood boil with indignation.

"Pat Murphy! say what you please about me, — call me all manner of names; but there is one thing you must not do, — you must never insult the name of my mother, no never, never, never!" — looking to heaven, as if to say his prayers, and standing like a rock.

"I will insult both you and your mother!" said Pat, giving him a blow.

Then Ned, like a tiger, chafed and foamed, and, striking his fists together, leaped at his foe, and struck him first on the nose, which sent him reeling, then on the temples, which felled him to the earth, then pounced upon him, and gave him blow after blow, till the blood burst from Pat's nose, and Ned's fist was all covered with blood.

"Oh, murther! murther!" cried old Mag Murphy, as she saw the fight from her window, and burst out of the house in a rage, with broom in hand, and her dog at her heels, to join in the fray. "Murther! murther! they be killin' my poor Patrick! my dear little saint! my honest boy! By my soul, and Saint Bridget, he shan't be killed right before my eyes. Help, help, help! Police, police!" Then she seized one of Ned's legs, while he lay upon Pat, and the dog seized the other leg; and, as they pulled, the dog growled, and she cried, "Police, police! Murther, murther!" Then the street windows rose, and doors flew open, dogs came barking out; and men, women, and children, without hats or bonnets, came rushing, pell-mell, towards the fight, until at last a policeman appeared; and, breaking through the crowd, he seized the boys by the collar, and asked what was the matter.

"Plase sir, ye'r 'onor, this ere boy has been stealin' a slid," said Mag; "and, because Pat told h'm he stole it, he's fell a-foul of him, and bate him almost to dith. Poor boy! Don't cry, my dear Patrick. See the blood a-runnin' down his poor innocent face! Dare little saint, darlin' crather," she said, as she kissed him and hugged him. "He niver fights, nor stales, nor tills lies. See how he suffers like a martyr 'cause he tills the truth, and hurts nobody! Here comes the market-man, he what owns the slid; he will tell you if 'tain't his slid."

"Yes!" said Mr. David Nelson, "that is my sled: it was stolen from one of my market-boys." So he seized it, and carried it home; while Ned was held by the collar, and taken to the station-house, amidst a rabble crowd of ragged street-prowlers, of every age, sex, and kind; increasing in numbers as the motley throng advanced; filling up from every lane and alley with bare-headed, bare-legged, hooting, and yelling juvenile precocities, throwing sticks and mud and snow, till now the police stops a moment to silence the mob. When they saw the blood on Pat's face, and knew that the Yankee boy must have caused it, then they yelled worse than ever, crying, " Shoot him, kill him!" At last, when near the station-house, a squad of policemen appeared; then the tumult ceased, and the crowd skedaddled.

Ned is taken into the station-house; and Pat Murphy and old Mag Murphy are the only distinguished citizens who are allowed to come in, and help make out a case. Ned sees his perilous condition. Nothing but intercession with the policeman can save him. What hope has he? What feeling for an innocent boy has a policeman, who has been dealing with rascals a lifetime? What tears will awake his pity? What protestations of innocence will *he* believe? How can a man familiar with bolts and bars, and crime's deceits, judge of the pride of character, or self-respect; or the mortification and eternal stigma of being incarcerated for crime?

"I want to go home," said Ned, bursting into tears. "I promised mother I would return early." — "You go home!" said Mr. Kelly sarcastically. "I guess you will go home: you have been too long on the street to talk of home now. I have got you this time, and I shall hold you for trial." — "Yis, yer 'onor, hold him fast, hold tight the dreadful crather," said old Mag, in a rage. "He's no father; he's in the strate all the liv'-long day; he's fightin' and stealin', and tellin' lies about folks all the blissid time. He's lied about me. He says I stole, and Pat stole. Yis, Pat stole, he says, — this dare latle saint of his mother! Poor Patrick! And, 'cause Pat told him he stole that ere slid, then he fell a-foul of him, and bate him almost to dith. Poor Pat! my angel! mother's dear, darlin' boy!"

Then Ned seized the policeman's hand, and fell upon his knees to attest his innocence. "O sir! believe me, when I tell you I never stole that sled. I found it at my door, with my name marked on it. I never stole any thing in my life. I am no thief. I am not idle in the street. I work for my poor, sick mother. Please, sir, let me go."

"'Taint so!" says old Mag, stamping her foot. "He did stale it; and I will appear in court, and swear to it."

"Hear me," says Ned. "I am an innocent child, innocent as the day is long. I would not wrong anybody for the world. I am poor; I have no father to protect me; my mother is dying!"

"'Taint so!" says Mag; "I seed her in the street a few days ago: she hain't dyin' no how!"

"Oh, hear me, sir!" says Ned. "You are my only friend; look in pity upon me; do not lock me up: it will disgrace me for life, it will kill my poor mother. Do any thing else with me, but do not put me in prison. Starve me; strip me naked in the cold; whip me till my veins burst; blister my back with burdens, and my feet with running; let my hands be palsied with toil, but let them never be disgraced by a chain, or barred by a prison. Let me walk erect, and hold up my head in innocence; and let me shake this poor fatherless land of toil, and say, 'It still is free!"

"By Saint Patrick!" says Mag, " his hand has been frae too long, it has, sir! Jist see poor Pat's face, heh!"

"Oh that I were a child of yours!" said Ned, " then you would love me, and pity me, and hear my prayers. Oh that I was a servant of yours! to wait on you, and do your bidding, and be truthful to you, and show you that even a poor street-boy may have an honest heart. May your children never want a father to protect them, and may they never be poor! Alas! I fear you have no children, you look so coldly on me. Would that you had one only child, one little boy about my age, with bright blue eyes, and sunny face, and tender heart, to climb up into your lap, and hug you, and kiss you so as I do now!" (Mr. Kelly thrusting him away.) "Oh, do not thrust me away! Let me love you as I would a father, for I have no father to love; let me call you more than a father,— even a friend! I cannot go into that dark cell. I cannot be locked up in this dungeon. I cannot stay away from my mother,— no, no! You must let me go; you will let me go, I know you will! O Mr. Kelly! be my dear friend. You are the only man in the world that can help me. Angels shall bless you; orphans shall love you. You will save me, I know you will,— let me kiss your hand. " Better kiss Pat Murphy's hand!" said Kelly, twitching away his hand. " That's so!" says Mag. " Patrick Kelly, ye is a gintleman every inch of ye; yis ye ba, a right blissid gintleman!"

"Oh, hear me, Mr. Kelly! I did wrong to strike Pat Murphy (my mother will blame me); but my mother will forgive me, and God will forgive me, and none but you so hard as not to forgive me. But I feel you will forgive me; yes, I know you will. I have something here," (smiting his breast) "that tells me you are a man. You would not blast an orphan's prospects; you would not hurt the innocent; you would not break a mother's heart? Then don't let me go to the courts; don't have it said I have been in jail! If your heart were stone, you would

"I cannot go into that dark cell! I cannot be locked up in a dungeon! I cannot stay away from my sick mother! No! no! Mr. Kelly. My mother is dying. You must let me go! You will let me go; I know you will. Throw off the Policeman; put on the Man! and let me go!" Page 102.

feel for me; if your eyes were balls of glass, they would weep. Oh, let me off! you never shall see me fightin' again. I am no fighter; I would not hurt a worm. Let me off, and I will show you how true I will be, how thankful to you; and how a poor, sick, dying mother, will bless you!"

"I see," said Mr. Kelly, "that your mother has taught you better things than to fight and steal. If you are thoroughly punished for this, it will be a lesson to you," putting a key in the lock, and opening the iron door to one of the cells.

"O Mr. Kelly! you will not turn that key on me! you will not lock me in there! The creaking of the door makes me shudder; its very look frightens me; the angry lock scares me; the sound of the turning key pierces my heart! I cannot go in there; I cannot be behind those bars! I cannot go out with irons upon my wrists. Let me see your wrists. There are no irons on them, no mark of irons; no red blistered streak of shame. Oh, how those irons would weep, to be put on my hands! Ah! their weeping mouths would refuse to close upon me, their jaws would set at sight of so cruel an intent. My hands are as innocent as yours, Mr. Kelly! Look at them! they have done no crime; they ought not to be bound. Oh, how my mother would weep, and angels would weep, and you would weep (you couldn't help weeping), if you should fasten me in there! I heard you sigh a moment ago, and the tears fell. You had some little feeling; your heart was not all of stone; no, it was not. You thought of your boy in my place, and you did weep; yes, I saw the tear: now pity me, sir! now take advantage of the occasion just now that your heart is tender.; now throw off the policeman, put on the man, catch at pity, let your victim go. Heaven will smile on the deed; God will bless you; and this poor, weeping, fatherless boy on his knees at your feet, pleading for forgiveness, shall rise up and bless you, and say that the jail hath been robbed of its prey, and a helpless orphan rescued from doom."

"But I must lock you up for one night, and you can have your trial in the morning," said Kelly.

"One night, one night! did you say? one night in jail, one night in a dungeon! one night away from my mother,— my poor sick mother! Oh, sir! I was never away from her a single night in my life. One night from my mother, now that she is sick and dying, and has no helper! Is this my gratitude for all her sacrifices for me?

Can I leave her without a fire? Have I a heart to do it?"

"You *must* leave her," said Kelly, seizing him by the arm, and dragging him to the cell, while Ned cried and shrieked, as the door closed in upon him, "O my mother, my mother! She is freezing, starving, dying, all alone, her Eddie far away. O mother, mother! Eddie will come home; he won't stay away! Do not cry, mother; Eddie will come home! Do not die this night, do not die before he comes! He is coming, he will come; yes, he will. He has not gone away to leave you without a fire: he will come. O mother! mother!"

CHAPTER X.

INTRODUCTION TO MRS. SOPHIA NEVINS, NED'S MOTHER.

PAT MURPHY'S wounds not being fatal, he left the police-station in high glee, rejoicing that he had cleared the street at last from that thorn in the flesh to evil-doers,—Ned Nevins. Skipping and jumping, he scampered off to Mrs. Nevins's house in Orange Lane; and, passing through the entry passage-way, he came to the door where the sick woman lay. Then, in malicious frolic, he placed his lips to the keyhole, and bawled out, "Ned's in prison! Poor Ned, the beak has got him!" Then, uttering a fiendish shriek, he ran through the passage, out of the house undiscovered. Soon he came back again to the keyhole; and, placing his hands over his lips to make a doleful sound, he cried, "Poor Eddie, darling boy! Eddie won't come to-night, he's"— but this sentence was cut short by an Irish woman from another door in the passage-way, who cried,—

"Out, ye young rascal! don't be tormentin' that poor sick crather. She be a-most did now. Away wid ye'r, you scamp, or I'll be arter puttin' the police on ye'r track: be gone, and let the poor crather die asey." Now, as a rush of other women was seen coming pell-mell towards him, Pat, with his coat-tail standing horizontally in the air, took to his heels, and fled.

Let us enter the room of Mrs. Sophia Nevins. It is on the north side of the house, — a room which a sunbeam never penetrated, and scarcely ever a ray of comfort or hope. The sun rises and sets, but casts no cheering beam on her face. Men come and go as regularly as the week passes; but they are not messengers of mercy: they come to collect rent, or to hurry up the neglected sewing-work. Within ten feet from her head, the Worcester trains, rumbling with passengers and heavy freight, pass every few minutes, shaking the building with hideous jar, and piercing the ear of the dying with the whistles' shriek.

Mrs. Nevins is asleep; she has at last found a drug that stupefies her, and makes her insensible. She heard not, or heeded not, the sound at the keyhole; and the rumbling cars startle her but for a moment, unless when some unusual sound occurs, such as the creaking of wheels, or grating of the brakes: these noises seem to pierce her soul. Strange place for a woman of her education and refinement! But poverty, like an armed man, hath forced her step by step to this. She could still have been in comfort, and perhaps in affluence, if she would have parted with her child; but this she could not do. A strange infatuation possessed her: she would not part with it for the world. Every eye that gazed upon it made her jealous; and every offer for its adoption aroused her anger. She could hear it call no other person "Mother;" no, not in heaven. By parting with it, she could be restored to society; but, by clinging to it, she could revel in its love, and drink in the ocean of its charms. By night, it was her only comfort and solace. As it lay in her bosom, and its little heart throbbed by hers, all care and sorrow were banished away. Its sparkling eyes, imaging nothing but love; its tiny hands playfully tangling in her curls, and clapping together in glee; its prattling voice, cooing in loving innocence, and crowing over imagined victories; its rosy cheek, its alabaster forehead, and its silken locks, — all awakened sensations of extreme delight. Where that child was, there was her paradise.

When the time came that she must be parted from it, or be ostracised, then banishment seemed but a holiday choice. So long as these little arms were clinging to her neck, these tiny feet were dancing in her lap, these eyelet gems were gleaming in her face, these ruby lips were printing one kiss upon her cheek, and receiving a thousand kisses in return, so long as she could hear its cries, and pity its tears, and relieve its wants, she was supremely happy.

What will not love accomplish? It nerves the arm of toil to perform herculean tasks; it strengthens weary feet, and shortens the longest journey; it lightens the load of care, and makes labor but a pastime; it looks the eagle blind, and espies sails of hope farther off than the half-discovered topsail seen by a wrecked mariner while drifting on his mast.

It tastes luxuries in the crumbs of a mouldy crust; it hears seraphic minstrelsy in the simplest speech; it feels a rapture at the slightest touch, and glows with ardor at the smallest sense or sound. Such were the feelings of Sophia Nevins.

But an educated, refined, delicate female, unaccustomed to toil, cannot endure fatigue like a muscular Margaret or a Bridget. Health must finally fail, and finance be wanting. There she lies a martyr: she is but the wreck of her former self, yet beautiful in ruins. See that wide forehead, that high and noble brow, that Grecian nose, that chin of firmness, that mouth of eloquence, and those temples of ideality! With such endowments, she must have succeeded, if she only had health. But here the parents were to blame.

Why did they keep her in the embroidery-room, like a caged bird, undeveloped in physical frame, planting seeds of death with no thought of future contingencies? Oh! it was for society, for fashion's sake. A curse on the fashion that can cramp and distort the mothers of our race, and convert their progeny into dwarfs! Let every woman of the land have physical exercise; let every muscle be developed, and the lungs have full play, if they are to produce vigorous men.

Here lies a victim of parental softness and false pride. By disease planted in childhood, her constitution yielded and broke at the first touch of labor. Oh, what a leap she has made, in jumping from affluence to this den of poverty and crime!

She sleeps! It is a delirious sleep. She sighs, and groans; the tears flow; and she cries, " O Eddie! why do you not come, when your mother is so sick? O Eddie! how can you stay away from your mother?'" Then she becomes quiet again.

See those Irish women gather around her! One of them watches the trunk, as if to get hold of it, then looks around the room to see if there is nothing else to steal. Alas! there are no valuables left. The room is almost bare. One thing after another has been pawned or sold, until there remains one old bedtick filled with shavings, on which she lies; a few torn coverlids, bearing the mark of her youthful needle-work, but now not half enough to keep her warm; a broken stove, and a few dishes, on which meat is still waiting for Eddie's meal; two broken-backed chairs, an old table, and a few other articles, not worth enough to pay an auctioneer for his services. In her trunk are a number of mementoes, which she will keep till she dies, though she may starve to death for want of their worth in money. Also on her hand is a ring, which, she says, has never been off her finger since first placed there by the hand of him, her betrayer, who may find it in her coffin.

"She'll niver ba any bater, she ba almost did, poor crather!" said a thievish Irish woman by her side, as she felt of her pulse, and gazed intently upon the ring as if soon to make it her prize.

"Yis! she will ba bater," said a benevolent old lady with pipe in her mouth. "I has sane her worse nor this, and sane her mends herself, and gits up agin, sure. She ba only worried 'cause Eddie don't come. Sha's in a sort of a drowse like now. When sha twitches and jerks, you can hear her talk in her slape: sha talks 'bout nuthin but Eddie, at all, at all. Oh, how sha loves that ere boy! sha sames sorter crazy arter him."

Now the Irish women are silent for a moment in watching Mrs. Nevins, when she broke forth in sobs and groans:—

"O Eddie! how can you treat me so?" she said, half awake, half asleep, and half deranged; with tears streaming down her cheeks, and wetting her pillow. "You never served me so before. I will forgive you if you will but come back. Do come back, my boy."

Then she thrust out her pale hand, as if to place it on his head, but, alas! there was no Eddie there.

"O my boy! you are not here. Ah, me! I fear Eddie must be killed: where can he be? O Eddie, Eddie! Why am I brought to this? Speak, ye tattered rags of my distress; speak, ye shreds of poverty; speak, ye relics of better days, — has it come to this? Have I not suffered enough?"

"O thou pale ghost of despair! have I not become a slave of thy fortunes? Cans't thou not say, 'Hold, enough'? Have I not been wedded to thee by indissoluble ties of adversity? I have combed thy shredded locks, and kissed thy beaded brow; I have been crushed at thy feet, and wallowed in thy foam; I have drank thy sighs, and fed upon thy tears; I have echoed thy groans, and tuned my heart's minstrelsy to thy wails; I have looked into thy face until my features have shaped themselves to thine image. I am a child of despair, — his own adopted child, grown under his shadow, nurtured in his dungeon, and fed by his poisonous breath."

"O my God! if there be mercy in store for a poor wretch like me, oh, pity me, and save my fatherless boy!"

With these exclamations, she fell back upon her couch, senseless and exhausted.

CHAPTER XI.

NED A PENITENT PRISONER. — HIS COMPANIONS IN THE BLACK MARIA.

"THERE, Ned, is your place for the present," said Patrick Kelly, the policeman, as he thrust him into the cell. "You have had your last street-fight, and stolen your last sled. The street is no place for you; to-morrow you will see an institution better than is found in Orange Lane."

Then he slammed-to the iron gate with a frightful jar, that echoed through the whole building; then seized the key, and thrust it ino the lock with such terrible sternness, that Ned fainted in his cell. How long he lay there, he knew not; for time had lost its reckoning with him.

Little by little he came to his senses, and opened his bewildered eyes; but when he saw the bars and grates, and realized where he was, he shrieked and groaned and shuddered and swooned again. Oh, what a piteous wail burst from that young, innocent heart when he thought of his awful condition! Such shrieks and wails ought to make the very stones weep, and the bolts yield; and none but a butcher or jailer could look coldly on.

As he slowly rose from the stone floor, and reached out his hands for succor, he instinctively began to pray. But now a double blackness settled upon his brow, not of a dizzy brain only, but the blackness of despair. How could he pray? He had broken his mother's precepts, and broken the law of God: he felt himself lost, lost! As whitest garments show quickest the stain, so the purest at heart are often most troubled with conscience. Ned felt condemned; every peccadillo of his life rose in frightful apparition before him; every petty quarrel with his schoolmates, every deception towards his mother, every pin or penny that he had purloined from her, now stared him in the face. He thought he must be guilty, or God would not have suffered him to be thrust into prison. His hair bristled with horror, awful sounds were ringing in his ears, doleful eyes seemed peering through the darkness, gibbering spirits were taunting him; and his blood ran cold with fright.

Amidst the awful gloom, he seemed sliding down an inclined plane, at the top of which he saw his mother looking down upon him, and weeping, and crying, "O Eddie, Eddie! has it come to this? O my precious Eddie! are you lost?" And, at the bottom of the plane, he saw surging billows rolling and foaming with doleful murmurings, like those he had pictured in his infancy concerning the gulf of perdition.

Down, down, he settled on the slippery plane, striving with outstretched arms to rise; but all in vain. And now the breath from the infernal regions strikes his cheek; and the cold, beaded sweat drops from his brow. O horror of horrors! blackness made hideous, and shapes and images frightful, by a distorted and overtaxed brain!

At last he falls into a drowse, a fitful, terrible drowse. He twitches and jerks, and dreams of hell. In a moment, he appears to be conversing with spirits lost. His lips move, and his tongue jabbers: he startles at fancy's imagery like a maniac.

The first spirit which he met was one like his own,—one who had struck the fatal blow, and had left the victim dead at his feet. The blood was still upon his hand, and could never be effaced. His name was Charley Nesbitt. In a moment of anger, he had done the deed, and now had an eternity to repent of it.

"O Ned, my old playmate! have you come

to this horrible place? Where are the teachings of your mother?" and then he vanished.

Ned was horrified, and wished to flee; but the heavy grasp of the nightmare held him fast: there was no escape.

Next he saw a drunkard, with cup in hand, wandering on the shores, seeking for drink. To every cindered rock, he cried "Drink, drink! give me drink! for I am mad with thirst." But every stream that come oozing out from the rock only added fuel to the fire of his thirst. He took the acrid draught, then madly cried for more, then drank again, then cursed the draught; and thus existence was continued, for he was not allowed to die. When he saw Ned, he stopped and stared, and cried "What! is it you, Eddie? you, here? what have you done?" Then Ned burst into a flood of tears. He sobbed and cried in his sleep, and shook with groans; but he could not break from the spell.

Now he saw the miser, with muck-rake in hand, compelled to scrape over the refuse and marl of this devastated region, in like manner as Ned had been compelled to dig at the coal-dump. The miser was shrivelled into deformity. His head was large; but his waist was like a wasp's: he had no heart left. What a change in his fortune! He seemed desirous to speak to

Ned; but Ned crouched down breathlessly still, until his attention was turned away.

Then he saw the oppressor of the poor, having a voracious appetite, but no food. His eyes looked pitifully upwards, his mouth was open, his jaws were lank, he cried continually, "Meat, meat!" but there was no meat to be had. Thus the maw-worm of appetite was gnawing upon his vitals day after day, where the "worm dieth not, and the fire is not quenched."

Now he sees the profane man, the blasphemer, compelled to repeat the oaths and imprecations, and perjuries and blasphemies, which he indulged in while on earth. The task is hard, for he has no heart for the work; but the law is inexorable, and must be obeyed. Now comes such a thunder-clap of shrieks and oaths and blasphemies, as if Pandemonium itself had split its ribs of adamant, and burst with its own explosion. At the hideous sound, Ned, shuddering, shrieked, and pitched from his bunk out on to the stone floor, and awoke. The noise was, however, not imaginary, but real; for, in the adjoining cells, were men afflicted with the delirium-tremens. Hence the yells that aroused Ned from his dreams, and drove him from his bunk.

It is midnight. Hark! A carriage is heard to halt before the station-house. The outer doors open: now the key is heard in the cell-doors, as one by one they open. Now it touches the lock of Ned's cell, as the name of Edward Nevins is called. Now the men with delirium-tremens appear. There is also a murderer, a robber, an incendiary, and a street-walker. They are all hand-cuffed and marched out, and hustled into the Black Maria together, and locked in, with no guard inside to prevent the maniacs from murdering the innocent. Oh, what company for a tender-hearted, innocent, lamb-like child, such as Eddie Nevins!

But Eddie thinks not of his company; his thoughts are two deeply centred on himself. They may swear and howl and fight, and bite each other's thumbs off, as they have been known to do; but he heeds them not. Oh the thoughts that swell his breast! Does he now pass over these streets for the last time? Ah! what will that mother do now? She forsook home and friends and wealth, and hid herself in poverty, that she might live with her darling boy.

If Eddie Nevins had no secret hope of being acquitted, he would rather die than live, — rather die than be parted from his mother.

Now the carriage arrives at the Tombs, and empties itself of its dreadful load. One by one the prisoners come out of the Black Maria. They are met by a squad of policemen, and marched to their cells for the rest of the night. What a bedlam do these Tombs present! As the culprits are here only to await trial, and many of them too intoxicated to keep still, strict prison-discipline cannot be expected.

There is a crazy prostitute, singing bawdy songs, and rolling out obscene language like a flood. There are men with delirium-tremens, fighting with ghosts and spirits infernal. Some are butting their heads against the walls until the blood gushes out. One is striving to cut his throat; others require straps upon them to prevent violence. There is a young man crazed for the first time. He sings and howls, and prays and swears, in a medley of piety and profanity, more like a fiend than a son of pious parents. Five persons, whose stomachs are overloaded with drink, are retching at the same time. There are forty-five in all. Twenty are charged with drunkenness; ten for thieving; ten for night-walking; and five are boys of the street.

What company for a child of prayer! What a school for a boy who had never before seen a court-room, or visited a prisoner's cell! What processes of hardening go on here! How fast a person may lose his self-respect and manhood! My God! is there no better place than this for the unfortunate children of neglect? O ye philanthropists, awake to the calls of the street-boys! Let every neighborhood form itself into a committee of the whole, to look after them, and give them a helping hand, before they are driven beyond the reach of help and hope.

Now daylight peeps into those cells. Some are a little sobered, and awaking to the awful sense of their condition. Others are still noisy, boisterous, and crazed. Some are crying for drink, drink, drink! as if their very existence depended upon the cooling draught of water. Nine o'clock arrives; and this den of human fiends rattles with the keys of the jailer, and cell after cell is opened, as each culprit's name is called; and a procession is formed of reeking, filthy, abject wretches. They march up the stone stairs, Ned Nevins in the midst, and sit down in the prisoners' dock for examination. The dock is about six feet lower than the court-room floor; so that the prisoners are hid from public view, except such as are called to rise, and take the prisoner's stand for trial. Sometimes a friend of the accused is allowed to look over into the dock to recognize his fellow; but not often. At any rate, there is no sympathizing friend bending over to offer encouragement to Ned Nevins. Such a friend would be as the face of an angel bending over the battlements of heaven. Alas for the poor boy! this is not a court of love and mercy, but of justice.

CHAPTER XII.

MR. BENEDICT'S ARGUMENT WITH SOLOMON LEVI.

"GOOD morning," said Mr. Theophilus Benedict, entering the counting-room of Solomon Levi, the Jew. "Good morning, sir. I have called to solicit aid for a few destitute children. I thought you might like to share in the blessing of aiding them." — "Ah, Mitter Benedict!" replied Solomon, "you come to te wrong place. You hash got into te wrong shop, I guess, heh? I keeps te moneys to let: I no gives tem vay, heh? Where be te profits if I gives te moneys vay, heh?" — "But," said Mr. Benedict, "out of your abundance, you can spare a little for the Lord's poor, and you will lay up treasures in heaven." — "No, not I, Mitter Benedict. I puts my treasures in te iron box, vhere I can gits him vhen I vants him."

"But thieves may steal, or fire consume them," said Mr. Benedict. "You had better make deposits in the Bank of Heaven." — "Ah, Mitter Benedict! I makes no sich 'posits. I risk him in te iron box. I fear te checks on tat bank vhat you speaks of be no goot. I no possible can shave tem: tay no goot wit te brokers. Tay say to me, 'Solomon, vaht ish tat you hash got, heh?' Ten I says, 'I don'ts know, Mynheer. Tay be von of Mitter Benedict's checks on te bank vhat he speaks of.' Ten tay say, 'Tish no goot: te peoples no like tish kind of stocks. Tay no like tish paper. Tay likes te hard moneys.'" — "But somebody must support these famishing, neglected children." — "Yah, yah! let tem go to te poor-house: it be better for tem and me too." "No, Mr. Levi, it is not better for them, nor you either. The State is a hard step-mother. She holds her children with a hard grasp. They do not become affectionate by her embrace." — "Vell, vhat of tat? vhat does I cares for 'fection, heh? If she keeps tem from stealin', tat be enough."

"But, hear me, sir. It is for *your* interest as well as theirs that I speak. A little timely assistance *now* may save you a round sum in taxes *by and by*. Aid a boy now in getting on his feet, or finding a home, and you save the State all future expense. To support a person in the almshouse or jail costs two hundred dollars a year. To continue that support during an ordinary life costs many thousands. To find a good home for a child will not cost twenty dollars. There are as many families wishing to adopt children as there are children to be adopted. Thousands of desolate hearts are praying for an angel to come to them in shape of some dear little orphan. To give this child a home before he becomes vitiated carries a blessing to some childless fireside, and saves the child to the State. In fifty years, the State of Massachusetts has expended about eighteen million dollars for supporting her dependent and criminal classes. Could these classes have been made productive instead of dependent, they would have added to the wealth of the State five times eighteen million. In nine years, the State has expended for juvenile delinquents at Westborough and other places eight hundred and fifty thousand dollars; being on an average of four hundred and ninety-four dollars per head. Supposing that one out of four of these delinquents does really reform, then the cost of actual reforms will be a thousand nine hundred and sixty-seven dollars per head. The State has not wealth enough to reform its culprits at that price." — "Ish tat possible? How te moneys be squandered! Vhy, Mitter Benedict! how tings be conducted, heh?" "Yes, Mr. Levi, there are men in Boston who will give next to nothing in charities, but who pay thousands of dollars a year in taxes to support criminals; and, if they did but know it, nearly all of this tax may be avoided."—"'Voided, voided! did ye say? 'Void taxes? Vhy, Mitter Benedict! ish tar any vay to 'void tese big taxes?"

"There is, Mr. Levi, a way to avoid three-fourths of them."—"Tree-fourts, tree-fourts! did ye say? Vell tat vash goot! Ye be's von goot financier: pray tell how ish tat done, heh?"— "It is done in a way you may little expect."

"Tut, tut, Mitter Benedict! Don't talk 'bout expect! I don't cares a bit how ish be done, only so 'tis done, and te speculation saves my moneys."—"Then I will tell you: it is done by the power of the gospel of our Lord Jesus Christ."—"Oh, out on ye talk! Hang te deceiver! I don't believes tat! No, not a word of it" (scratching his head, and stamping his feet). "Te gospel be von big humbug. Show me von single gospel-cure, I ten talk mit ye."—"Well, Mr. Levi, let me speak of old Puritan times. When these colonies were young, they were governed almost wholly by the precepts of the gospel. Their founders were men of God. Taxes were small, and crimes rare. Rev. Nathaniel Ward wrote, that he lived twelve years among them, and saw no drunkard, and heard but one oath. Now oaths are as frequent as the ticking of the clock, and drunkards as numerous as an army of rebels."

"But your gospel makes bigots, and hangs witches," said the Jew.

"True, there may have been some over-zealous ones who have resorted to the uncharitableness of barbarism to promote their ends. But this belongs to the age of barbarism rather than to the gospel itself. Now, sir, let me tell you a little about that gospel which you so much despise and hate. The gospel makes honest men and worthy citizens; it protects life and limb, enhances the price of property, reduces taxes, makes the pauper a supporter of himself and six; turns breweries into bakeries, gaming-houses into prayer-rooms, brothels into family sanctuaries; makes the desert of poverty be glad, and the wilderness to blossom as the rose. It is better than all police institutions for reforming culprits and preventing crime. Law and policemen make eye-servants; but the gospel changes the heart, and reforms the character and life.

Oh, what a glorious instrument for overturning the iniquity of the world! Let every policeman try it, every magistrate judge by its decisions, every politician abide by its precepts, every family altar be dedicated to its service, every child trained to its instruction, every mother guided by its spirit, every father consecrated upon its altar, and where would be the culprits, the poor-houses, the jails, the arsenals? and where the need of the thousands of watchmen to protect our dwellings?"—"Vell, tat ish true; but so it would be if men would obey to law of Moses," replied the Jew.

"No, sir! life and immortality are fully revealed only in the gospel, and through our Lord Jesus Christ. The law of Moses never taught the art of free government, liberty, equality, fraternity, and the individual nobility of man. It was not a promoter of universal education, and of the arts and the sciences. It had no power to change the heart: no law has power to change the heart. Law may demand the penalty,—an eye for an eye, tooth for tooth, burning for burning; but the heart may still remain unchanged. Restitution will not change the heart: the thief may restore the five dollars which he has stolen, and still be a thief. Repentance will not change the heart: a man may repent, and still remain unconverted, unregenerate. Nothing but the spirit of Christ, through the blood of the atonement, can change the heart. Christ only can do the work; and he is able to save to the uttermost,—a dying thief, a wicked Manasseh, a treacherous Judas,—save to the very ends of the earth all that will come unto him. Hail, holy Jesus, Son of God, Prince of peace, King of kings, Lord of lords! let the whole earth submit to thy reign, let kings and potentates bow to thee! and all hearts adore thee! Let the mountain of the Lord's house be established upon the tops of the mountains, and let all nations come unto it."— "Tut, tut, tut!" said the Jew, "your gospel make von big set of hypocrites."

"Yes," said Mr. Benedict, "all good currency will have its counterfeit. One out of twelve may be spurious, but the other eleven-twelfths shall be the salt of the earth. Yes, sir! the gospel that, with a few poor unlettered fishermen as its apostles, could overturn the religion of the whole Roman Empire,— a religion supported by imperial authority, by poets and philosophers the most noted of any age or clime, and by the customs of a thousand years; the gospel that could overturn such a religion, rooted so deeply in the hearts of all classes, and sanctioned by so long usage, and upheld so firmly by the imperial power,— that gospel can yet overturn the imperial power of sin, dry up the fountains of iniquity, bid the captive of lust and appetite go free, and restore Boston, the once Puritan Boston, to its primeval state; when no drunkard shall be found in all its borders, no profane swearer be heard in its streets." — "Tush, Mitter Benedict! avay vit ye prophecy! Stick to te facts. Tell me vhat goot te gospel now be to Boston, heh! How much money does him bring to Boston, heh? How much sin does him stop, heh?"

"Very well, let me tell you, Mr. Levi, Boston owes its prosperity to the gospel. Religion promotes honesty, honesty begets confidence, and confidence is the soul of trade. By winning public confidence, Boston has become the second city in wealth on the continent. The gospel makes the gambler throw away his cards, the drunkard his cups, the miser his avarice, the thief his propensity for stealing, and the trader his tricks of deceit."—"Vell, vell! avay mit yer teories; let us have te facts. Who be te persons made bitter by yer gospel, heh?"

"You and I are made better by it. If you were born in heathendom, your property would be unsafe; and you would not have the respect for moral virtue that you do now."—"Yes; but who has been converted by it? who be regenerated? vhat ye call it?"

"Well, I will tell you. There is a man living on the same street with you who was taken from the jail, while his family was supported by charity, and brought to the church of God. He is now converted, is an honest man, and earns fifteen dollars a week; so the gospel saves to the State the support of him and his family, and adds to the public wealth the amount of his wages besides." — "Vell, tat be goot, tat be von goot gospel. Be tar any more such converts, heh?"

"Yes, there are scores of such, and hundreds of less flagrant cases reclaimed by the churches, missions, and sabbath schools, of Boston. And, what is a hundred times better than all this, there are thousands and tens of thousands of persons prevented from the first step in crime by these institutions. It is hard to stop sliding in the middle of the hill: you must not start, or you must go to the bottom. That which prevents starting in a career of vice is the most useful. Though the gospel may reclaim ten thousand persons from the error of their ways, yet double that number uncontaminated, who have been prevented from entering into vice, have the greater reason to rejoice at the gospel's power."

CHAPTER XIII.

COURT-SCENE. — NED'S TRIAL AND NARROW ESCAPE.

THE court is called, and Edward Nevins stands on the upper step of the prisoners' dock. His head reaches just above the railing. He sees a court-room full of staring eyes; but no eye is looking kindly towards him. Behind him, down in the dock, are some forty prisoners awaiting trial; some of them still under the influence of strong drink; some with blackened eyes and bruised faces; most of them are the refuse and offscourings of the city. Ned is also in no plight to win favor or gain sympathy. His head is aching and whirling with the loss of sleep, and crazed with excitement. He was arrested in his ragged clothes: his knotty hair stands on end, his eyes are wild and glaring, his face sooty, and his whole appearance forbidding in the extreme.

Some of the spectators whisper, "There is a young rogue; you can see the mischief in his eye." Ned's chances of escape appear rather slim. To his right are the friends of the criminals, awaiting the calling of the prisoners' names, so as to intercede for them. But there is no kind intercessor for Ned Nevins,—no sister to tell the story of the plot laid against him, no father to give bail to court for his good behavior, no weeping mother to pawn the tattered clothing from her back to pay his fine. His mother was dying in Orange Lane: she could not relieve him. He stands alone to vindicate his innocence against the machinations of old Mag Murphy.

Ned was but a poor newsboy. What chance has he for mercy, or even justice? Before him are seated the judge and his clerk; the centre of the hall is filled by lawyers, conversing about their various clients; but a penniless street-boy, having no money to fee them, is too small an object to arrest their attention: therefore his case will probably be hurried through as soon as possible. The clerk rises, with a warrant in one hand, and a pen in the other. The pen is just filled with ink, ready to write the sentence in a moment; for the cases are many, and matters must be hurried up. He evidently thinks the boy had better plead guilty at once to save time, and be sent off to the Island immediately; for his forbidding looks condemn him.

He said, "Edward Nevins, you are charged with three counts: first, for being idle and disorderly; second, for stealing a sled belonging to one David Nelson; and, third, for an assault upon Patrick Murphy." Now the clerk looks at the boy, then puts his pen to the document, as if to write the sentence, even before it be pronounced by the judge: for he knows by long experience what to write if the boy says "guilty," as most likely he will; for what does he know about court-rules? He has been taught confession from his infancy, and learned it in his catechism, and has practised it continually towards God and his mother. Why not confess now, and let the court have an easy time of it? He will get off quicker, if not better. Then it is so easy to write on the document, "Sentenced this day, to House of Correction or Industry or Reform-School or School-Ship, for six months, or two years, or during minority. It is only for the boy to say "guilty," as he has said a thousand times to his mother; and the thing is done.

The clerk said to Ned, with his pen touching the warrant, "Are you guilty, or not guilty?" And, to his great astonishment, the little culprit had the audacity to say, "Not guilty." The clerk, with wondering eyes, looked towards the prisoner, thinking he must have misunderstood him, and repeated the question; but the boy answered firmly, "Not guilty." Alas for the poor salaried clerk! The boy was resolved to assert his rights. The document fell from the clerk's hands; his pen of ink was lost! He had to proceed to trial before recording sentence.

He said, "Let the following witnesses be called, — Patrick Kelly, David Nelson, Margaret Murphy, and Patrick Murphy. Hold up your right hands. Do you severally solemnly swear that the evidence you shall give to this court be the truth, the whole truth, and nothing but the truth, — so help you God? As many of you as are Catholics, kiss this Bible. Mr. Kelly, please state to the court what you know concerning the prisoner at the bar."

Now, Kelly was a little "over the bay;" therefore he exhibited a trifle more of the *naïveté* than he intended. "If it plase yer 'onor," said Kelly, "I knows nuthin' good of him. He is in the strate most of the time. He has no father, an' the boys be pickin' at him all the time. I think he would be better off at the Island; then the boys wouldn't have no one to fall a-foul on."

"Do you know who's to blame?" said the judge, "he or the boys?"

"Well, sir, if it plase yer 'onor, I suppose the

boys be to blame; for they pitch into him so, 'cause he has no father to protect him, and 'cause his mother be a bad woman what keeps a bad house."

"*She ain't a bad woman!*" cried Ned, at the top of his voice, his eyes rolling, his muscles twitching, and his whole frame giving signs of tremendous excitement. "She ain't a bad woman; and he that says she be a bad woman lies; and *I will tell him so to his face!*"

"Hush, hush, my boy!" said the judge, in gentle tones, becoming more and more interested in the case. "Keep still, my lad. You shall have a fair trial, and you shall be allowed by and by to speak for yourself." Then, turning to the policeman, he said, "Why don't you arrest the boys, instead of Edward Nevins?"

"Well, sir, yer 'onor, there be so many on 'em, I should have the whole neighborhood down on me; and I should be in danger of *my own dear life.* So I think it best to quiet 'em by seizing on the weakest, and gitting him out of the way."

"Well, what about the sled?" asked the judge. "Oh, sir! yer 'onor, I knows nuthin' at all, at all about that, 'cept what these are folks says; and, as to the fightin', I didn't see when it commenced, nor who is to blame." The judge said, "That will do; let David Nelson be called. "Mr. Nelson, do you recognize that sled as your property?" inquired the judge, after the sled had been shown him by Kelly. "I do, your honor. It was stolen from one of the boys, while delivering his basket of provisions from my store." — "Do you know any thing about the prisoner at the bar?" said the judge; "any thing that would tend to criminate him?" — "No, your honor: I have no recollection of him whatever." — "Let Margaret Murphy take the witness-stand. Now, Margaret, tell the court what you know concerning the prisoner at the bar." — "An' may it plase yer 'onor," says old Mag, "I knows much about him, the dreadful crathur, — more than I wants to know about him. He be a stalin' and lyin' and fightin' all the blissid time. He says I stole, an' Pat stole; an' he struck Pat, an' grabbed him by the throat, and fisted him: an' I thought, on my soul, he would kill him, poor Patrick, my dare, darlin' boy! There he ba, yer 'onor, almost did, poor darlin' boy! Oh, dear, oh, dear! Boo, hoo, hoo!" and her fat sides shook, and her rum-blotched cheeks glowed with passion, and she felt for her handkerchief to wipe away her crocodile-tears; for she had an object in getting Ned sent away. She had another suit in court, at which he was to be a witness; besides, this affair of the meat and sled might turn out to her serious disadvantage if Ned be acquitted.

Patrick Murphy is called. "Patrick, tell the court how the quarrel commenced," said the judge. "An' may it plase yer 'onor," said Pat, "I seed Ned Nevins comin' near my house with a slid an' a basket of coal. I knowed he stole the slid, so I told him so." — "How did you know?" said the judge. "I knowed it belonged to Mr. Nelson, the provision-man. "How did you know that?" asked the judge quickly. "'Cause I had seen it at his store, and knowed he had lost it." — "How did you know he had lost it?" — "'Cause, sir, yer 'onor, I seed his boy go along with it, playin' with his dog; then I seed him come back, an' say he had lost it." — "Didn't you steal it?" asked the judge sternly. "No, sir! I didn't." Then old Mag sprang upon her feet in a great fluster, and said, "*No, sir! yer 'onor, no! Niver a bit ov a slid did he iver stale! No, niver, niver!* He ba one of the bist of boys that iver lived: yis, he ba! He wouldn't stale a copper! No, sir! he wouldn't!" — "Sit down, Margaret," said the court. "We are questioning your *son*, not you." She sat down in terrible agitation, stamping her foot, shaking her fist, wiping her face, and declaring that they were trying to ruin her poor innocent boy. "Now,

Patrick," said the judge, "Didn't you cut that name on the bottom of the sled?" — "Well, sir, if I did, I didn't stale it," says Pat. "Then you acknowledge that you did cut it, do you?" — "*No, sir!*" said old Mag, jumping up, and shaking her clinched hand in Pat's face with the gesticulations of a fury, — "no, sir! yer 'onor. He niver didn't do no sich a thing!" Then rolling her owlish eyes at Pat, and puffing and wheezing, — "Let the police take that woman into custody for contempt of court," interrupted the judge. "Now, Patrick," he continued, "let me see your jack-knife." Then looking at it, and pointing to the blade, "I observe that the point of this blade is gone. How did you break that knife? Is not that the point in that sled, where you cut the name?" — "Yis, sir, I cut the name; but I didn't stale the slid." — "Well," said the judge, "that is enough for the present. You may sit down."

Then the judge said, turning to Ned, "Now, Edward, you can state to the court what means you have for getting a living, and why you should not be sent to one of the public institutions. It is evident that you did not steal the sled; but are you idle and disorderly in the streets?"

Poor Ned! He was in a hard place. He didn't

know how to commence to address a court: he didn't know what to say, he was so sick and dizzy and frightened; but, with a faltering voice, he began, "I be, sir, Mr. Judge, a poor fatherless boy. My mother be long sick. I don't know but she be dead since yesterday. I thought I seed her spirit come to my cell last night, and look at me; then she turned away, and wouldn't speak to me. Then I cried 'cause mother wouldn't speak to me, nor kiss me, 'cause I was so wicked. Then I thought it couldn't be my mother; for she would speak to me, and weep for me, and pray for me, when I had been naughty; and she would forgive me. She used to say, 'I will forgive you, my darling, now go to sleep;'. then she used to tuck me up warm, and kiss me, and say, 'Good night, Eddie; I hope Eddie will sleep good.' But I couldn't sleep last night; no, I couldn't sleep in that dreadful place."

"That is not the question, my lad," said the judge, interrupting him: "I want to know what you do for a living." — "Well, sir, I picks coal in the mornin', and sell papers in the evenin'; and sometimes I carries out baskets for a provision-man. I ain't idle, and I don't fight. My mother says, 'If I do no wrong, somethin' good will come to me.' I earns a dollar some days; and I picks up sticks and coal enough for all my mother's fires." — "Don't you go the theatre, and spend your money?"

"No, sir! I never went to the theatre in my life. I goes nowhere but to work and to bed."

"Don't you go to school?" — "Yes, sir: I forgits that. I goes four nights a week to Franklin night-school."

"What do you learn there?" — "I reads and spells, and writes and ciphers, and studies gography; and sometimes, when the city men comes to see us, I speaks pieces."

"Why don't you want to go to the Island, or to Westborough?" — "'Cause, sir, there be bad boys there. I shall learn bad things, and I don't want the name of it. Mother says I must be 'spectable, and keep a good name; then folks will trust me, and help me, and love me. I fear, if she knows that I have been in jail, she will die: she will think I have been bad, when I ain't."

Then the judge turned to the assembly, and asked, "Is Uncle Cook in the room?"

Now, Uncle Cook is chaplain of the jail, and guardian of all boys who are discharged on probation from the police court.

"Uncle Cook," said the judge, "here is a boy too innocent to be arrested, too proud to go to the poor-house, too self-reliant for a charity-school, too noble-spirited to beg, and ashamed to be mean. Please take his name and residence, and have him report himself to you once a week for the next three months; and I will put him on probation for that time. If he gets into another difficulty, report him to the court. I believe that boy is yet to make his mark in the world."

Then Uncle Cook and the officers and lawyers gave him some money to set him up with papers; and Mr. David Nelson bade him call at his store, and promised to give him employment part of the time. (Little did Mr. Nelson think who the boy was that he was inviting to his house.)

Upon gaining the street, Ned thanked God from the lowest depths of his heart. Tears of gratitude rolled down his cheeks. Purchasing his papers, he started for home, crying, "Here's the Heral', Jirnil, Trav'ler, 'Ranscrip'," with a voice made sweeter by the sorrows through which he had passed.

CHAPTER XIV.

SOLOMON LEVI AND DAVID NELSON.

"NOW, Mr. Levi, how can we settle?" said David Nelson, sitting in a private room in the Parker House, whither they had retired to take some refreshments, and to adjust their accounts. Mr. Nelson was a grocer and provision-dealer. Solomon Levi was a clothier and a broker. The boys called him "Old Sol."

"Settle!" said Sol, seizing a glass of lager-beer. "I tink our accounts vash 'bout even, von for von. I clothes your family, and ye's feeds mine. Vhat tink you, Mr. Nelson?" lifting his glass to his lips with a patronizing smile. "I think it's hard times," said Mr. Nelson, "and I've got to shave mighty close this year." — "Shave close? Yah, yah!" said Sol. "Shave close! I guess ye's been shaving mighty close tese 'ere ten year, heh? Vhat a pile of stocks ye's got! heh?" "Yes," said Mr. Nelson; "the Lord has prospered me somewhat." — "Tut, tut, tut!" said Sol; "don't say ish be te Lord; more like ish be von devil, vhat help ye, heh? Ye made yer pile by short veights, I guess, a little. Didn't ye? Yah, yah!"

"Well, never mind that," said Mr. Nelson; "let us resume our business. You say that I must *feed* your family, and you *clothe* mine, do you? What a loose way of doing business! Besides, I have only one to clothe in your line, and you have ten to feed! Oh, fiddle-sticks! Which side be the devil on in such a case?"

Here they were interrupted by a rap at the door. "Come in," said Sol; when the door opened, and in came Bill Bowlegs, Sol's overseer of needle-work, — a large, two-fisted, coarse-grained, mink-eyed, hobbling Anakim. "Here, Mr. Levi, is the account you ordered me to bring," said Bill, cringingly handing him a paper. "Very vell, Bill. I vash engaged at dis time. You can go for de present," pointing to the door. So Bill swung his swaggering frame out of the room. His locomotion was not the best. His legs seemed to have been bent by a superabundant weight upon them in early life; but his savage manners, his hard heart, his cruelty to inferiors, and his fawning obsequiousness towards superiors, made him a fit tool for Old Sol to elect chief of staff in his war on the female constitution.

"There," said Sol, "tat be von man tat ish vorth his veight in gold! See vhat an eye he hash got, heh? De Yankee gals no cheat him, no how. He see de slack vork and de loose stitches as far as de hawk see von chicken. Tay don't pull te vool over his eyes; tay don't come it over him wit tar tears and sobs. He goes for makin' moneys. Yes, sar: he make ye have von big pile of moneys,—gold moneys, silver moneys, and tousand-dollar greenbacks, heh?"

"But he's not cruel to the poor girls, is he?" said Mr. Nelson. "Tut, tut!" said the Jew, jocosely. "None of yer pious cant, none of yer meetin' talk. He hash to be cruel, or ve makes no moneys. He is von big voman-killer. He sees, vhen te blue comes under te eye, and tay coughs, and te blood comes from te lungs, and tay be pale and sick, tat tay don't draw te stitches tight. Ten he rap te table, and stamps his foot (here the Jew acted the part in comic imitation); ten he look at te vork, and scowl jist as if he be mad; ten he tear te stitches; ten he look at te voman vith tat big black eye of his, tat lightnin'-flash, and he transfer te stitches of tat vork right to her side, so tat she die. He hash killed more vomen in Boston tan te var hash men of Boston."

"Oh the wretch!" said Mr. Nelson: "he's

murdered them!"—"Vel, no; not quite so bat as tat: he not 'sactly murthered tem, but killed tem by inches,—stitched tem to death."—"But," said Mr. Nelson, "they were not obliged to work for him."—"Vel, no; tays not 'sactly obleeged to vork: but you see tay hash to vork or starve; and starvin ish not te most pleasantest ting for te stomach, you know: so tay choose to vork rather tan starve."

"Starve in Boston! good heavens! is it possible?"—"Hush, hush, David! don't get excited. You see tar be so many vomen clamoring for vork, dat ve give 'em just vhat ve please, say about von-fourth vhat te Government give us for te vork; den ve just pocket te other tree-fourts, and tats vhat make us contractors te rich nabobs on State Street, heh?"—"And is there no remedy?"—"Vel, yah! tar ish two remedy: von ish for te vomen to vork in te kitchen, and te other be for tem to sell tar virtue for hire. But you see te Yankee gal ish too proud to do te housework, and she be too virtuous to sell herself for te moneys. By te powers of Moses! how she hold on to her principles, heh? Not all te gold in te mint will purchase te virtue of some of tese Yankee gals."

"Very well," said Mr. Nelson, "is not pride of character helpful to moral sentiment?"—"Hush,

hush yer preachin! don't talk of sentiment. I talks about moneys, tats all; moneys, sar, nothin' but moneys! does ye hear?" — "Well, then, let us take a financial view of the matter," said Mr. Nelson. "If these women are too proud to beg, and too high-minded to go to the poorhouse, then the State saves by their pride half a million of dollars a year; and you don't have to pay taxes for them." — "Vel, yah! tat ish sound reason, tat vas goot; pride be von goot ting, yah, yah!" — "Now," continued Mr. Nelson, "you say they might save themselves by selling their virtue; but would they live longer by a vicious life than by a virtuous one? Does not vice kill more than double the number that the needle does, after all?" — "Vel, I suppose so; but ten it be sorter pleasanter to be flattered up a leetle, and dress fine, and all tat." — "Ah, sir! but what of the hereafter? what of?" — "Hush, hush! didn't I tell ye none of yer preachin'? I be von Sadducee. I believes in neither angel nor spirit; I be von Jew, sir; I loves moneys. You has yer steeples and meetins' and Sundays. I has von Got, and von Sabbath; and tat ish enough for me."

Now they were interrupted by another knock at the door, when in came a rum-crimsoned Irishwoman, with an old shawl over her head, her arms almost bare, with both hands extended and held together, begging for alms. How she got by the porters in the hall is a mystery. "Plase, seer, will ye ba so keend as to give a poor lone woman a cint? I 'as had nuthin' to ate; I ba starvin', seer. I 'as put nuthin' betwane these ere dyin' lips all this ere blissid livelong day" (then wiping her lips, for she had just been eating), — "jist a cint, only a cint, seer; plase give me a cint, an' may all the saints be arter blissin' ye for helpin' a poor sick crather! and may ye niver ba poor!"—"Away from this door!" cried a porter, who was passing that way. "Go down stairs! How came you here? Haven't you been fed half a dozen times to-day? You are half drunk now. Down with you!"

"See there!" said Nelson. "Now judge ye which deserves the most sympathy, — the honest needlewoman, too proud to beg and too honest to deceive, or these foreign paupers, crowding our streets, and teaching their progeny nothing but deceit and lies. Europe has emptied herself of her scum and filth, and her foul stomach has vomited them to our shores. Look at the children of France! one out of every thirteen are illegitimate; look at England's lower classes! one out of six a pauper; look at Italy's beggars!—and will you sneer at the pride and virtue of American women, the soul of our independence, and the glory of our race? God forbid, sir!"—"Oh, no!" said the Jew; "I loves virtue, I loves independence; and I don't love to pay taxes: therefore, I must say, America be von goot country."

At this juncture, Mr. Benedict came in. "Gentlemen," he said, "I have come to solicit your aid for a benevolent object: I know you must approve of it."

"Yah!" said the Jew. "You came to see Mr. Nelson, I guess, heh? Tat be te gentleman: he's been just preachin to me some of tis doctrine, he's te man."

"But," said Nelson, "if you have come after money, Mr. Levi is the man: he has the golden pile, and more than he can spend in a lifetime." "No!" said the Jew,—"no, I's not! I be von poor man: ish be Mr. Nelson vhat ye vant."

At this cool reception, Mr. Benedict left, without stating his object, feeling that gifts of charity from such men would not bless the giver; for God loveth the cheerful giver. These were not the men to be a blessing to the world for elevating their race.

"Now, David," said the Jew, "as you seem to have a leetle touch of te pious, where do you go to church?"—"Nowhere," said Nelson, his face coloring. "Nowhere! ha, ha! I guess ye does, or ye vouldn't talk pious in tis strain." — " Well," said Mr. Nelson, " I hire a seat for my wife ; but I seldom go myself, except to the colored church at the West End. The churches are so cold and formal, and the colored people so earnest and devotional, that I often go and listen to them. In fact " (looking up, and putting his hand on his breast), " I have often thought to ask them to pray for me ; for I am such a sinner."

"Yah, yah! You be a sinner, heh? Vel, I guess ye vas. I tought someting ailed ye; come, cheer up, and take a little more brandy." — " No, I can't now ; I have something here that liquor can't wash out." — " By Moses and all te prophets! if ye ain't jist ready to become a Metodist or a Millerite ! Vhy, vhat's te matter, David ? " — " Well, to tell the truth," said David, " I'm not situated the best in the world." — ' Vhy, ye ain't goin' to sign over, and burst up, be's ye ? " — " No, not that." — " Lost childers ? " — " No." — " Lost property ? " — " No." — " Wife sick ? " — No, she's not exactly sick ; but " —

" Ah ! now I has got ye : she be cross, and scold, heh ? Yah, yah! tat it ? " — " Well, I haven't done just right in my life " — " Haven't ye ? Vhy, ye haven't murdered nobody, has ye?"—"No, not exactly murdered, but coming plaguy near to it: truth is, I didn't marry the woman I was promised to."—"Oh, tush! vhat of tat? Tis voman bring ye von big pile of moneys, didn't she?"—"Yes, she had money enough; but"—"Tush, tush! ye's got von goot home, and von goot wife, and all te goot tings required in tis life. She be virtuous, be she?"

"Yes, she is virtuous; that is, if there be any virtue in making a man a perfect slave. Oh, what a lot I have had! what a slave I have been! what a fool in my choice! There is the girl of my first love, that amiable little angel, all love and all mercy, making poverty itself a paradise, whose heart I broke when I made her promise never to show her face to me again, if I would but leave a legacy for her boy. Ah, poor girl! her shadow is ever on my track, her image ever before me. Whenever I see a woman veiled and crushed, ashamed to show her face, walking these back and by streets, I think of her and her cruel fate. I am haunted, God is angry, hell is gaping, fiends are sporting over my doom. Life is a burden, death would be a relief" (here the Jew strove to interrupt him, but Nelson continued), "unless I can be rid of this torture, this undying sting, this burning shame that palsies my faculties, poisons my soul, and blights my hopes. Gold is nothing: all the gold in the world could purchase but an Aceldama of blood. O conscience, thou stern avenger! I feel thy tightening cord around my neck; and like a penitent Judas, throwing the accursed silver at Jewish feet, I seize the rope, and, bidding farewell to earth, swing in mid air between hope and despair, heaven and hell! Angels, pity me!" he said, rising to his feet, and thrusting his hands to his neck as one in delirium-tremens, striving to tear away the tightening noose of an imaginary cord that choked his utterance.

CHAPTER XV.

DEATH OF NED'S MOTHER, IN ORANGE LANE.

MORNING came. Mrs. Nevins had been refreshed by sleep. The delirium of the opiates had passed, and she upbraided herself for giving way to despondency. Had not God promised to be the widow's God, and a father to the fatherless? Had he ever failed her? Was he not a present help in time of trouble? Could she despair? True, she had lost her boy; he was never absent from her a night before: but new trials must awaken new trusts, and elicit new endeavors. With an iron will and firm faith, she leaned all the weight of her soul on God in prayer, and went to sleep. After this, she was so much strengthened, that she thought to sit up in her bed, and finish the last pair of drawers hanging on the chair. Foolish thought! she was too near her grave. Yet, rallying her expiring energies, she threw her old shawl over her shoulders, and, procuring some tea of an Irishwoman, she began to sew. The stitches went hard, her brain whirled, her eyes darkened, and she fell back on her bed for a moment; then, taking a little more tea to give her strength, she tried again.

At this moment, the rent agent came in to collect the week's rent. "O sir!" she cried, " you have come one day too soon. What shall I do? how can I get the money?" — "I don't know," he said: " that is your look-out, not mine. I must have it, and have it to-day." — "Oh, spare me, sir! My boy has been gone all night: he didn't bring me his coppers as usual, and my work is not finished. I tried, sir, yes, indeed I have, this morning I've tried hard to finish it, but have failed. Oh, sir! what can I do?" — "Don't know," said he gruffly; " but I must have it mighty soon, or you leave the house."

At this, she thought of one more relic of happier days in her trunk: so she asked the Irishwoman to pawn it for a dollar, and give it to him; and thus she drove the wolf once more from her door.

Soon the Jew's man, Mr. Bowlegs, came for the sewing-work. "Not done, heh? I thought as much. These 'ere sewin'-women are allers fallin' down on their beds, and givin' up, and sayin' they can't do the work: git up, marm, and let us see your work." Then he seized one garment, and then another; and, finding the stitches of one a little loose, he began to rip it, and then, with a savage jerk, he tore the garment almost from end to end. "Ah, marm! that's the way you do your work, heh?" flashing his keen black eye like lightning.

At this, the poor woman gave a shriek and a cough: her lungs gave way again; the blood came to her lips, and she fainted. How long she lay in that state, whether a day or an hour, she knew not, for she lay in the land of shadows, on the brink of the spirit-world. Finally she opened her eyes for a moment, and gazed towards the window, and stared at the light, then shuddered, and fell back as if shrinking from some hideous object. Perhaps the light of life was hateful to her; but she was a Christian, and ought not to hate any thing God had made. Now Ned Nevins, just returning from the court, came undiscovered into the room. He saw his mother repining and despairing, in an agony of grief. The big tears stole from her sunken eyes, and rolled down her pale cheek: sighs gushed forth, and her bosom heaved with deep emotion. Her ruling passion was strong in death: that passion was the love she had for her absent boy. He saw her lips move; she muttered unintelligible sounds, then, when reviving a little, she mentioned his name. What a sight for the poor persecuted boy! He felt that he was the cause of all this grief. Oh, the anguish of his soul! Could he ever forgive himself for this night's absence?

"O Eddie! my dear, darling boy! Why don't you come, Eddie?" she said. "Your mother is dying: can't I see you before I die? Where can he be?"

Then the noble-hearted boy flew to her side, and stretched his arms over her pillow as if to beat back the shades of death from her brow, and said, "O mother! do not cry. You can see me. Eddie is here: look up, mother! see me! here I am!"

Then she opened her eyes, and stared in bewilderment, as if afraid to trust her senses. There was her boy bending over her pillow, almost palsied and petrified with fright.

"O mother, my dear mother! have I killed you? have I broken your poor heart, mother? I aint guilty, mother; no, I ain't; indeed I ain't. Eddie is as innocent as a lamb. Look up, and believe me, mother!" Then he threw his arms around her neck, and kissed her hollow cheek, and smoothed her pillow, and sighed and sobbed, and longed to die with her; for what were life to him without a mother?

"O Eddie! is it you? Have you come? Where have you been? Why could you leave me? why serve me so?" she said; then looked steadily into his face for reply. Ah! what a look was that for the poor boy! — that kind, upbraiding look; — that look of truth, honesty, justice, love, mercy. He quailed before it, and covered his face for shame. Then he kneeled, and seized hold of her white hand, and kissed it, and cried, "O mother, forgive me this time! forgive me, mother! forgive me before you die! you must forgive me!" then, seizing her hand more tightly, and kissing it again and again, "I shall die, mother, if you don't forgive me!"

"I do forgive you, my child; but pray tell me where you have been?" she said, looking eagerly at him.

"Now, mother," he said in a subdued tone, as if fearing to speak, "you won't blame me, you wont cry if I tell you, will you, mother?"

"I'll try not to, my tender-hearted boy; " but — but — but; " then, giving a deep sigh with her choked utterance she continued: "I fear there is something wrong. Oh! tell me, my boy, and relieve me from this anxious suspense;" and the tears gushed copiously from her eyes. "Tell mother, Eddie, why didn't you come home with the coal, when you knew how much I needed it? I fear you sold it, and squandered the money."

"Oh, no, mother! Eddie wouldn't dare to do

such a thing. I — I — I couldn't come home," said he, stammering. "Ah! my boy, what has happened? where have you been? Mother is afraid you have been wicked."

"No, I ain't been wicked, mother: I been 'bused and persecuted." — "Why, Eddie, dear, tell me! What has befallen you?" The poor boy, trembling in every joint, dropped his head by her side, threw his arm around her emaciated form, and strove to hide his face in her bosom, as he gasped, "O mother, don't let it kill you! Oh! must I tell you, *Eddie was locked up last night?*" — "My God!" she shrieked, clasping her hands, and rising in her bed, and gazing wildly at him, "*has my Eddie been in jail?* Is he disgraced? Is he ruined? O my God! must I drink this cup also? Can I die with the thought that my boy is a criminal? Oh, no, no! It can't be possible. There must be some palliating circumstances. Tell mother all about the matter, my own dear, darling child," clasping him closer to her bosom.

"Well, mother, I met Pat Murphy, and he said I stole that sled; but I didn't care much for that. Then he struck me, and knocked off my hat, and called me hard names. Then I said, 'Let me alone; let me go home to my poor sick mother, for she wants the coal.' Then he laughed at me, and thrust his finger in my face, and sneered, and said, "Your mother, heh? Ha, ha! She's one of 'em! That's so!" Here Ned choked up; he couldn't speak for tears and sobs, he was so completely overwhelmed with feelings of pity and rage. Then straightening up, and wiping his eyes, he burst forth indignantly, "Mother, can you believe that he would dare to do it? He said that you, my mother, was a *bad woman!*"

"Well, my child, what of that? What if he did? Does that make it so?" said Mrs. Nevins, coolly. Then Ned, rising in a rage, replied, "'What of that? what of that?' do you say? Do you think I could look on, and have that done to my mother? No, no, my dear mother! no, never, so long as there was a bone left in these knuckles, and I had power to strike! No, I couldn't: so I gave the great moping lubber what he deserved: yes, I did, and I would do it agin." Then he chafed, and rolled his fiery eyes, and cried and raged for some moments.

"O my child! you should not fight; you have lost every thing, and gained nothing; besides, it is unchristian."

"Unchristian or not, I couldn't see my mother abused, and I wouldn't."

"But you've paid dear for it, I fear."

"Yes, I have, mother; but it may be the last

time that I ever shall have an opportunity to do it for you on earth."

"Well, my child, I forgive you this time: but do be careful in the future; be careful, and govern your passions, and do not fight."

And now, kind reader, the scene changes; one of our characters leaves the stage of action; the hour of departure is at hand.

Mrs. Sophia Nevins requests her boy to kneel by her side while she places her hand upon his head, and utters her last vocal prayer. Death is sealing up the portals of her senses; but the sight of the soul is unobscured. Her boy is to be set afloat on the tide-wave of a great city: the police are watching him with an evil eye. Raising herself in bed, and placing her hands upon his head, she prays: —

"Father of the fatherless: here is the boy thou gavest me; I leave him in thy hands. I asked not for him; but, having received him, thanked thee, and have given my life for his. Love constrained me: I do not repent the sacrifice. He is a lamb, with no shepherd to guide him. The crimes of this city already break in upon his soul, and the suspicious eyes of the watchman mark him as their prey. What but a superhuman power can save him? Be thou, O God! more than a mother. Check his wanderings; forgive his errors.

"He now mounts the giddy wave, and starts on life's fearful voyage alone. A mother's hand hath led him to the shore of youthful responsibility: he embarks on temptation's sea without chart or pilot. Take thou the helm, O God! When storms of persecution rage, may he find a haven in thee! High rolling on the tide of this great city of iniquity, let guardian spirits pilot him over the shoals of deceit and crime. A wandering Ulysses, may he chain himself to the mast of firmness, and stop his ears to the voice of the sirens! Hear a mother's prayer. Save him from a drunkard's doom and a felon's fate. Amen."

Then, turning towards her child, she said, "Child of my prayers, adieu! a long adieu! Weep not for me. Your loss is my gain. I go where the wicked cease from troubling, and the weary are at rest. When the Lord maketh inquisition for blood, he forgetteth not the cry of the humble. Although clouds and darkness are round about him, yet righteousness and judgment are the habitation of his throne. I commit you to his care. I fear you will miss me. Farewell!"

Soon after this, she breathed her last; and Edward Nevins felt for the first time in his life what it was to be an orphan, penniless, friendless, alone, in the house of death. He gazed around the room, and saw the mementoes of her refined taste. There were the pots of faded flowers still standing near the window; and there the few small pictures hanging upon the wall; and there the old trunk, which he would not dare to open at present, containing some little precious memorials; and there was the mother's Bible, a fountain of blessings, a well of consolations, from whose unfailing promises she drew, for her spiritual thirst, waters of unceasing comfort in time of trouble. They all spoke of things that were. He was alone with death.

CHAPTER XVI.

FUNERAL. — NED THE ONLY MOURNER. — APPEAL FOR THE NEEDLEWOMAN.

THE city hearse arrives before a door in Orange Lane. A box is carried out and placed in it, and a single mourner attends the funeral. That mourner is Ned Nevins, following the hearse for a time, then riding upon the seat with the driver. Through the crowded streets the hearse hurries unceremoniously along, passing by a multitude of carriages, omnibuses, cars, and throngs of people; but nobody knew, or apparently cared, what was within, save that lone sentinel-child upon the seat, turning his sad thoughts within, reflecting on the love of her who was gone, and on his own abject and forlorn condition.

Finally the driver condescended to ask him a few questions; and, turning to the boy, he said, "What ailed your mother, my lad?" — "She sewed herself to death, sir." — "Sewed herself to death? Why, what was that for?" — "For me, sir," said the boy, with tears in his eyes. "For you? Couldn't you do any thing for yourself?" — "Yes, sir: but it was too late; she had almost killed herself stitchin' before I knew it." — "Who did she get her work from?" — "From Solomon Levi, the Jew, sir." — "Wouldn't he help her in her need?" — "No, sir: he said that all his sewing-women were about alike, sick and dyin', and he wouldn't help none of them; they'd better all go to the poor-house." — "And wouldn't your mother have been alive now if she had gone to the poor-house?" "I suppose she would; but she said she rather die than go." — "Why?" — "Because it would be disgraceful."—"Had she no friends?"—"She might have had, she said; but she forsook them all for me: so she wore a veil when she went out, and tried to keep close, and wouldn't tell where her folks lived." — "Had you no father?" —"Don't know, sir." Now the tears started afresh; and the boy began to move nervously about, and seemed desirous to change the subject.

Mount-Hope Cemetery is at last reached. They enter the Potter's Field, a place set apart for the burial of the city's poor. Two men are standing, with shovels in hand, waiting for the hearse to arrive: then they pile in the boxes one upon the other; for the trench is already dug, and the coffins were made before the breath had left the body. The work is a mere matter of business with these men: they cannot be expected to feel like other men. Ned felt every jar of the coffin to pierce his soul: he wondered how these men could handle a coffin so roughly. Each grating sound of the box, as it was drawn from the hearse, made him shudder; for there was the only one in the world that ever loved him: she was all tenderness and affection, and he would have her buried with gentle hands.

He saw her placed in the lower tier of the trench; but what was the number of the box, and where to find her again, he could not tell, and will not know till doomsday. Poor child! he had no grave over which to plant the flowers still blooming at home, and moisten them with his tears; no tomb to mark the spot where his dear mother lay. The earth is thrown back and levelled over the coffins as the trench is extended, the front of the boxes left bare until new ones arrive; and thus saint and sinner, the virtuous and the vicious, citizens and strangers, white and black, are inextricably mixed, and the grass made greener from the united dust of their remains. Such is the pauper's funeral, such the orphan's fate, such the needlewoman's end!

Hear, ye inhuman landlords! ye who have grown rich on the life-blood of the poor and neglected; ye who have streets called after your names, and those names a terror to the unfortunate tenants! If there be future retribution for oppressing the Lord's poor, verily you shall drink the dregs of the cup.

Arise, ye needlewomen of America! and demand proper employment and remunerative wages. Come thundering at the door of public opinion and popular prejudice, and say, "Give us a chance for our lives, give us place, give us work, give us wages! If we are fit for places now occupied by men, give us those places: if we can earn as much as men, then give us men's wages!"

Rise, and seize the yard-stick, and drive out every ribbon-monger and tape-seller from behind the counter; drive him from every shop and store where small wares are sold! Arise! seize the composing-stick, set the types, and stand by the writing-desk; drive out the able-bodied men; let them do heavier work. Arise, ye gifted ones! grasp the pen, and join the multitude of your sex in riding on the triumphal car of authorship. Seize the chisel: let the cold, inanimate marble be made to speak, and breathe thoughts big with immortality.

Let another Harriet Hosmer appear with her Zenobia, another Louisa Lander with her Virginia Dare, and another Miss Whitney with her Godiva! Let another Emma Stebbins arise with her statue of Massachusetts' great educator, Horace Mann! Let another Miss Mitchell appear to measure the distances of the fixed stars, and weigh the planets in their courses!

Arise, ye teachers, ye public educators! hold your place in the schoolroom; make yourselves equal to men in your profession; then demand men's wages, or proper remuneration.

Arise, ye operatives of the mill, at the spindle, the loom, the factory, the shop, the store, the counting-room, the printing-office, and every place of female labor! Let there be one general, universal strike for woman's rights. Arise, then, ye who mould the minds of youth; ye who are almost absolute over hearts and homes; ye who sway the sceptre over men's hearts, and play the despot and act the petty tyrant at will; ye whose united pleadings never failed in any revolution; rise! move heaven and earth by your prayers!

Radical changes demand radical efforts. Arise, then, and let superhuman efforts be put forth! Humanity demands it; civilization demands it; Christianity demands it. God Almighty demands that every yoke be broken, and the oppressed go free.

O ye sordid contractors! hear the cry of the wretched and dying, with your vile work still in their hands.

Hark from under the altar the cry of the souls of those who have been martyred by this unnatural system of labor, saying, "How long, O Lord holy and true, dost thou not judge and avenge our blood on them that dwell on the earth?" Up, up, up, ye women of America! Strike for your rights; dash the cup of sorrow from bleeding lips! Elevate the condition, health, and hopes of woman. Up! and give her equal position in labor; up! and make labor honorable as well as remunerative; up! and battle for the right: make woman feel her nobility; let her become self-reliant, heroic, independent, indomitable.

Up! and rouse the conscience of the nation. Let dishonest contractors, revelling in wealth, spending thousands at fashionable watering-places, sailing to Europe, and travelling the world round, on your earnings, feel the stings of an indignant, broken-hearted race. "Upon what meat doth this our Cæsar feed, that he hath grown so great?"

Let the pale consumptive hold up to her destroyers the glittering weapon of her death, that conscience-stinging needle, as one through whose eye the scriptural camel might as easily pass, as for them to think of entering the kingdom of heaven. Let the ghosts of the departed, with bony fingers, bleeding lips, fiery tongues, and glaring eyes, figures of dying consumptives, speak of long-endured wrongs, which, though buried, are never forgotten.

All humanity demands that you act. The coming generation, children yet to be, demand that the mothers of our race be well developed, strong, and vigorous; that they be equal to men, and eligible to every high position. Thousands of women who have no employment demand your action. Ten thousand needlewomen of this city, starving on their scanty pittance, pale, haggard, with skeleton forms, eyes sunken, cheeks blanched and hollow, lungs consuming, sides aching, flesh teeming, filling thousands of graves every year, demand that place be given to woman, and that her labor be remunerative.

Six thousand cyprians, flaunting the streets of Boston and its suburbs, many of whom have been starved to submission, to dishonor and crime, by the unnatural and arbitrary rules of labor, — these degraded, abandoned victims of poverty, oppression, and temptation, demand your help. Their average life is four years.

Fifteen hundred of them die annually, — a long procession, extending hand to hand, reaching more than a mile ; and their ranks in the serried columns of garlanded victims, marching to the sacrificial pyre, are filled by fresh supplies. Fifteen hecatombs of New England's daughters to supply the lustful fires of one city ! Fifteen hundred fair virgins, many of them from vestal fires on mountain, hill, and river side, daughters of parental hope and prayer, coming fresh from the sanctity of their country homes, to be offered on the funeral pyres of intemperance, prostitution, and homicide ! Oh, what a drain of life, and nerve, and virtue, and innocence, and hope, and heaven, to make this horrible sacrifice !

Shudder, ye demons ! howl, ye lost ! Let hell echo back her groans, and death utter shrieks of horror, that Boston, the pious city of the Puritans, the intellectual Colossus, the pioneer of all reforms, the pride of the whole earth, — that she allows the grinding wheels of the Juggernaut of oppression, the crushing heel of Mammon, and the baleful fires of Moloch, to crush, torture, and devour so many of her fair children, right in sight of her schools, her courts, her altars, and under the eaves of her sanctuaries !

Up, ye women of America ! Let your voices

be heard for the oppressed! Tens of thousands of the unfallen fair, now struggling for a livelihood, demand your aid. An ounce of prevention now is worth a thousand pounds of cure. Oh, awake, awake!

CHAPTER XVII.

NED A NIGHT IN THE STREET. — VISION OF HIS MOTHER.

"HERE'S the Heral', Jirnil', Trav'ler, 'Ranscrip', five 'clock, last 'dition,'" never sounded from newsboy's lips in more melancholy strains than from those of Ned Nevins on returning from his mother's funeral. He stood at the corners of the streets, crying his papers in such piteous tones of despondency as must compel the stones to cry out, and the angels to weep; yet he found but few purchasers. What did the jostling crowd care for the cries of a ragged street-boy? Who knew whether he were an honest boy, or a thief? Who would take the trouble to inquire into his condition? What were his wants? what his conflicts? what sorrows had broken his young heart? Away with such thoughts! He was but a coal-picker, a newsboy, an orphan. There was no kind-hearted Mr. Benedict to look into his case: that gentleman is too busy on his other objects of charity; he may never cross his track again. Night is coming on; but gloom thicker than night gathers round him. His papers are not sold. He dare not go home: he has a superstitious dread of sleeping in the room and on the bed where his mother died. Blacker than darkness itself seemed his prospect. Trembling, shivering, too horrified to weep, and too high-minded to beg, he still cries in piteous strains, "Here's the Heral', Jirnil, Trav'ler, 'Ranscrip', five 'clock, last "dition; but his pitiful voice, echoing back from walls of brick and hearts of stone, awakens but little response.

Hunger and excitement are at last doing their work. Dizzy blackness overshadows his brow; his brain reels; the houses seem whirling round his head. He faints, and falls upon the hard, cold stones of the sidewalk. The fit is but for a moment, however: with a strong will he rallies; for he fears the police may be on his track, and take him to the lock-up, or send him to the Island: then farewell to all his hopes; he can never visit his home again. But he rises in a minute, and scrabbles up his papers, and looks around to see if still he is free; if there be no police coming to take him; and if, when the dread of death is passed, he may yet visit the sad memorials of his lamented mother, and read her old Bible in Orange Lane. Not to attract the police by the eager gaze of the crowd, he musters up his courage, and starts off, crying, "Here's the Heral', Jirnil, Trav'ler, 'Ranscrip', five 'clock, last 'dition," but in a subdued, broken tone, that told too well the afflicting sorrows of a motherless, friendless child.

The stars are peeping out on the placid waters of Boston Harbor. The vast forests of shipping, representing every nation and every clime, are still as death, save the mournful whistle of the wind through the cordage, and the low murmuring ripples of the waves that warble to the sleeping crews requiems of peace to their slumbers. The wholesale-business parts of the city are emptied of their population. The surging tide of human beings ebbing and flowing — tides that roll in with the sun, and go out with the sun — has receded; only now and then a single team, or a single footstep, is heard on the pavement. The great stone warehouses, with all their treasures from India, are closed; their fronts, with cold sculptured bas-reliefs, have no sympathy for the poor: they stand frowning on an orphan shivering at their doors. Gladly would Ned rest his weary limbs beneath their cold steps, or in some old cart by the forbidden stable; but he has no blanket, and the weather is cold.

Looking at the stars as his only comforters, he

passes up State Street, by the banking-houses, where fortunes are made and lost in an hour by the fate of war, or the price of gold; but now all is silent and dark, save where, by the dim light, the private watchman is guarding the vaulted millions. Ah, how acceptable to him would be a few shillings of that hoarded treasure! But he must not covet nor complain. Sadly and lonely he wends his weary way to the court-house, and seats himself upon the cold stone steps of that modern bastile. What a chill comes over him when recollecting the night once spent in the Tombs below! How coolly is justice meted out here! Colder than the rock on which he sits, already freezing his garments to its side, is the very place of justice. What tears have been shed over these steps! what sighs and groans, that have made the welkin ring! What sinking hearts have passed over them, never to come out with hope! What sad partings have been witnessed here! How many a youth has learned here, for the first time, the appalling nature of crime, when it was too late! How many have been crushed forever by too severe a sentence on the first slight offence! Within is the judgment-seat. Before this seat, forty persons often appear in a day, two hundred a week, ten thousand a year. What a multitude for little Suffolk County!

Just over there is Judge Ames's office, where boys are sentenced to the School-ship, and from thence to the sea, never perhaps to return. Here is the room where broken-hearted wives, becoming insane, are sentenced to the asylum; and here is the court of the truant-officers, where truant and vagrant boys are disposed of, and sent to the various institutions.

By and by the Black Maria will appear with its midnight freight. Oh, what horror the thought of it brings to Ned! recollections of his one night's ride appal him. He would not see it: the sight of it is too dreadful. He must flee; the police may espy him brooding over these cold steps; he must escape; and away he goes.

It is half-past eleven o'clock: the crowds from the theatres are coming out, and filling the sidewalks. "Here's the Heral', Jirnil, Trav'ler, 'Ranscrip'. Paper, sir? half-price, only two cents! Paper, sir? last edition. Paper, sir?" but no response.

What crowds attend these theatres! and how few attend a prayer-meeting, or even the preaching on the sabbath, in Boston!

Greater crowds are found in the two thousand drinking-saloons, even on the sabbath, than are found in the churches. What harvests those saloons are reaping! How many families are made desolate! And these gambling hells! See, there! a fight at the door of one of them; a man is shot. The police comes, and take the parties to the station-house.

Ned now stands at the doors of the dance-halls in North Street. As the blotched and jaded wretches come pouring out, and reel towards their homes, staggering out of hall after hall, filling the streets with howls and hoots, what a picture of hell! The faithful boy plies his calling, however, and cries, "Here's the Heral'! Paper, sir? half-price, only one cent! Paper, sir?" But who is there among these degraded beings that would read a paper at that late hour? Baffled in his last hope, the poor boy travels back again, like a spirit doomed, finding no rest for the soles of his feet.

It is the dead of night. The bell of the Old South strikes one; and the bells of Hollis Street and Castle Street answer the sound — "ding, dong" — like a funeral knell. Silence reigns. Now is the time for burglars and incendiaries. Spirits of evil roam the earth, and now is the time for Ned's temptation. Cold, hungry, and fatigued, with nerves weak, and no protector, he may seem an easy prey.

An angel appeared to the boy, — an angel of

darkness, in human shape. Coming behind the boy, he said, in mournful tones, "Pity me, young lad; hear the tale of my woe." Ned started up to see if there were any in the world more to be pitied than himself. The tempter continued, "Listen to my complaint. Like you, I am an exile and a wanderer. I have no rest day nor night; I roam these streets with unblessed feet, a deserter from truth. I am doomed to expiate my crimes by banishment from hope." Here Ned began to suspect that all was not right. But the tempter continued, "I am more sinned against than sinning. The world owes me a living; that living I must have; and the world owes you a living. Why do you pine and starve in the streets? See, these narrow windows! A boy of your size can enter there! See that water-spout! you could climb that: it is the ladder to wealth; untold treasures lie before you. Look at this watch, and this purse of gold! Look at this match! strike that match, and, by the throne of Lucifer, you have a fortune!"

He was about to proceed further, but Ned could not entertain the first idea of crime: he closed his ears, and turned and ran away. He ran until out of breath; and, for a long time, he dare not look back, the shape and sound of the terrible tempter so horrified his soul.

He stopped not until he arrived on the coal-dump at the ocean side, where his mother used to meet him, and help him carry home his basket of coal. Would she not again pity him on that lone strand? His sorrows were great: none but a mother could feel his grief. He turned towards the sky, and saw one particular star looking down upon him. He gazed upon its twinkling, as so many smiles from heaven. Ah! he took it for his ever-vigilant mother, shining from the watch-towers of the spirit-world.

But he saw the star pass beneath a cloud; then he sighed and wept, thinking that she veiled her face because he listened to the voice of the tempter. A shadow continued on his brow; but when the star emerged from the cloud, shining brighter than before, he was comforted.

He looked into the water, and saw the same star: it seemed on the rolling wave to be coming towards him. Beautiful sight! perhaps his mother was once more to visit him on that desolate shore. O rapturous thought! Oh the joy of his soul! He seemed to hear her voice over the wave, saying, "Eddie, I come." He heard it speak in every ripple. Its music was sweeter than the voice of many waters sounding in the paradise of God.

But, alas for him! After looking on the wave a long while, and seeing the white form receding and disappearing far away without casting one pitying look upon him, then he knew that it was not his mother: no, it could not be; for however severely he had been tempted, or however far he had wandered from her precepts, yet she would have approached him, and prayed for him, or soothed him with some word of comfort in that lone hour of solitude and despair. No, it was not, it could not be, his mother.

Now he fell upon his knees, and wept and prayed. He prayed long and loud. The winds, and the voices of the sea, mingled with his cries; but, high above them all, went the spirit of that prayer to the ear of the God of Sabaoth. And the God of heaven, the Father of the fatherless, the widow's God, heard him and comforted him; and, as from heaven itself, this text came to him, "Yea, though I walk through the valley of the shadow of death, I will fear no evil; for thou art with me: thy rod and thy staff they comfort me." While praying, he heard the fire-bells ring. He arose from his knees, and found that the fire was in the same district where he had met the tempter an hour before. Ah! some poor mortal had done the deed; somebody had struck the fatal match, and become ruined for life. He thanked God that he had escaped: he cheered up, and took courage for the future. Now the morning-star is rising, the silence of night is breaking, the streets echo with the sound of busy life. Market-wagons are coming in from the country; physicians and night-watchers, and printers and reporters for the morning papers, are returning home: daylight appears, and Ned Nevins is still in the street.

CHAPTER XVIII.

NED'S FIRST FLOGGING BY DAVID NELSON, WHO IS INCITED TO CRUELTY BY MRS. NELSON.

"WHO comes dar?" says Dinah Lee, the contraband cook of Mrs. Nelson, to Ned Nevius, as he rapped at the kitchen-door, with meat-basket in hand. "Oh, it be's you, Ned! ye's brought de meat fur de dinner, heh? La sus! what a leetle bit ob a dinner dis ere be for all de folks, heh? Dar ain't 'nuff for Massa Nelson hisself alone; den dar be Missus Nelson, and leetle Nellie too; and den dar be myself. La sus! I wants to eat somethin', I guess. Jerusalem! dem folks thinks I don't wants nuthin'. See dat ar leetle piece ob meat; den see dem ar leetle 'taters, and dem few beets and turnips! La! dar ain't so much as Massa Lee used to gib to his dog Cæsar. Golly! I shall hab to tie a string to de meat to keep him in de pot; for him all bile away, an' I lose him; and Massa Nelson he say, 'Whar am de meat, Dinah?' Den I say, 'Dunknow, Massa Nelson, guess him be all gone to de gravy.' La sus! what stingy folks you Yankees be, heh!" As Ned was well acquainted with Mrs. Nelson's parsimony, he smiled approvingly, but made no reply, for his heart was sick at the death of his mother. Now Dinah Lee was a young contraband, recently brought from Fortress Monroe. Whether she came from the estate of the rebel general, Robert E. Lee, or some other Lee, is not stated. At any rate, she was somewhat dissatisfied with the narrow limits of her new domicil, and the still narrower souls of her employers. She had been used to large rooms, wide door-yards, plenty of stores for cooking, and more generous diet than she found at Mrs. Nelson's. "La sus!" she continued, "I cant see how you Yankees lib, nohow: ye don't hab nuthin' to cook, ye don't have nuthin' to eat, and ye don't hab no room to do nuthin'. See dis ere leetle door-yard! dar ain't room 'nuff in it to stretch a clothes-line nohow you fix him; and dis ere leetle kitchen,—'cant turn round in it wid a mug of milk. Yah, yah, yah! See how 'nurious Missus Nelson be! She"—Here Ned stopped her. "You don't mean 'nurious," said he; "you don't mean 'nurious, you mean *penurious*."—"Yes, *pe*nurious," said Dinah, with a drawl on the first syllable, and a contemptuous toss of the head. "Yer thinks ye knows a sight;

but ye ain't so smart as ye thinks ye be." Then she continued, " See how Missus Nelson lock up eber ding! She lock up de flour, an' de meal, an' de sugar, an' de 'lasses, an' de spoons; can't make no hoe-cake, no johnny-cakes nor slap-jacks, nor pies, nor puddins, nor nuthin'. She fights de semtress, 'cause she ask too much; she drives off de chamber-maid, 'cause de poor girl wants her pay. She sells ebber ding she can, 'cause she wants to be rich; an' she no gib nuthin' to de poor. All de poor might be a-starvin' an' she'd no help 'em. She sells de bones to de junk-man, an' de rags to de ragman, an' de grease to de soapman; an' I werrily believe she drown poor pussy in de wash-tub, to get rid ob feedin' her. La sus! she'd"—

"Hush, hush! what are you talking so long for?" says Mrs. Nelson, opening the parlor-door, and coming to the kitchen-stairs. "What do you mean by keeping that boy from his work, Dinah?"—"La sus, Missus!" says Dinah, "don't hurry me, den I's work de cheaper. I's only pickin' up de bones to put in de basket; Massa Nelson he hab sent for um. I's looking for to see if dar be no meat on um." Then, with a sly chuckle, "Meat on um!" says Dinah to Ned Nevins, "meat on um!" holding up a dry bone: "I guess dar nebber be no meat on um; no not 'nuff to tempt de mouse."—"Less talk and more work there, you child of Erebus! hurry up, and let him begone!" says Mrs. Nelson, entering the parlor, and closing the door. Let us follow her, while Ned goes and comes on his journeys, weary and fatigued by grief and exposure.

"Tink, tink, tink! one, two! one, two! one, two, three! tink, tink, tink!" sounded in the parlor, as Nellie Nelson sat before the new piano, watching the last tedious moments of the closing hour. "Now Nellie," said Mrs. Nelson gravely, "as your lesson is ended, I have another to teach you. It is exceedingly vulgar for you to mix so much with those poor children and servant-girls as you do: you make too free with them altogether. We are soon to move to Chester Park, and you must commence to learn your dignity and importance: you are our only daughter; did you think of that?"—"Yes, ma'am," said Nellie; "but I want to love somebody. I has no pussy now; and brother Willie and sister Jennie are both dead; and it be so dreadful hard to tink, tink, tink at the piano all the livelong day, and to study out the hard words you make me learn. Oh, it is so lonesome!"—"Lonesome or not," said Mrs. Nelson, "you *must* keep good society, and avoid these poor children."—"Why, mother? Why ain't they just as good as rich children? There is Susie Pinkham; she got the medal in the Franklin School; her mother washes for us: and there is Nellie Stedman; she took the prize in the sabbath school; her mother does our sewing now: and there is poor Ned Nevins" — "Stop!" says Mrs. Nelson, "I will not have that boy's name mentioned in my presence. You have flattered him and pitied him too much; you have talked with him, and asked him about his mother; and you have given him cake, and tried to help him carry out his basket, and looked so sorrowfully on his old rags, that I have been actually ashamed of you." — "Why, mother? what hurt is there in helping the poor?" — "No particular hurt, if you can only learn to keep away from them, and let them know their place." At this moment, a tumult was heard in the yard.

"Don't strike me!" said Ned Nevins to Mr. Nelson, as he stood in Mr. Nelson's back yard, holding up his hands to ward off the blows. "Don't strike me in this manner: you don't know who you are beating, sir! I am no Irish beggar, to be knocked about like a dog! *My mother said, if I do no wrong, something good will come to me.* I never was whipped in my life: I scorn it. You would not dare to strike me if I had a father to protect me; yet because I am a helpless, fatherless boy, ye think ye may beat me like a slave. No, sir! stop that! I'll stand for my rights!"

"Rights, rights! Ha, ha! You've got rights, have ye?" said Mr. Nelson, ironically. "You poor vagabond, you've got rights, I suppose, to destroy my property; and I, poor silly mortal, must just grin and bear it, and have no redress. Yes! you can break, burn, or steal; and I, forsooth, must look calmly on, and pay the bills: blame me, young lad, if I haven't rights too! *Might makes right!* I tell you, I'll take the pay out of your hide, you poor snivelling, simpering drone!

Then he fell unmercifully upon the weeping boy, with stick in hand, and gave him stroke after stroke, with a sound that echoed through the yard, and brought Mrs. Nelson to the window. "Oh, mercy!" said Mrs. Nelson, clinching her hands, and shaking her false curls in a rage. "We shall have all our property destroyed by these heathenish beggar-boys. See there! a basket has fallen, and two or three bottles of old Madeira are broken. Oh the careless brat, the impudent scamp! let him sweat for it," she continued. "That's right, Mr. Nelson! be a man once in your life! stand up for your rights, and teach him a lesson which he will remember. Oh, dear!" she said, sighing in an hysterical fit; "oh, dear! what shall we do with these good-for-nothing, ragged urchins, these pests to decent society? I do hope we shall be rid of them when we arrive at our new mansion in Chester Park."

Mr. Nelson, encouraged for once in his life by the sympathies of his not over-affectionate wife, felt the spirit of her advice to nerve him on; and he redoubled his blows, till the flesh of the poor boy was bruised and torn.

"La sus!" says Dinah, running to the window, and gazing at the sight. "Dat ar be jest likes what us niggers has been used to get in old Virginny, heh? Does ye Yankees beat de poor sarvants like dat?" — "Hush, hush your mouth, you black slave! hold your tattling tongue!" cried Mrs. Nelson, anxious to vent her spleen in some way, hitting her a knock on the head. "La sus, Missus Nelson! ye needn't be a-knockin' me; it don't hurt none: I is got used to dat." — "Then I will strike you harder till it does hurt" (hitting her another knock); "and you shall know your place, and keep your tongue still." — "O Missus! it wont do no good to strike me: I knows my place now! It only makes me feel wusser, an' kind ob hateful like! Gingoes! it makes me mad I hates everybody, I do; I hates myself; den I bumps my head 'ginst de doorposts, and strikes myself, and bangs myself, and bites my lips; den I tinks what a fool I was to act so."—"Then you must hold your tongue, do better, and mind your work; then you won't get hit," said Mrs. Nelson. "Do better! did ye say? La sus! It ain't de *doin'*, Missus; it ain't *doin' better: it is bein' in de way when de gun goes off!*"

This last expression raised the anger of Mrs. Nelson to fever-heat: she clinched her hands; she chafed and scowled, and bit her lips, to think of her false position; she burst into a paroxysm of tears upon discovering that she could not subdue the poor unlettered dependant whom she despised. Rising in rage, she was about to vent her vengeance in more terrible demonstrations, when little Nellie, interposing her delicate form, with hands upraised in supplication, her face bedewed with tears, fell down before her, and cried, "Don't, mother, don't strike her: she will be good! I know she will."—"No, I's shan't be good nuther! I's ugly! I feels wicked as I can lib."—"But you will be *good to me?*" said Nellie, with such angelic grace and tone, that might have touched a heart of stone. You know it's wrong to talk and act so, Dinah: you will be good to me?"—"No I's won't bes good to nobody. I feels like murder when I seed that poor boy whipped so hard. O Jemima!

how I shudder; I bes all bilin' ober wid winegar! Tarnation, how I feels!" working herself into a passion, and showing her big lips, and grating her white ivory teeth, with a jar that startled Nellie from her seat. "O Dinah!" said Nellie, "you make me shudder and tremble, when you show so much temper. O Dinah! how can you be so wicked?" seizing hold of Dinah's hand, and trying to allay her anger by gentle touches of affection. "Not be good to me, when I have been so good to you, and taught you to read, and say your prayers, and love you so?"

"Don't say *love*," says Mrs. Nelson, scornfully; say *like* or cared for: you can't *love* a person that is so low and vulgar." — "Yes, I can, mother: I love everybody in the world. I love you, I love papa, and I love poor Ned Nevins; and I love Dinah, I do: don't I love you, Dinah?" she said, throwing the magic spell of her loving glance upon the poor despised contraband, and exorcising, as by a magician's wand, the evil spirits from her nature. "La sus! I guess you do lub me, Nellie;" falling on her knees before her, and throwing her arms around Nellie's waist. "I guess ye does, Nellie. Ye can lub a poor nigger, I knows ye can: yer leetle heart be full of lub for ebberbody. I wouldn't stay in Massa Nelson's house two minutes, if it warn't for you, Nellie.

You reads stories to me, an' shows me de pictures, an' tells me how de Yankees lib, an' what de childers learns when da goes to school, an' talks about de Bible an' Jesus, an' de childers of Isralum in bondage, an' says prayers for me, den I be so happy;" then grasping her hands tighter around the child's waist, and hugging her little innocent breast closely to her dark face, with a heart overflowing with gratitude, she blubbered out the big tears, and sobbed, and cried like a baby. Her feelings were overcome; she was completely subdued, and became as gentle as a lamb. Such is the power of love, even the love of a little child, to subdue the stubborn will of the apparently incorrigible.

Meanwhile, Ned Nevins, with a sorrowful heart and sad countenance, was proceeding with his work, thinking continually of the death of his mother, and of the shame and mortification of being whipped; but telling no one of his sorrows, not even Nellie, whom he saw watching him on the staircase, with an eye of pity, that made his heart overflow with gratitude to God for sending him one friend that could weep at his distress. Strengthened by the thought, he went trudging up stairs, with his boxes of goods and baskets of wine, to the garret, which was now used as a store-room for speculative purposes, as goods were rising in value.

"Oh dear, what work!" said Mrs. Nelson. "These boxes make so much litter and dirt, and these street-boys are so careless and offensive. I do hope we shall have no such doings as these when we get to our new mansion. Then she turned away, consoling herself with the encouraging prospects of her new domicil, her future *sanctum sanctorum,* in the select precincts of Chester Park.

CHAPTER XIX.

NED'S SICKNESS. — ANGEL WATCHER. — ANGEL OF THE STAIRCASE.

MORNING came to Mr. Nelson's, but no Ned Nevins. What could this mean? Ned had been usually as punctual as the sun on the dial. A flash of conviction struck Mr. Nelson's mind, that all was not right. Yesterday's proceedings might have been a little too severe for the poor boy; especially after learning the death of Ned's mother, and of Ned's exposure all night in the street. How could the boy have toiled the day after that exposure as he did for him? What wonder if he had dropped a basket, or broken a bottle? As he sat down to dinner, he said, "Mrs. Nelson, my dear, hadn't we better send and inquire after Ned? Perhaps he is sick; I must have somebody to do my work."

"No!" said she angrily, showing her disgust for him, and scowling her face. "Get a man, a respectable man, to do your work; let us have no more of these beggar-boys."

"But do you know," said Mr. Nelson, that he has lost his mother?"—"Well, what of that? Perhaps the mother was no help to him; let him go to the poor-house; what do you care?"

"But, my dear, I fear we were too severe with him yesterday; I wish Dinah to go and see."

"Don't know whar Ned libs," said Dinah, gruffly. "Perhaps Nellie knows," said Mr. Nelson. "There, 'tis again!" said Mrs. Nelson, shaking herself in quite a rage. "You must get our dear little Nellie's name mixed up again with that beggar-boy, Ned Nevins. Good heavens! when will you learn the dignity of your position, Mr. Nelson? When shall we be free from vulgarisms? Oh! when shall we get to Chester Park?"

The truth is, Nellie did know where Ned lived, for he had told her. And, more than this, Nellie had seen, beneath that tattered garb of his, a boy of true merit,—a generous, aspiring, noble heart. Ned had felt that he had a friend in her; for she watched him intently when he came with his basket, and inquired particularly after his health, and that of his poor mother, and slily divided her sugar toys with him, and sent little tokens to his mother. And, when he received that mortifying castigation, his heart would have broken, he would have yielded to despair, for it was the most humiliating calamity that had ever befallen him; but there was one eye that looked on, and pitied him, — one little angel face that stood at the window, and saw, and wept. In her tears, he felt strengthened: each tear to him was as the weight of a talent in the balance of his grief. And when watching with longing eye and sympathizing look his weary toil, and sharing in her young heart the burden of his sorrow, she stole in upon the stairs, unseen by her jealous mother, and spoke a kind word to him, as he bore the heavy boxes to the attic, and said, "Are you not tired, Eddie? Can't I help you?" Oh, what magic in those words! What rays of comfort glittered in the face, half veiled by dark ringlets! what beams of hope in those pitying, love-inspiring eyes! Ah! this world could not be a prison-house of woe, with one such little angel in it as Nellie Nelson. Her face was as an angel of mercy; by her gentle look, weariness was dispelled, sickness forgotten, pain banished, the grave hid, hope inspired; she was an angel of the staircase. Yet what had Ned done to deserve her smiles, her pity, her love?

He was only a poor orphan street-boy, tattered, dejected. Besides, he had no mother now to talk to Nellie about, and nothing to command her attention. He went to his home on the night of his flogging, sad and disheartened. Oh the mortification, the chagrin, of being whipped! Sick and weary, he sought his couch: he had no fear of home now, and no dread of the bed on which his mother lay. He was too sick for reflection; he fell upon the bed, and went to sleep. But sleep could not restore his health; that had been too much shattered by watchings and exposures, and by the heavy blows of Mr. Nelson. Fitful dreams troubled him; horrid phantoms appeared, shapes of terror; the room was whirling round; the rattling of the engine, with its long train of cars, rolling all night near the head of his bed, seemed as the engine of death bearing multitudes to the tomb. The very bed beneath him seemed whirling round, and bearing him down, down, to some bottomless gulf below. Horrid fright! At last, he found some of the opiates that induced his mother to sleep, and he fell heavily on his couch to sleep again. This time he slept a long sleep, one that seemed to know no waking. One of the Irishwomen of the house said, as she looked in upon him, "Poor boy! it ba almost over with the dare little crather; he will soon ba with his mother, darling child."

At eleven o'clock he rallied a little, just the time when Mr. Nelson wanted him most; but he fell back to sleep again, lay closer to the bed, hugged the pillow, breathed heavier, and lay more stupid than ever. Finally he rallied again, and woke; but, looking towards the light, he sighed and fell back, as if he would seek the shades below, and be with his mother. Why should he desire to live longer? What reason had he to hope? Yet there was one object to inspire his hope, one that loved him still, — one lone star that shone upon him in his desolation, when all other constellations of the universe were dim. That star was Nellie Nelson; and that star was now shining right down in his face; but he was asleep, and knew it not. Ah! could it be that she was in that squalid room in Orange Lane? Yes, there she stood, a lone watcher, a spirit pure as a snowflake lit from heaven; in voiceless silence she stood, gazing on the care-worn features of the sleeping boy. Her dark, penetrating eyes were as a deep well of sympathy; they watered in pity as she gazed. Her little half-concealed bosom heaved above her low silk waist, and beat in harmony with his deep sighs; and her tender sympathies shuddered at the suppressed sobs of his over-burdened heart. In modest diffidence she stood, her long black curls falling gracefully over her snow white shoulders, vying with silks and gauze, and golden necklace, to hide from public gaze the blushing beauty of the form that had deigned to weep.

Ah, what a form was that to be seen amidst the infernal surroundings of Orange Lane! Profane wretches and rude boys stood silent and aghast when she approached; old men stepped modestly back to give way for the fairy footsteps of her tripping feet; and old hags bowed their diminished heads in shame and reverential awe at seeing a young Madonna enter these long infected, God-forsaken abodes of vice.

What a contrast to Ned Nevins! She was born in affluence; he in most abject poverty. She was clothed in silks and gold; he in rags. Her couch was the richest that gold could purchase; his was a bed of shavings, covered by thin, tattered bed-quilts, but quilted by a mother's hand in her happier days. Nellie Nelson stood in that dark room, a child of fairest prospects, garbed in costliest attire, the picture of happiness itself. Yet she was not content, while she saw suffering that her gentle hand could relieve. She bent over the bed, placing her lips close to his cheek, and her soft hand upon his forehead, and said, as she breathed in dulcet cadences upon his dull ear, "O Eddie! be you sick?" As the gentle voice struck his sleeping ear, Ned started in his slumbers, as if it were the voice of his mother. Then muttering some unintelligible sounds in his dreams, he sighed heavily, and said, "Oh, no, it is not my mother! No: I have no mother! Eddie has no mother now!" Then turning over in his bed, with a shudder. and a groan, he slept on, without opening his eyes. O happy sleep! if it could but hide his pain, or obliterate his woes. Then the vigilant watcher by his side again said, "O Eddie, be you sick? hear me, Eddie, Nellie has come!" but, as she shook his shoulder to wake him, she only started the pain in his bruised frame, and turned the course of his dreams into the channel of yesterday's proceedings. "Don't strike me, Mr. Nelson! don't strike me! I never was whipped in my life!" he murmured on. "O Eddie!" cried the weeping girl, "It is not Mr. Nelson! it is Nellie Nelson, Eddie, your friend Nellie. She has come to see if you were sick; wake up, Eddie!"

Ned awoke, he opened his eyes, he stared, but he could not believe his senses: he dare not speak. There was the little angel of the staircase, the Peri of beauty, bending over him, like hope over the dying. Her face was suffused as by an April shower; her cheeks were flushed as by the rainbow of promise; and now the sun of her smiles, breaking through the thick clouds of suspense, shone into his waking eyes like the light of heaven.

With gentle grace, she threw her arms around his neck, and kissed his cheek, and said, " O Eddie, be you sick? I thought you was sick, so I sent Dinah back to get you some broth; now you must look up, and see me, for she will be here in a few minutes, and then I must go." Ned at first thought an angel had been sent him, through the prayers of his mother; but, when he saw that it was Nellie, he blushed to think of the state of his room for such a visitor, and of his own unworthiness. "O Nellie!" he said, "how did you find the way here to this terrible place? What will your mother say? I know she hates me; and Mr. Nelson would not have struck me if he had cared for me."

"But my father is sorry for it," said Nellie; "and when I told him about your poor mother, how she died, and no one went to the funeral, and how sad and lonely you was, and how you must feel after being whipped, then my father cried, and said, ' Poor boy! Dinah must go and see him.' But, as Dinah didn't know the way, I came with her: so you see my father has some feeling for you after all. Then, Eddie, dear Eddie! if you knew how much I feel for you, then you would want to live for my sake," she said, weeping. Then she bent over in anxious suspense, as if fishing for pearls in the deep of ocean; and, when she caught a glimpse of his eye, she seemed to have found the long-sought gem; then with kisses and caresses she brings the submerged treasure to the light of day by the net of her love. She kisses him again and again, while her silken tresses fall luxuriantly over his pale features, awakening hope, and leaving him in a maze of happy bewilderment. "O Nellie!" said Ned, lifting up her head from his cheek, and looking into her eyes, "how can you care for or pity me, when your mother is so opposed to me? What merits have I, that you should pity me? I am but a poor orphan street-boy. It would be a shame for you to know me in society, or speak my name before your mother. Oh! do not bestow your pity on me: I can never repay it."

"Pity you!" says Nellie, "why? I can pity anybody. I can pity you, and help you; and that will wrong nobody. Pity don't cost any thing."

"But," said Ned, "I am not worthy of your pity or anybody's pity; I broke the precepts of my faithful mother, and got into a fight, and disgraced myself by being locked up; then I am poor, and have no chance for learning, and no way to get money; and I don't want to disgrace you, dear Nellie, by having it said you ever cared for or pitied me." — " But you will not always be so poor." — " Oh, I don't know, Nellie! that all rests with my heavenly Father."

"No, you cannot be poor; you will have work, and lay up something, and buy a home; then I will come and see you, Eddie." — "Ah, Nellie! I fear that is too much to hope; yet my mother said, *if I do no wrong, somethin' good will come to me.*" — " No, it is not too much to hope; for God will help you, Eddie; he will give you friends, and a place to live in, and success; for you have been so faithful to your poor mother, and you have such a tender heart, and are so good and truthful. My dear Eddie," she said, giving him a kiss, " oh, how I love you, Eddie! you seem just like a brother to me. God will give you friends; yes, I know he will, and you will yet be happy."

" O Nellie, I thank you for thinking so well of me, and coming to see me. I wish I were as good as you think me. Your kind words are medicine to my soul, and your smiles better than the light of day : I fear you have done too much for your own good."

" Ah, Eddie! I have done nothing for you : I wish I could do something. When I am gone, I shall think of you; I want you to think of me;

and we will think of each other when we say our prayers to-night. If I am not allowed to see you to-morrow, when you come with the basket, then I will place my white pocket handkerchief at the window, so you may know that I remember you."—"O Nellie! how kind you are! how can I repay you?"—"By praying for me, Eddie, and asking God to give me as good a heart as you have got." At this moment, Dinah came into the room, with her pail of smoking broth, crying "La sus! Missus Nelson didn't want me to warm it, nor heat it at all; but I guess I would a leetle." The words were scarcely out from her lips when Mrs. Nelson appeared also at the door, much excited. At sight of her, Ned's face colored, for it had been quite pale; his heart went pit-a-pat; he trembled. Oh, how he pitied poor Nellie! he could not see her suffer for him; he could not see her punished. No! he would rather die in his bed.

"Ah, my daughter! that is the way you do, is it?" said Mrs. Nelson. "You send Dinah away, so that you can stay here, in this dirty room, surrounded by these low Irish, heh? just as if you were not Mr. David Nelson's only daughter! yes, soon to be daughter of David Nelson, Esq., of Chester Park. O! O! O!" wringing her hands, and shuddering in a kind of *genteel horror!*

CHAPTER XX.

MRS. NELSON'S VISIT TO MRS. NOODLE IN CHESTER PARK.

"COME, Nellie!" said Mrs. Nelson, "we shall be late. The carriage is at the door. We are to make our visit of inspection to Mrs. Noodle's mansion in Chester Park to-day. I hope the ride will improve your health, my dear."

Nellie went with fearful apprehensions, pained at her mother's Chester-Park mania. She trembled to see how cruel, tyrannical, and heartless her mother became, when aspiring after the vanities of high life: she sickened at the thought. One spark of tender feeling, one token of Dinah's gratitude, one loving look from Eddie, would outweigh them all.

Now Mrs. Noodle is averse to receiving visits from any but the select few of upper-tendom. Her husband died after acquiring a fortune in a business which would not bear the scrutiny of the present State constabulary; leaving her in affluence. Her dwelling is magnificently furnished; every thing is *comme il faut,* betokening wealth. Mrs. Noodle lives alone, has three servants, is proud, vain, simple, and selfish. In her former humble condition in life, her education had been sadly neglected. One could scarcely recognize a scrub-woman of the North End in the now fashionable lady of Chester Park. Mrs. Noodle has been to Europe. What she saw, she don't remember; what she went for, she didn't know, except it was to please her son, and be classed among the *élite!* (Pardon me, she don't know what that word means.) The truth is, she didn't carry knowledge enough with her to bring any back. She couldn't see London for the houses; she couldn't see Saint Paul's, on account of the massive walls; and she couldn't see the Alps, on account of the mountains. Paris had so many hard names, she couldn't remember one of them. Her journey was as wearisome and sickening as in early days her scrubbing over the wash-tub was pleasant and healthful.

She saw one object, however, which she remembered: that was a redoubtable *live Lord.* Whether he had wings like a cherubim, or horns like the teraphim, she had not the penetration to discover, neither could she remember.

Books, paintings, and statuary, she had no taste for. A leaf plucked from the tomb of Virgil awakened no poetic sensation; but a sight of a piece of the queen's candle transported her into ecstasies. She was no reader, except of a few short articles in the evening paper, and in the Ladies' "Magazine of Fashion." She had a photograph album, containing likenesses of a few royal personages, and of herself, her son and his daughter, and the poodle-dog, but studiously omitting all her poor relations.

She kept a diary; but what she could put into it is a mystery. She spent her time in watching servants, in locking and unlocking closets and store-rooms, to deal out carefully weighed stores for cooking, and in opening servants' trunks to see if they had not stolen something. Each day she arranged her silver-ware in a different position, thus making seven dispositions of it a week. If a scratch should befall one of the articles, she would most likely set it down in her diary as a sign of general decay, and of the untrustiness of servants.

Mrs. Noodle's appetite is not so good as when she in early life exercised at manual labor: she is somewhat troubled with those genteel complaints, — *ennui* and dyspepsia.

Lest the servants be troubled in the same way, she feeds them short, and drives them hard. The luxury of pie, cake, or puddings, they do not enjoy, except when visitors appear (and that is not often), or when the young Noodles come to spend the day with grandma. Then there may be a few fragments left for the servants.

What she does not have in meats, she makes up in display. Her table is elegantly set with China-ware, bearing her initials, and silver-ware lined with gold. Imaginary ills prevent her partaking of any but the plainest food. All she has for the morning meal is a piece of toast and a cup of tea. For dinner, she has a cup of tea and a plate of beans.

See Mrs. Noodle seated alone at her table, sole possessor of all this glitter and gold, "monarch of all she surveys." No poor relations annoy her; no greedy eye covets her meal; there she sits alone in her glory. She taps her foot upon a concealed spring in the floor, and her obsequious man, Shrugs, appears, with the air of an *attaché*. His whole attire is *recherché*, with white satin vest, white neck-tie, and gloves to correspond. He takes his station behind his mistress; she nods her head; Shrugs proceeds to the speaking tube, gives the order, and forthwith the dumb-waiter is heard slowly rising from the basement, bearing the anticipated meal.

Wonderful to tell! it bears only a cup of tea! a plate of beans! Shrugs takes them upon a silver salver to the table. Bowing obsequiously, he retires, awaiting further orders.

O luxury! what a display over a plate of beans! What magnificent pomp! Three servants and a *dumb*-waiter called into requisition to supply a plate of beans!

Such aping after aristocratic show and foreign customs is unprofitable and un-American. Such a waste of time and labor demoralizes both the serving and the served. These persons should be employed in more useful household or mechanical work. Of what use are they in the world? What sciences, arts, or philanthropic efforts, would such a system of labor develop?

But Mrs. Noodle was entirely swallowed up in self. She had a convulsive abhorrence of missionaries, and philanthropists: the very thought of them alarmed her. If a collector called to collect funds for the poor or the orphans, she immediately went into hysterics, and asked for water to prevent her from fainting.

A ring is heard at Mrs. Noodle's door, and the man Shrugs, in white gloves, appears. "Is Mrs. Noodle in?"—"No, madam! she's not in!" says he, coloring.

"Yes, she is in!" cried the kitchen maid: "I wouldn't lie for nobody."

"Oh, yes!" said Shrugs, "she is in; but she is *very particularly* engaged!"

"So am I engaged! and was engaged to Mr David Nelson twenty years ago! Tell your mistress that *Mrs. Nelson*, wife of David Nelson, Esq., of the firm of Nelson & Co., sojourning in Chester Park, is at the door."

Now, Mrs. Noodle, hearing the loud conversation, opened the door of her sitting-room, to listen a moment, when in comes Shrugs, crying, "Whew, Mrs. Noodle! *My Lady Nelson* is at the door! *Lord Nelson's wife!* I guess. Oh! Kezia, princess royal! how she struts!" Then out came Mrs. Noodle, very anxious to see her distinguished guest, and to make an apology.

"Pardon me for detaining you so long, Mrs. Nelson: there are so many *vulgar people* calling now a days, we must *make a distinction*, you know!"

"Certainly, certainly! Mrs. Noodle, "a *great distinction!*"

"Then you appreciate my position?" — "Appreciate it? Mercy on me! I don't know why I shouldn't, Mrs. Noodle: I have nothing but beggars and peddlers and street-boys calling all the time." — "Oh you are not an English lady, then?" — "Not exactly, though Mr. Nelson is of English descent." — "Ah! I thought I might renew my happy acquaintance with some distinguished personage of England." — "I am very sorry to disappoint you, Mrs. Noodle; but I have heard so much of your splendid mansion, and your superb furniture, I have come to solicit an examination of them, preparatory to furnishing one for myself in Chester Park." — "Then you intend to reside among us, Mrs. Nelson, do you?"

"Certainly: that is the height of my ambition. I long for the pure, serene air, the refined, genteel society, of Chester Park. My present dwelling and surroundings are not at all congenial. Nellie is our only child: her aspirations have greatly deteriorated; her sympathies have already taken a bias towards the poor and degraded. La, me! don't you think my daughter would rather be playing in the dirt with street-children than to be here to-day!" — "Oh, shocking!" said Mrs. Noodle; "I scarcely can believe it; but such are the fruits of mingling in low society." — "Yes, Mrs. Noodle, to-day she would rather be in her old dress, teaching Dinah in the kitchen, than to be attired genteelly, as you see her there. Why, Nellie! where are your gloves, child? It's the strangest thing in the world you can't keep your gloves on a minute. Hold up your head: why do you stoop so?"

"Well, ma, I can't help it," said Nellie, placing

her hand upon her side. "I feel too tight here." —"Pshaw!" replied her mother, petulantly, "you are always crying about being too tightly laced. But we are detaining you, Mrs. Noodle: will you be kind enough to show us over the house?"

"With all my heart, Mrs. Nelson. You shall see every thing for yourself." Then Mrs. Noodle escorted her inquisitive Yankee visitor from room to room, elated at the opportunity (for she was but too happy to display all her riches); and like Hezekiah of old, showing his treasures to the spies of Babylon, she kept nothing back.

There were the cold, frescoed walls, echoing to every sound but that of joy; the rich, heavy cashmere and brocade curtains, adorning the windows, but excluding the beautiful sunlight of God's love. There were rosewood tables, chairs, and side-board, sofas, ottomans, and a magnificent escritoire of the same costly material, which, however, was never used for literary purposes. There was the parlor-grand piano, silent as the grave. No heavenly strains or angelic sounds were heard emanating from its silver chords; for Mrs. Noodle had no music in her soul. There were the long looking-glasses, elaborately set in polished rosewood; and the chandeliers, sparkling with a thousand glittering jets, as the light reflected upon the pendants. The carpets were of the best foreign manufacture, — Brussels, Turkey, &c.; home-productions being too vulgar for a Noodle.

"Oh, how magnificent!" says Mrs. Nelson. "Superb! elegant! Why, Mrs. Noodle, like the Queen of Sheba, I may say, 'The half hath not been told. You must be the happiest mortal living.'"

"Yes, I ought to be, I can't help being happy; but — but — if — and (hesitating). Yes, I am; but" —

"Away with your buts and ifs, Mrs. Noodle! who can be happier than you?" — "But servants are troublesome, you know: they require so much watching, are so deceitful and dishonest. I cannot trust them even with the sugar for my tea. I keep my keys by my side all the day long, looking after servants, locking and unlocking. Ah, me! I sometimes wish myself back to my humble home again."

"Tush, tush! Mrs. Noodle. Think what *society* you have here, magnificent society! Oh the select, the *élite* society of Chester Park!"

"Yes! Mrs. Nelson; but Chester Park is waning." — "Waning, Mrs. Noodle, how? What do you mean?" — "Why, there are so many butchers and bakers crowding in." (Mrs. Nelson took this as a rebuke to herself; for her husband was a provision-dealer.)

At this moment, Nellie cried, "Oh! take me away from this dreadful place. O my head, my head!" The poor child became dizzy while gazing upon all this vain show and useless parade. She grew faint, and called for Dinah, and asked to be carried home. She was shocked at her mother's pride and heartlessness. That mother seemed forgetful of all tender ties, willing to sacrifice even Nellie herself upon the altar of pride and vain glory.

Nellie could not consent to the offering. Her heart sickened, her cheeks grew pallid; she called for water, and, throwing up her hands, she cried, "I am faint, mother. Oh! take me away from this dreadful place: it feels so cold and deathlike. Oh! *do* take me home, where Dinah will bathe my head." And she fell senseless upon the floor.

The engine which Nellie heard at Ned Nevins's house in Orange Lane seemed rumbling by. Ah! the sound of that swift messenger was premonitory of death. The winged car was approaching for her departure. Poor child! she is too delicate for earth, too unselfish to live in this age of traffic, where hearts are bought and sold, and gold is adored as God.

The fainting girl was taken up in the arms of Shrugs, and borne to the carriage, and carried back to her more congenial home: while the trembling mother began to ponder on the first premonitory lessons of vanity, on the instability of all earthly hopes and prospects, and on her first, though not very pleasant, associations with Noodledom, in Chester Park.

CHAPTER XXI.

ANNIVERSARY MEETINGS. — ADDRESSES BY THE GOVERNOR, MAYOR, WENDELL PHILLIPS, ETC.

A SERIES of anniversary meetings commenced in Franklin School Building, Jan. 17, 1864. The pastor opened the meeting with prayer, and commenced to read the report, when the Governor arrived.

As Gov. Andrew approached the altar, the children of the sabbath school rose with a song of welcome, and very prettily sang, "Happy Greeting." The Governor remained standing until the song was ended, then began to address, first the children, then the adult members, of the Mission.

One thing he regretted: the boys of the night school were debarred the privilege of meeting on this occasion. They were to have a separate meeting: he wished it were otherwise. He desired to stand on a platform wide enough to embrace philanthropic men of every creed. He would grasp the hand of Father Healy,

Father Williams, and Bishop Fitzpatrick, and say, "Let us all work together for our common humanity." He had great respect for those men. But a system that will not fraternize with Christian men, and is opposed to free schools, a free press, and free discussion, is un-American, and at variance with the genius of our institutions.

SPEECH OF JUDGE RUSSELL.— Judge Russell's name is a household word. Among all philanthropic names, none appear so often before the public, few take in so wide a grasp of charity, and none is more acceptable, because no man can better say the right thing at the right time. If the ladies of the great New-England Fair wish to make an announcement, Judge Russell's silvery voice must tell the silver story.

This morning he had just come from the School Ship, where he meets almost every sabbath morning to address a hundred and sixty boys. He said his text was a salt-water text: he would speak from lessons of the morning. The iron steamship "Caledonia" lay, full of holes, almost a wreck in Boston Harbor. She, through a false compass, had struck on Cape Cod. Conscience may become false, like the needle that will not traverse ; then comes the wreck of character. A beautiful ship in the harbor was loading for China: her freight and her armament were described, and compared with such as are needed for the voyage of life. In that ship there may be one wormy timber. The carpenter has thought to hide it from sight; no one discovers its weakness till at sea, when a storm comes; then the worm-eaten timber gives way, and the ship goes down. So may one spot on your character, one sinful habit, destroy the hopes of a lifetime. He instanced "The Chesapeake." This beautiful steamer was sailing gently by our shores, when suddenly a company of pirates from within seized her, and made her their prey. Your foes most to be feared are not those from without, but traitor thoughts from within. Many such lessons he related. and with telling effect.

EX-MAYOR QUINCY'S ADDRESS. — Hon. Josiah Quincy said our country is a grand Union Mission; our soldiers bear the light of the gospel of freedom and civilization to a worse than heathen land. Virginia's governor had boasted that she was exempt from the pestilence of free schools. Twenty thousand of her white population could not read. Darker statistics, and more startling facts, came from States farther south.

He then portrayed a Christian character in life and in death. It was more easy to die a Christian's death than to live a Christian's life. He related scenes in the life and death of Horace Mann and John Quincy Adams, and concluded by saying, that we do not prize the golden opportunities we have for doing good.

When Mr. Eldridge, of the School Ship, spoke of retiring from teaching the boys there, Mr. Quincy rose, and replied in tears, "No, never! do not retire from so noble a work. Heaven will smile upon you; God will bless you: it is the noblest work of all the earth."

MEETING OF THE NEWSBOYS. — No little excitement occurred Monday evening, during the exhibition of the newsboys, and the delivery of addresses to them by Ex-Mayor Wightman, Wendell Phillips, and Mr. Philbrick, Superintendent of Public Schools. The boys expected a treat, and they came in high glee. They had been promised a chance to speak on the same stage with these notables, one after the other, — now a newsboy, now a mayor; now a coal-picker, now the principal of the schools; now a boot-shiner, and now the one whom Mr. Beecher calls "the most admirable orator of the world." They appreciated the importance of the occasion, and were determined to do their best. The first boy called to speak, however, did not come to time. The laugh of his companions, and the staring eyes of the audience, frightened him. But the master of the exhibition, himself a graduate of the Mission, was not easily discouraged. He had counted much on his reputation, and scorned a failure. He aroused them by his eloquence, then called for a volunteer. Up rose a hand; the spell was broken: a boy rose to speak, and shouts followed. The boy went through with his piece admirably, and came down from the stage amidst vociferous and tumultuous applause. Several boys followed him, to the great delight of the audience. Then came forward the boy who failed at first, and by his clear, correct, and pathetic enunciation, actually beat them all. Indeed, the recitations of the boys were the greater charm of the evening.

What could awaken more interest than two hundred street-boys, — fifty-one without a father, many of them without employment, and nearly all of them started on the highway of either appetite or lust, or crime? They were to be a menagerie of wild tigers let loose on this city, or to be tamed, and schooled for useful citizens. The eyes of the whole city were upon them. Who could draw a crowd, or awaken public interest, like them? Day before this, the Governor, the Judge of the Superior Court, and Boston's most eloquent Ex-Mayor, all had spoken for the Mission. All were noted orators; yet they had failed to attract the crowd or win the attention elicited by these untutored boys of the street. They were the *foci* upon which centred the concentrated rays of pity, admiration, and hope. In them, hunger cried for bread, innocence demanded protection, instinct spurned bad example, conscience fought against temptation, and genius was struggling for the light. They seemed to say, " Give us a chance, or we will make you trouble; school us and care for us, or we will cost you dear."

It takes genius even to sell a paper. These boys are geniuses: the truth is, they know too much. Who has brighter instincts? Who can find a flaw quicker, or catch at a slipping word? Who meets your rebuke with a keener repartee? Who can upset your argument by a more palpable hit? Their wits have been sharpened by hunger, and ground on the stone of self-reliance and exposure. Who, then, would wish to talk to such a crowd, or hope to keep their restless tongues and feet still?

MAYOR'S WIGHTMAN'S SPEECH. — Two representative men, of antagonistic political principles, were to meet on the same stage, and address them, — Mayor Wightman the conservative, and Wendell Phillips the radical. These two party-leaders, antagonistic as lions, were to meet as lambs; yet how could they speak together in the same cause? for they had had sore differences. When the storm of war was brewing, Mayor Wightman saw its dreaded thunderbolts: and, knowing its cause, he laid it at the feet of the abolitionists. As a prophet, he saw our commerce swept from the sea, our property wasted, and our land deluged in blood. He dreaded the coming catastrophe. Standing at the head of a great conservative constituency, composed of the wealth and power of Boston, he said, "Boston must be purged; these fanatics must be put down; Tremont Temple shall be closed." Alas for him! his mandate was like Mrs. Partington's broom against the ocean: the tempest lowered, and thundered on, and soon the tide of war swept into its vortex men of all political creeds. Now we see the conservative and radical striking hands together, as we shall soon see, in our distracted country, the South and North striking hands, and embracing and kissing each other. But will Mr. Wightman hold these boys? Yes, as conservatism holds the peace of society. He will hold them by not stirring their passions; he will hold them negatively. When he rose, the dignity of his official position commanded respect ; and his subject, though not exciting. was entertaining. He was as cool before that volcanic pile of human passion as a Cambridge professor over his fossils. His philosophical teachings, presented with ocular demonstrations, were plain, simple, and instructive. For half an hour, the boys listened, most of them attentively. He could say at the close, what but few speakers could say before such a crowd, "I kept them still, and held their attention."

WENDELL PHILLIPS AND THE NEWSBOYS. — Wendell Phillips is a prophet born before his time. Living in this or any other age, he must necessarily say unpalatable things. He sees coming peril while other eyes are seared; he sounds alarm when his words, like those of Lot to his sons-in-law, appear as "one that mocked." Before him sat the children of that foreign immigration which is soon to rule us, or we are to Americanize it. Boston is fast yielding to the foreign vote, and it requires not even a prophet to see the coming struggle. Hence Mr. Phillips's interest. It was quarter to nine o'clock when he rose to speak. For two long, weary hours these wild, restless, unmanageable boys had been confined, with no relief, no ventilation for their pent-up spirits. They were uneasy as mice in a trap: what man would dare speak to them now? They had heard, however, so much of Mr. Phillips's fame, they were prepared for a moment, out of mere curiosity, to keep silent.

He looked upon them like a father. His countenance was benignant; benevolence beamed from his eye. How amiable! Is this the much-dreaded Wendell Phillips? How delicate his hand; how feminine his complexion; how sweet the tones of his voice; how clear his accent; how deliberate in speech! This the terrible political ranter, that has dissevered peaceful states, and shaken to its centre a united continent? Yes, that is the man. Then his looks deceive us. By the soft drop of his leaden words, we should suspect that he had but little flint and fire within, and should place him in the ladies' parlor rather than in the arena of political strife.

He must have two natures, the meek and the ferocious. Thus far, however, he has shown nothing but meekness. But meekness will not hold that nervous, restless pile of bone and sinew long, and ferocity would forfeit their confidence. What, then, will hold them? Nothing but genius. Is he the man for that? Let us see.

Said Mr. Phillips, "We are all in one ship; we

have one common interest; we go down with
you, or you make the voyage with us. We owe
you much; you owe us much. Many of you are
newsboys. Free schools make newsboys; without education, no one would buy a paper. You
could not live in Paris or London. Mind
makes the man; thoughts build a nation. Who
made the first steamboat?"—" Robert Fulton,"
answered a dozen voices. " Then Robert Fulton
made these United States."—" Boo-hoo-hoo! I
don't believe that," shouted several voices. " Let
me tell you, boys, what you can do if you will
try. Theodore Parker purchased his first book
by picking whortleberries; my classmate in college spent the first shilling he ever earned for a
book. Now let me tell you of two other boys
who have lived in Boston. One was the son of
wealth, whose father doted so much on him that
he had his son's portrait painted on the large
panel of almost every door in the house. The
house was a splendid mansion, the finest in the
city, and the panels were made expressly for the
portraits. Let me tell you the fate of that son:
he died in the poorhouse. The other was a boy
who came in from the country without a dollar,
and asked to stay for two weeks at a store where
they had already a boy: he wished to stay until
he could get a situation. At the end of two

weeks, the merchant, seeing that he had made himself useful, determined to keep him and the other boy also. Soon this boy became a partner, and in ten years he bought out his partner, and is now the richest man in Boston, building his house on Beacon Street. There is hope, then, for you, — hope for any boy who will try.

"Who commands at Charleston?" — "Gillmore," was the reply. "Do you know about his guns?" No answer. "Well, I will tell you. They will send a shot five miles: Mr. Parrott, the inventor of them, was a poor New-Hampshire boy. His thoughts were worth fifty thousand men. Stevenson, the first locomotive builder, was worth a hundred thousand men. You see then, that the character and brains make men. Do you know Gen. Butler?" — "Yes, sir!" — "Yes, sir!" — "Yes, sir-ee!" — "Well, I see you do." By this time all had waked up in earnest; the noise became difficult of suppression; the sexton became alarmed for the safety of the seats, and the policeman came forward to make arrests. "Let them alone," said Mr. Phillips: "I will take care of them. I was asking you about Gen. Butler. He is the coming man of America. When hewing his way from Annapolis to the defence of Washington, he saw a broken engine, and asked if any man among his troops could repair it. Suddenly a man sprang from the ranks, and said, 'I can do it, for I helped make it.' — 'Can any man repair this track?' — 'I can,' cried a voice, 'for I helped build the Fitchburg Railroad.' On another occasion, the general and all his troops on board a ship came near going down by the treachery of a pilot. 'Is there any man that can steer this ship?' cried the General. 'Yes,' replied a soldier; 'I am from Marblehead, and I can steer it round the world.'

"These soldiers are New-England boys, and they carry the free schools with them: their very hands are taught to think. There are more brains in the hands of a New-England boy than in the heads of the European populace." This caused some sensation, as most of these boys are of foreign descent, and free schools are looked upon with suspicion. Mr. Phillips continued, "Our shops and our mills are taught to think: New England thinks for Boston, and Boston thinks for the world.

"You, then, are Americans; you are Boston boys."—"No! we ain't!" shouted a score of voices; "We are from Ireland, the auld Emerald Isle!" Great confusion, much shouting and stamping. "It is all over now," thought almost every one except Mr. Phillips. He had been accustomed to confusion and tumult, in old antislavery times. Indeed he delighted in the excitement; he courted the conflict that he might win the victory: but how shall he regain his lost ground? how win back his audience? Ward Beecher had no harder task in striving to convert the secesh sympathizers of a Liverpool mob to the interests of the North, than Wendell Phillips had in striving 'to Americanize his audience, or convert young Ireland into young America.

He was not to be disconcerted, however, though the spectators were terribly frightened; neither was he the man to attempt to brow-beat these rebellious spirits into submission. He must parley with them, and play with them in medals of their own coin; then he must bide his time. Before their shouts for Ireland had fully died away, he cried out, at the top of his voice, "Did you ever hear of Daniel O'Connell?" Tremendous shouts, and clapping of hands, and every demonstration of applause. "I will tell you a story about him."

The tide had now turned in his favor: he saw that he had their attention; and, as he was personally acquainted with Ireland's distinguished patriot, he wove that man's history into his discourse, side by side with Washington.

He mixed the characters so closely, and

EFFECT OF WENDELL PHILLIPS' SPEECH, IN AMERICANIZING THE IRISH.
"There is our flag. Will you keep it? will you keep it?"
"Yes! yes! yes! we will! hurrah! bully! tiger!" Page 227.

jumped so often from one country to the other, that in their applause they scarcely knew which country they were cheering. They thought it was all good; " First-rate! bully for you!" Now was his time to hit again upon the glories of America. This time he was most successful. The asylum for the oppressed of all nations, the hope of an enslaved world, now distracted and torn by slavery and civil war, looked to her adopted children for sympathy and support. Should she look in vain? Shall freedom or slavery triumph? "*You are to be the future rulers of this great nation; will you prove worthy?*" Deafening applause! and cries, " Yes, we will." This touched the key note of their aspirations. The idea of ruling is a Hibernian instinct; and the thought of ruling this great nation is a tall consideration. Now they became as demonstrative and hilarious as some of the newly naturalized on election day. He said, pointing to the star-spangled banner over the stage, "*There is our flag, will you keep it? will you keep it?*" — "Yes, yes, yes! we will! hurrah! bully! tiger!" The excitement and applause that followed baffle description. Suffice it to say, his was a triumph, and a triumph on the radical side. He portrayed the evils of this city, especially that of strong drink, and bore down upon vice, until he made it appear hideous.

He related the story of Thomas Benton, concerning his mother, on temperance, and thrilled their young hearts by anecdotes and illustrations, until near ten o'clock, and held their attention to the last.

CHAPTER XXII.

SNOWBALL RIOT. — APPEAL TO THE RIOTERS.

WO hundred noisy, boisterous boys are waiting at the iron gates of Franklin building for admission. The crowd soon increases, until it seems as if the courts and lanes of Boston have emptied themselves of their juvenile delinquents.

There are representatives from Orange Lane, Carney Place, Hamburg Street, Federal Street, and Fort Hill, whose conditions say, "Let Boston beware: she sleeps on a volcano! Educate us, and care for us, or look for thefts, mobs, murders, and conflagrations." The police have not yet arrived: the crowd becomes obstreperous.

Now some ladies and gentlemen pass the crowd to enter the building; when, plump, plump, plump, the snowballs strike against the door before them, and dash into their faces. "Oh dear! they are killing me; I am all covered with snow; open the door, let me in; I shall die!" cries one lady, leading half a dozen others, who are muttering the same complaint. "Oh the rascals! they ought to be hung," cries another: "they have spoiled my new bonnet." Still another, "Oh dear! the snow is running down my neck. Oh! my bosom is full of snow." — "That's so," said her discarded lover by her side; "it was always cold, and full of snow: I hope it may freeze." — "Don't cry," said her present gallant. "You are out of the storm now. I will protect you." Now a company of teachers approach, and they fare but little better.

"Oh dear! they will murder us. Well, this is our reward for teaching them." Now comes the sexton, against whom the boys have a particular spite. He is a strong, stalwart man, one of the best to keep a congregation of irreverent young men in order. But a crowd of obstreperous boys out of doors, in the dark, with snowballs in hand, waiting for a mark, are not so easily managed. When he passed, "Bo, ho, ho!" sounded along the line; but they stood back, fearing to cross his track. When he came near the door, however, with back towards them, then, *whang, bang! how the snowballs flew!* This time prudence was the better part of valor, and he, too, had to flee like a woman. "There, there!" he cried, shaking off the snow as he came in: "this is what you get for helping these Irish scalawags. Our pastor forsakes his flock to teach these ragamuffins, who will soon rise up, and cut his throat to pay for it. When you have been sexton five years in this building, as I have been, then you will get your eyes open." Now another company rush for the door, and well they may; for a shower of balls come whizzing by, like rebel bullets. Soon the police appear, and order is restored: the boys march into their seats, to be addressed by several gentlemen. It is well, perhaps, for the boys, that the speakers did not witness the riot; for then they might have felt more like *dressing* than *ad*-dressing them.

Rev. R. C. Waterston rose to speak. He started night schools in Boston, thirty years ago. What a change in thirty years! Whole streets and neighborhoods have given way to the foreign population; ancient land-marks are fast disappearing; Puritanism is becoming a thing of the past. America's destiny rests on the tide-wave of foreign immigration: the problem of her future is involved in these boys. Now is the time to solve the question, — shall they overwhelm us? or shall we Americanize them?

Most of them are Catholics, averse to free schools and American ideas. Puritan principles are an offence unto them: their watchword is, "Papacy and Democracy."

They are tooth and nail against what are called reforms,—against police bills, Maine Laws, negro suffrage, and abolitionists. Such being the material of Mr. Waterston's audience, how could he control them? He rose to speak, but they would not listen: in vain were the efforts of the police; the feet of the smaller boys went clitter clatter, and their tongues went gibber jabber; while the larger boys were more malicious. He said, "Most of you are American boys, are you not?"—"No sir, we are from Ireland."—"Then let me tell you what I saw in Ireland." So he painted Irish scenes, and told Irish tales, until he got their attention, then produced his *coup de maître* in a way they little expected. "Boys!" said he, "hear me for a moment: I am going to pray." This opened their ears, and awakened their ideas; for they are more averse to Protestant prayers than to free schools. "Hear me, boys: I want you all to keep still." Then came murmurs of evident dissatisfaction. "Boys! you don't know what I mean: I am going to pray for my old friend Bishop Fitzpatrick, who is dangerously ill." At the sound of "Bishop Fitzpatrick," a flash came over that audience, and in a twinkling the tumult ceased: every foot was still, every whisper hushed. Could it be that they were charmed to silence by the name of a priest? Yes, the key of their destiny is found in the hand of the priest.

Mr. Waterston took advantage of this: he prayed for the bishop, the priests, and the boys; then he went through with his speech without interruption.

SUPERINTENDENT'S APPEAL. — Then the Superintendent of the Mission arose, and said, "Boys, I am ashamed of your conduct at the gate this night. You have disgraced yourselves in the estimation of your teachers' and the public. Think what these teachers have done for you? Many of them have perilled their health and lives for you. Think of those, who, in poverty and want, have come, even from beds of sickness, to teach you, such has been their love for you. Think of that one who lost her reason solely by teaching you: she is now conversing with ideal images on the wall. She became too anxious for your good; you have driven her mad by your ill conduct.

And what have I not suffered also by your insults? When I first opened this school, I was hooted and stoned in the streets. The boys that I have most favored have often been the most ungrateful. You have prejudiced the people that worship here against you; and I alone have to bear the responsibility of your deportment. You have divided my church, injured the cause of Christ, turned my brethren against me; driven sleep from mine eyes, health from my body, rest from my mind, friends from my bosom, and comfort from my soul, except that comfort and satisfaction one feels in being right, and doing good under any circumstances. And why is this? Have I ever treated you unkindly? Have I ever laid violent hands upon you, or allowed any teacher to do it? Have I ever striven to proselyte, or turn you from your religion? Have I not said, Go to your own church on the sabbath, keep out of the street, be honest, be respectable? The religion that makes men honest is the best, whatever be its creed. Have I not been true to my promise? Have I not taught you, fed you, clothed you, and given you homes, and cared for you like a father? And what is my reward for these ceaseless toils? You can remunerate me in no way, except by being thankful. Even this you refuse: some of you heap insult upon ingratitude. Yet, with all these discouragements, I do not cease to labor for you, and bear with you, and pray for you, because my Saviour, whom I strive to follow, is long-suffering, full of compassion, and of tender mercy.

Never do I kneel by my bedside at night, without praying for the poor fatherless boys of my school, and the poor orphans of the street. When it storms, I think how can the poor shivering newsboy sell his papers to-day? What will he have to eat? and what will his poor mother do for want of the few coppers he brings her? And the coal-picker and the shavings-boy,—what will they do in the cold snow-storm? And the market-boy, with wet feet and heavy basket, travelling all day in the rain and sleet, until almost ready to drop down, not daring to say he is faint or sick or cold, lest he lose his place, and his mother have no bread? I ask my heavenly Father to pity you, and feed you, and clothe you, and give you homes and friends and fire this cold winter. I ask him to provide for you as he does for the birds, and to give you friends that will care for you, and help you, and love you, and teach you things that are for your good.

I feel for you, and pity you, when I remember how lonely and sad I felt when a boy; how I wished for a friend, some one that would love and pity me; how I wept when I became fatherless, at the tender age of four years; how I repined at being turned out of doors in the snows of winter; how I grasped my mother's hand, and cried as she led me wandering through

December's snow to the nearest shelter; how thankful I was for an old store to live in, and even a crust of bread; how I wept when I saw my mother in that store, and thought she would die; how I shuddered at seeing the drifting snow, like a winding sheet, beat through the clapboards, and cover her sick bed; how I came home from school, and went into the woods for sticks to heat her gruel, and wept and sighed alone; how I kneeled on the cold snow by the side of my hand-sled, and prayed to God amidst the whistling of winds in the forest trees, prayed for some sign of comfort and hope; how my young soul wrestled and struggled for light and hope in the cold breezes of that dark evening; how I asked God to send me friends and food and fuel, to let my mother live, to make me a good boy, never to trouble her poor heart any more; how she rose from her sick bed, and set a light in the window to light me home; how happy I was on returning to find that friends had come to my relief, and were watching by her side; how grateful I was for every favor; how thankful for a smile, a word, a look; how I took my hat off, and bowed to anybody that would look kindly on me; how I trembled when anybody passed me coldly by, and would not speak; how I treasured up the little tokens of early friendship; how I loved the little boys and girls of the school, and shared my little stores with them; how I tasted of the apple with them, and found it sweeter than any fruit I have eaten since; how glad I felt when I had made anybody happy. When I think of this, I am paid for all the sacrifices I have made for you, and all the insults I have borne. I shall continue to help you, and pray for you, though you may be unthankful. I teach you for the love of doing good, and not for any earthly reward."

He closed amid breathless silence, while many a streak was furrowed on the smutty faces of these boys by falling tears. From this time forth, the character of the school was completely changed. There were no more riots, or insults of any kind to superintendent or teachers: and a more grateful and obedient class of boys, as far as their knowledge and habits of life would allow, is not often found. For the next three months, it was but a pleasure to teach them: they were grateful for the smallest favors; their progress was encouraging; their exhibition in declamation was a grand success; their deportment was respectful to all. When the term closed, the boys parted with their teachers very tenderly, following some of them to their homes, thanking them again and again, and begging to be admitted to their classes the next season.

Not a little of this change was produced by J. D. Philbrick, Esq., Superintendent of Public Schools. By several addresses to the boys, he showed them that his heart yearned to see them elevated and encouraged. His views were broad enough to embrace the whole population, and to reach every child. He told them of his early efforts to acquire an education, in a country town of New Hampshire; his privations and scanty advantages by the log fire in the old country fireplace. He then related instances of his experience during his long residence as a teacher in Boston. He instanced several candy peddlers and newsboys, who had risen to wealth and eminence. One was a wholesale merchant in Franklin Street; one lived on Beacon Street; one had graduated at the Latin schoool, had studied French, and was now having a large salary in a French house of New York. He would like to have all these boys go to the day school; but, if they could not do that, then let them do the next best thing,— let them study here.

Alderman Nash stated what accident determined his course when a youth, and made him leave the broad-axe of the ship-carpenter in Plymouth County to tend store in Boston. He said the reason of his success in that store was, that he never attended theatres, nor even spent his time in ice-cream saloons; but he improved his leisure hours in study at home. Being in the public councils of the city for many years, he had endeavored to spread popular education, and, as far as possible, to reach every class.

Joseph Story stated, that, when President of the Common Council of Boston, he visited the ragged schools of London. Boston, with regard to its ignorant and abject poor of foreign birth, was fast becoming a second London. He had done all in his power to elevate the foreign population, and stay the tide of pauperism and crime. He spoke hopefully to the boys, encouraged them by many an anecdote, and filled their young hearts with much enthusiasm. After the addresses, the boys partook of their refreshments, and were dismissed. Thus closed a series of anniversary meetings.

CHAPTER XXIII.

A LOT ON THE AVENUE. — MYSTERIOUS EPISTLE.

"LA sus!" said Dinah Lee, as she loooked out of Mr. Nelson's window, and saw a carriage drive up. "La sus! if dey ain't bringin' poor Nellie in de arms! Oh, how pale she looks! I guess she be dyin'."
Then she flew to the door to meet her, and help her in. Nellie was sick and faint; yet she knew Dinah, and reached out her hand as if longing to find a friend. Dinah kissed the hand, with tender words of endearment, then, gathering up the faded form in her arms, bore her to her little bed; while Mrs. Nelson retired into the sitting-room to cogitate on her rather dubious prospects at Chester Park. The carriage had scarcely left, when another sound was heard at the door. It was from Mr. Nelson: he was intoxicated, muttering imprecations, and fumbling to find his latch-key At last he rang the bell, and Dinah opened the door. "Wife, I'm come! ain't ye glad to see me?" said Mr. Nelson, staggering in. "La sus! I ain't

your wife!" says Dinah: "I ain't nobody's wife; I nebber was married, and I ain't goin' to be, no how." — "Oh! beg yer pardon, 'scuse me, Dinah, I was not lookin'. Where is she? Ah! here is Mrs. Nelson; yes, here she is. Wife, ain't ye glad to see me?" — "*Wife?*" said Mrs. Nelson, contemptuously, and with unmistakable emphasis, "*wife? wife?* do you call me? you might as well call me *old woman*. Why don't you say *Mrs. Nelson?*"—"Oh! 'scuse me, hic, hic, *Mrs. Nelson!*" as he reeled forward to pat her on the cheek, "'scuse me, my dear, my chick, my gentle duck!" — "Duck! do you say? Don't call me duck, you goose, you! Keep your distance, sir."— "Oh! don't be too hard with your old beau, my dear. I've been makin' a purchase for you, I have." — "Have you?" she said, starting up, and changing her tone, not a little anxious to know what he had purchased; for she feared the effect of his bargaining, and feared that she might be made penniless any day by the machinations of Solomon Levi, the old Jew.

"Yes, I've made a purchase for ye; but I guess I won't tell ye jist now, hic, hic!" — "Oh, do tell me!" said she in pathetic strains; "do tell me what you have purchased!"—"Ah! you are comin' to a little, my dear, heh? Ha, ha! I thought I could fetch you. Well, I have purchased a *lot*." — "A lot," said she, more excited than ever, — "a lot! Well, is it in Chester Park?" — "No, madam, it is not in any park." — "Oh dear! then you have bought a lot without consulting me." — "Can't help it: the bargain is made." — "Oh, do tell me!" said she, in exceedingly persuasive tones, — "do tell, where is the lot?" — "Well, madam, it is on the avenue." — "On the avenue? what avenue? Is it Commonwealth Avenue?" — "No, not exactly." — "What then? you know I wouldn't live on Harrison Avenue, nor Shawmut Avenue. What avenue is it?" — "Well, madam, it is Cypress Avenue." — "Cypress Avenue! Oh dear! I believe you want to kill me: what do you mean?" — "I mean just what I say, hic, hic." — "Do tell me where is the lot?" — "Then, if I must tell you, it is at Forest Hills, madam." — "Well, there!" said she, with the utmost scorn and contempt; "there! if the man hasn't bought a *graveyard!* I knew he wanted to *kill me.* Oh dear! *I shall die, I shall die!*" she said, crying piteously, and wringing her hands. "Very well," he said, turning upon his heels to go out, and rejoicing that he had got the advantage of her once in his life; "very well, madam; if you are so soon to die, it is well that I bought the lot, for we shall want to use it immediately, hic, hic!"

As he turned to go out, and drew his hand from his pocket in demonstrations of triumph, he inadvertently dropped a letter upon the floor, which Mrs. Nelson picked up, and read. The letter was from Ned's mother, Mrs. Sophia Nevins, written just before she died. The jealous woman was but too well pleased to get hold of the document, and devoured its contents in greedy haste.

"Mr. NELSON. Sir,—Ere this reaches you, I shall be in my grave. Borne down by grief, I die within a few blocks of your dwelling. Yet you know it not. Faithful to my vow, I have veiled my features from your sight, and have never interfered with her who has robbed me of my affianced lord. Yet my shadow has ever been upon your track: I have followed you from city to city, not in revenge, but in love. When you have prospered, I have rejoiced, though I had not a crust to eat. When you have erred, and resorted to strong drink, I have pitied you and prayed for you, though you seem to have had no pity on me. Oh how I repent that you ever stole into my reverend father's parlor! that you ever came into his church, and joined in his prayers! that you ever stole my heart! My life has been one long night of penitence and prayer. The pine-tree still whistles with the sighs I breathed when first I found myself a forsaken, useless thing. I said to father, "Do forgive me!" but he turned pale; his great heart heaved and sighed, and he never smiled again. The flowers still bloom with fragrance, and the rivulet still flows by the banks where we met; the robin and the wren still make their nests in what was then my father's yard: but my parents have died with broken hearts; they lie in premature graves. All they could give me was an education and a name: the name I wasted, and the education became useless. And now, all pale and chill amid the abject surroundings of Orange Lane, I have hid myself to die. I gaze out upon the stars, I think of you, I think of the past, I think of my fate; I see that unchanging north star, Cynosura, emblem of constancy, now looking down upon me, as when first we met at my father's home. I think how benignly it shone upon us through the lattice-work in the arbor of my father's garden, when we first took our evening walk. I think of the pledge you made me then and there; how your unsordid, youthful heart heaved and swelled with feeling; how your overflowing affections burst as a river over its banks; and how my poor heart was swallowed up in thine. All nature was in sympathy with us. The flowers were pouring forth their generous odors, the whippoorwill singing wantonly on a rock by our side; and the gentle brook, warbling melodiously over the pebbles through the orchard, and by the flowery banks in ripples, dashing amorously at our feet, sang of love. I was lost to time and sense. I had no heart of my own. All was thine: if I had had a thousand hearts, all should have been thine. Millions! in a moment! O rapturous hour! O delusive hope! You stood between me and my God: you was my God; I worshipped you, and received words from your lips as proofs of holy writ. Your glowing features looked as fair as the chaste moon, and your heart I thought as pure; and that fair orb herself seemed in radiant smiles of holy approval to answer back your caresses, as she kissed the bosom of the yielding waters carolling at our feet, with lips of ruby, purple, and gold. As the clustering grapes hung pendent on the vine, so you hung upon my answering bosom, undeceiving and undeceived. As the twining tendrils clung around the trellis, so I clung to you, hoping and giving hope. The gentle zephyrs bore our sympathetic whispers to the recording angel in the skies, and our mutual vows were plighted, as I thought, forever. The stars, to seal those vows, shone lustrously upon our upturned faces, as we sat, and saw the pointers of Ursa Major turning on their midnight round, circling, on the wheel of night, the polar star. Ah! little did I think of the bear behind those pointers, and less did I believe I was cherishing a bear in my bosom.

But that is past. The same star is there; but all else, all things with me, how changed! I was but a poor minister's daughter, loving, but not beloved; having no patrimony but a pure heart and a good name. Another, who had *money*, supplanted me; gold blinded your eyes; my fate was sealed. All I ask is, that you will remember your vow concerning my boy. If you have been unfaithful to me, oh, be not to him! He will present you the parchment and the ring. I loved him because he looked like you: if I parted with him, I felt lonely; if I clung to him, I had no place in society. Without him, I could teach and live; but with him I must pine and starve. I chose to do the latter: the work is nearly accomplished; food could not now be relished.

Yet I would not change conditions with her who should be your comfort and solace. She has been a thorn in your flesh, the plague of your heart, the torment of your life. Tormented at home, guilty in conscience, intemperate in habits, you seem accursed of God. Two of your children have died cripples: the other is too pure for earth, and will soon go. When Nellie is gone, remember my boy. Like a Sappho, have I loved you; like an Eloise, have I pined in banishment from you; and, like a discarded Josephine, have I been faithful to you to the last. Oh what a happy man I would have made you! Oh how I would have cherished and loved you! But I die in banishment, and on a bed of shavings. It is hard to die a pauper, but better than to break a vow. Like a Mary with the young child, I have fled to the Egypt of strangers, no more to return to the Jerusalem of my home. Farewell! my brain reels, my pen fails me, my lamp grows dim. Now, David, I leave you: a morsel from your table would have been sweet, but no more of that; remember my boy. Again adieu, a long adieu: no more shall I trouble you. I am going home; angels beckon me away: I see my father and my mother on the immortal shores, waving palms of welcome. Ah! they speak to me: they say, 'Come away, my child; thy lot has been hard; come up hither.' Oh! who would live always in such a world as this?"

> "Hark! they whisper: angels say,
> Sister spirit, come away:
> Lend, lend your wings! I mount, I fly!
> O grave! where is thy victory?"

Mrs. Nelson read the letter with horror and

astonishment. She saw herself pictured in her own true colors, and blushed at her moral deformity. What had her wretched life been, but a waste and a torment, both to herself and husband? Her imperious temper had made home a hell. She had been straining after unattainable objects, harassing and being harassed, duping and being duped, until her life and character had become as false as the showman's phantasmagoria. What were all her gatherings at balls and theatres and operas and masquerades now? Here was a poor woman starving for a crust, dying on a bed of shavings, yet having more peace of mind and solid comfort in one hour's holy communion with God than she had enjoyed in a lifetime. She confessed to herself, and said, "Oh what a loving wife this woman would have made for Mr. Nelson! while I have been only a vixen and a shrew. What wonder that he has left home, and resorted to strong drink? Is the prophecy true, that Nellie must die? Have all my hopes for preferment, and all my toils for wealth and fashion and place, been vain? Is it true, that peace and happiness and virtue are found among the lowly? Are boys of the street to be encouraged? Is Ned Nevins so near a relative? Was his mother this angel of gentleness and forbearance? If so, she was a thousand-fold better than Nellie's mother? Is this abject and penniless boy more virtuous than Mr. Nelson himself? May not I yet commence my own life anew, and win my husband back to peace and sobriety? Cannot I do some little good in the world by alleviating and elevating the race? Do not these street-boys present a glorious field for philanthropic labor? Then let me throw off this sham, and commence life anew and in earnest." Thus reasoned Mrs. Nelson. From that time forth, all was changed in her character and appearance: her haughtiness, pride, and arrogance disappeared; she was studiously determined to follow out her noble and heaven-inspired resolve, and, being possessed of a strong mind, succeeded.

CHAPTER XXIV.

NELLIE NELSON'S PLEA TO A HARD-HEARTED MOTHER. — THE MOTHER'S CONVERSION.

"WATER! a little water! Please, Dinah, give me a little water!" said Nellie Nelson, as she reached out her little hand from the bed, and made signs of want. Dinah no sooner heard the cry than she flew down stairs after the drink, happy in the opportunity of waiting on so sweet a child.

"Nellie, why didn't you ask me for water?" said Mrs. Nelson. "Why do you always call on Dinah?" — "Because, mamma, Dinah loves to do any thing for me; she wants to do it." — "And don't I love to do it, my child?" — "Yes, mamma; but you speak so sharp to me, and scold me when I talk about the poor children: you say I must not speak to them, nor help them, nor give them any of my toys; and you make me sit up so straight, and lace so tightly, and keep my gloves on every time I go out: it makes me sick; I don't feel happy, mamma, I don't." — "But you'll soon get used to it, then you will feel better." — "No, mamma, I fear I shall never be any better: I grow worse."

"Oh, don't say so, my child! you must get better: I shall die if I lose my Nellie. You are my only child: I cannot live without you, my darling. Do look up, and say you are gaining," giving her a kiss, and weeping. "You are better now! just a little better, are you not? Tell me."

"Oh, no, mamma! I have such terrible dreams: I can't live when I dream so; I feel dreadful." — "Pugh! dreams won't hurt you, my child: you can shake them off, and forget them any time." — "No, I can't, mamma: they seem really true, and appear again and again, in the same way; they alarm me, and I can't help it." — "Pray tell me what you are dreaming about?" — "I dreamed that I was dying, mamma, and then I went to heaven." — "Oh, don't talk about dying, my child! you will kill me, you will break my heart!"

"Then you don't want to hear me, mamma?" — "No, my child, I cannot hear you talk so: I don't believe in dreams. You must live, and see the flowers, and talk about birds, and play with the school-children." — "But you don't want me to play with any children but the children of Chester Park."

"Oh yes, my child! you may play with any children, and do any thing, and give away any thing you have, if you will not speak so sadly, and not talk about dying." — "But you wouldn't allow Ned Nevins to come into my room?" — "Yes, he may, my daughter; he may go all over the house, and play with you all the time; and he may come and live with you, if you want him here; and he shall be a brother to you, if you will but get well, and not talk about dying." — "Ah, that is what I dreamed, mother! I dreamed that I had died, and gone to heaven." — "Don't talk so, dear Nellie: you will kill me." — "Hear me, mother: I dreamed that you would not serve God, and be good to the poor, till I was gone; and when I had died, then you felt lonely and sad; then you took in Ned, and kept him here, to fill my place; then you cried, and began to pray, and wished you had been a Christian, and had helped the poor; then you became humble, and loved everybody, and was kind to papa, and joined the church, and loved Ned."

"But I can love Ned now, my child; and I can be kind and good, if you will but live." — "No, mamma, you can't be good yourself, your heart is so unbelieving and so hard." — "Who told you so? Who said my heart was hard? Who has filled your head with such thoughts?"

"Nobody, mother; but I fear you have not been born again?" — "What do you mean, my child? what are you talking about?" she said, angrily.

"I mean, mother, that you have not given up all for Christ, and have not become a Christian." — "How do you know that? How do you know what I have become? Ah, this is the fruit of those sabbath schools! they have taught you to hate your mother." — "No, mamma, I don't hate you; I love you all the time, and love you with all my heart: but I dreamed that my dear mamma would be lost in the great day of judgment, unless she were born again, unless she had her stubborn heart changed; then she would not see God, nor his angels, nor little Willie and Jennie, but she would be banished forever from his presence; then I cried in my sleep, and I prayed to the Lord to save my poor mother. I told the Lord, if mamma wouldn't be a Christian without it, then let Nellie die, and go to heaven, and be with Willie and Jennie, then mamma would want to come where we were; for she would be lonely on the earth, and would not worship the things of the world; and she would repent, and forsake her sins, and give her heart to God, and be good when I was gone, and she had no Nellie." — "I tell you I can be good now, and you must not die."

"No, mamma, you can't be good in your own strength; you can't change your own heart; none but Christ can make you a Christian; and I fear you are not humble enough to give Christ your heart, and will not do it till I die." — "Yes, I will," said the mother, as she turned away to weep. Then it was that the proud, imperious woman began to bow to the simple arguments of a child, and her stubborn heart began to yield to the inspirations of gospel truth. Angels were watching her decision. Oh, what a struggle was there between nature and grace! She fought like a tiger against conviction and submission; but fate seemed to corner her, God was angry with her, her child was in danger: if she lost that, all her schemes of ambition were foiled, and all her worldly hopes blighted.

She felt that she was a sinner. The simple words of the child brought conviction to her heart. The child seemed inspired, and would not leave the subject till the mother submitted. Yet how hard for an imperious, tyrannical woman to become as docile and submissive as the wolf and the leopard in millennial times, when "a little child shall lead them."

"O Nellie!" she said, "I want to be good: and, if you will not talk about dying, I will try to be good; but I can't do it in a moment. I must have time to think about it."

"Ah, mamma! if you put it off, you will fail, or you will try in your own strength; then you never can be a Christian. None but Jesus can do helpless sinners good. Come to Jesus, come just now." — "How can I, my child? It is easy for a little angel like you to come; but I am an aged and hardened sinner. My heart is corrupt: I fear there is no hope for me." — "Don't say so, mamma!" her little eyes brightening up with hope, and her countenance flushed with the fever of excitement, — "don't say there is no hope; for there is a promise for you, mamma. Think of the thief on the cross, think of wicked Manasseh! 'Whosoever will let him come.' *Will* you come? then you may come, and come just now." Then she reached out her little arms to embrace her mother; then threw them around her neck, and printed the warm kiss upon her cheek, and said, "O mamma! you don't know how I love you! I want to get well now; I want to live so as to make you happy." — "Now, Nellie, you please me. I want you to talk of living and getting well; for you don't know how you grieve me when you talk of dying."

"But, mamma, you should grieve because you are a sinner, and have no hope in Jesus, and cannot meet your little ones in heaven."

"I do grieve, my child, and would do any thing in the world to be a Christian." — "Then you would pray, mamma?"—"Yes, Nellie, I will pray. I will do any thing; I will give up all for Christ; I will give my little Nellie to him if he demands it" (hugging her, and giving her a kiss, and weeping bitterly). "Yes, Nellie, you are not too good to give to Jesus. O my darling, how I love you! how sweet your words have been to me!" kissing her again. "Oh that I may love Jesus as well as I do you!"—"You may, mamma, even now if you will pray to him, and give your heart to him, and trust him, and lay all in his hands. Come, mamma, kneel by my side, and pray God to forgive you, and save you just now: I never heard you pray in my life." —"Ah, Nellie! I can't pray now; you must excuse me."—"Then I fear that Christ will not receive you. If you are ashamed of him, he will be ashamed of you."

"I am not ashamed, my child; but it is hard to commence to pray so soon."—"Mamma! your heart cannot be right in the work. You say you will pray; but it is just to please me, I fear. Oh! you are not honest before God: may the Lord forgive you!"—"Oh, don't think so, my child! I am sincere. I will pray anywhere and any how, if I may be forgiven."

"Then pray right here, mamma!"—"I will, dear child; but how shall I begin, and what shall I say?"—"Say, 'Lord, be merciful to me a sinner! save, or I perish'!" Then that conscience-stricken mother bent her stout form by the bedside, and cried to God from the depths of an afflicted, broken heart, with an agony that seemed to move heaven and earth, as she said, "Be merciful unto me, O God! hear me for thy mercy's sake! O Lord, forgive my sins! give me a clean heart; renew a right spirit within me; give me back the health of my child if it be thy will; if not, give me grace to endure the sad bereavement! help me, O Lord, for I am weak and needy! forgive me, for I am a great sinner! I have sinned against heaven, and in thy sight, and am not worthy to take thy name upon my lips: save me, O Lord, for Jesus' sake! Amen."

She arose from prayer, when Nellie threw her arms around her neck, and said, "Now, mamma, I know you will be a Christian, you appear so earnest. Oh, how glad I be! how kind you look! how sweet our home will be! how happy papa will be when he sees you are trying to be good!"
— "But, my child, was I not good before?"—
"No, mamma, not as a Christian: you could not be good without Christ."

"Then I am determined to find Christ. I have lived long enough in my sins, and, from this time forth, I give up all for Christ."

"O mamma, how happy you make me! I feel like singing and praising God, I be so happy. Now let us sing, mamma." Then they sang,—

> "Oh! happy day that fixed my choice
> On thee, my Saviour and my God."

And for the first time in her life that proud woman's heart was humbled and subdued, like the heart of a little child. Christ and Nellie now lay near her heart, and earth's trifles and vanities appeared exceedingly small in her sight. To her the heavens were changed; there was no frowning cloud; God was good, God was love; the skies were beautiful, earth appeared lovely, its inhabitants were attractive; and she was starting on a life of new existence.

Oh, how anxious was she to enter the fields of missionary labor! they seemed white, and ready for harvest: the fields were great, but the laborers were few. How she loved the place of prayer! how sweet was her communion with God! How beautiful appeared the face of every child! rich or poor, it had the image of the divinity stamped upon it; how different to her eye now appeared the boys of the street! They had precious immortal souls, capable of being eternally happy or miserable. How hard was their lot! how small their advantages! how meagre their chances for truth and honesty! how short their probation for eternity! Should not every Christian philanthropist be up and doing? Her cry was, Awake! awake! Her zeal seemed as fire shut up in her bones: she could not forbear.

When Nellie should become sufficiently recovered, she was determined to visit the nightschool, and study the history and nature of those boys, and see what could be done for them. What a complete change had come over her! From an inveterate hater of the poor and needy, she now becomes a philanthropic enthusiast.

Welcome, thrice welcome, to the rich fields of holy endeavor! Let the blessings of the poor, and them who are ready to perish, be upon thee! Let the widow and the orphan rise up, and call thee blessed! Let the multitude of redeemed from the streets, the lanes, and the hovels, become stars in the crown of thy rejoicing in the kingdom of God, for ever and ever!

CHAPTER XXV.

MRS. NELSON'S VISIT TO NORTH STREET. — BLACK SEA AND ITS WAVES. — LOUISA LOVELL.

"WHOA, whoa! steady there, not so fast!" said the driver of a span of high-spirited horses, as they entered North Street, with a splendid carriage, containing a lady, with a policeman at her side. The top was thrown back, and the driver was ordered to move slowly. It was past ten o'clock: a thick mist hung over the city, and the lamps shone but dimly; but the dance-halls of North Street were in full blast. The uneasy coursers foamed, and champed the bit, and chafed; striving to advance more swiftly as the music from the halls greeted their ears, and the calls of the dancing-masters sounded from hall to hall. The breath of the steeds, mixed with the aqueous atmosphere and the mist of their perspiration, enveloped them in a fleecy cloud, telling that this slow pace was not their accustomed speed. Hurriedly had they passed from the South End, through Washington Street, by Faneuil Hall, to

North Street; and now to be suddenly checked, and compelled to walk at a slow tread, was contrary to their custom and their mettle. They seemed conscious that this was no place for fine carriages and respectable citizens, — no street through which fashionable pleasure-seekers would drive. They drew in their heads, and twitched on the bits, as if to loosen the reins, that they might hurry away from the scene; but they were held by a strong hand, for the orders were explicit. That lady in the carriage is Mrs. David Nelson, visiting North Street on a tour of inspection. What sights does she witness? What sounds salute her ears? A hundred creaking fiddles sound their doleful notes, a thousand erring feet answer to the call. Here the votaries of Bacchus and Venus hold their orgies; and vice, her high carnival. Here festering corruption holds perpetual symposiums. If Boston be the "hub of the universe," then North Street is the "hopper" of Boston. It is the hopper of a great grinding mill, greater in its effects than the mills of any legitimate corporation. Its business is to grind out fates and destinies, and tears and sighs and groans, and despairing agonies, and crush and devour human life. It first blinds the victims, then destroys. A strange infatuation urges them on: they dance like apples in the hopper, then sink at last by their own attrition. There are mills in the land for pulverizing quartz, and grinding grain, and crushing sugar-cane; and mills for triturating bones: but this life-consuming mill, with its thousand workmen, and its thousand sounds of horror, forced by steam-power from the brewery and the pit, does more than this, — it crushes and devours both the bodies and the souls of men.

If there be one place nearer the fiery lake than another, then North Street enjoys that bad pre-eminence. Situated but a few rods from State Street, which ranks next to Wall Street (the richest street in this new world) — behold, what a contrast! As Mrs. Nelson enters this location, she is forcibly reminded of Dante's "Inferno," with the inscription over the gate of hell, "*All hope abandon, ye who enter here!*" As Virgil conducted Dante through the seven gates of Limbo, and through the seven rounds of the nine circles of hell; so this policeman is prepared to conduct Mrs. Nelson through the petty Pandemonium of Boston's iniquity and crime. There is no need of old Charon the ferryman to bear these miserable beings over the river of death: they are passing over the waters of Acheron and Styx before respiration ceases, before their souls have left their bodies.

Mrs. Nelson arrives opposite Ferry Street. There is the Black Sea! with its waves rolling and foaming, and sending forth its own shame. In this Black Sea, the lamented Father Mason once preached and prayed, and stood like a dike against the tides of licentiousness; but now, alas! there is no dike, no gospel barrier, to check the waves of sin. We ministers, with fastidious nicety, may gather up our robes, and remove to the South End, to escape contamination; yet the evils do not lessen by our departure. Where Father Mason stood and toiled and fell, now J—— C—— calls forth his motley group of reeling victims to the dance. The call for the dance is as the charge to battle, where there is no escape, and no hope of victory. Further along are other halls, the *El Dorado*, *Bella Union*, *Sweet Home*, and *Strangers' Retreat*, — names suggestive, but, oh! how delusive to the unwary! Mrs. Nelson passes the various halls until she arrives at Commercial Street, then, returning through Fleet Street and Clark Street and Richmond Street, she prepares, with memorandum-book in hand, to enter some of these dark abodes, conducted by her guide. She is just the woman for the occasion. Resolute, of strong nerve and will, she is determined to probe the evils of Boston to the bottom. Let us follow her into one of these halls.

There stands the master of assemblies behind the bar,—a wide-shouldered, two-fisted individual, able to quell any disturbance which the poisonous contents of his decanters may excite. Near by, stands the fiddler, resining his bow and tuning his instrument. Beyond these men are a set of stalls and curtains, the latter of which we will not raise. Seated on broken benches, at either side of the room, is a motley crew of bloated men and painted women, black and white, mixed in most unreserved sociability. There is a son of Neptune leaning on the shoulder of a daughter of Venus; and, like Palinurus at the helm, he falls asleep at his post of danger. The vile compounds in the potations have worked disastrously for himself and his purse. "Who is that woman dressed in mourning?" asked Mrs. Nelson: "how saint-like she looks! she must be a missionary."—"No! not quite a missionary," said the policeman: "she is only acting as a guy; her mourning is put on and off to suit the occasion. She is a sympathetic character, mam! she attends temperance meetings, to weep over the misfortunes of the inebriate; sometimes she may be found in a prayer meeting, deeply affected; and in times of revival, when a stranger ministers in the sanctuary, she may be seen at the altar, weeping like a penitent. She has a tear in her left eye for all solemn occasions. She admires to be at funerals, and to mix with the mourners; she is exceedingly affectionate; she enters into the feelings of the unfortunate with a gusto."—"See! there is a young man leading her to a seat!" said Mrs. Nelson. "Yes!" said the policeman, "that young man is just in from California; he has lost some money of late: she pities and soothes him, and prescribes a balm for all his woes. Oh! the tears, the gentle sighs, the soft caresses, the heavings of that tender bosom! Jupiter and Juno! What lamb-like amiability of temper! But hold! see there! They pass into another room: the curtain falls."

We will not follow Mrs. Nelson and the policeman through all their perambulations; suffice it to say, that in this neighborhood may be found representatives of every profession of crime, from the boy stealing junk, the girl just being initiated, up to criminals older and of harder mould. There is a man who once moved in respectable society, but who in an evil hour plunged into intemperance and licentiousness, and here he ends his career. There is one educated for one of the learned professions: but, alas! his education is of no avail. There is a girl, daughter of a minister, reared in virtue and refinement: alas for her fate! But few of these persons, however, have ever moved in the higher walks of life. They are mostly, persons brought up in obscurity and degradation. They are diseased, demented, half idiotic, a corrupt progeny from corrupt parents, familiar with vice, foul mouthed, offensive, disgusting. If the out-side view be so distasteful, what must be the inside, — the hidden, unrevealed scenes of woe?

Let us follow Mrs. Nelson into the back cellar of one of these establishments. There lies a girl dying, — a girl of respectable connections, but now an outcast. Low, damp, and dismal is the place; a dim lamp shines upon a single watcher, who is uneasily waiting for the breath to leave, so that the dead-wagon may be called. What a place for a once refined and innocent girl to meet her Maker! The sound of the fiddle and the roll of the dance still go on in the front hall; but she heeds them not: her thoughts are far away among the New-Hampshire hills, where her mother and sister are vainly praying for her return. "Poor girl! Are you sick?" said Mrs. Nelson. Startled at the sound of a kind voice, she opened her eyes, and gazed a moment in bewilderment and wonder; then she covered her face, and wept, fearing that it might be the voice of her mother. "O, O, O!" she sobbed, with her hands covering her face. "I cannot see my mother here." — "It is not your mother," said Mrs. Nelson: "pray tell me your name." — "They call me Louisa Lovell; but that is the name of my shame," she said, covering her face again, and crying and sobbing aloud. "Do you think you will recover?" — "No: I cannot get well; I shall live but a few hours." — "Don't you want to send some word to your poor mother?" — "Oh, no! It would break her heart, it would kill her, and my poor sister too?" — "How came you here?" — "I was deceived, betrayed by one who said he was rich and single. He was neither. Finding myself lost, I floated on the surface for a time, then made a desperate plunge for the bottom. Here I have found it." — "What was your occupation?" — "I was a teacher in a private family, South." — "Did you ever profess religion?" — "When young, I professed to be converted, but was not: if I had been, I never should have been here." — "How long since your mother has heard from you?" — "Many months! don't speak of that! my mother prays for me in the name by which I was christened, — a name which she loves; and my sister still plays my favorite tunes upon my piano at home, vainly watching for my return." — "But you will send some kind word to them before you die?" — "No, never, never! I may have broken their hearts, by my neglect; but I will never disgrace them by a recital of my crimes."—" It would not be a disgrace, but a comfort to them, especially to know that you died penitent and hopeful."— "Ah! that is the trouble. God knows I am penitent enough: I have almost wept my eyes out; I have groaned my life away; but I have no hope, no hope!" (clasping her hands, and shrieking and groaning in despair.) "Do you pray?" —"No, I cannot pray: I dare not look my offended Maker in the face." Then, as if to change the subject, she said, "They tell us that persons given to this life live, on an average, four years; but I tell you most of them live but a few months. It would astonish you to see how suddenly and unceremoniously they go out of the world: they go out of sight as by a stroke. I could tell you of girls of sixteen, running away from a friendly home, who have been decoyed here, who have died almost immediately. And these people have such a knack of disguising the matter, in changing the names and ages of the victims, and removing them from place to place, so that the public know nothing of the actual murders committed here. Oh horror of horrors! How did I ever come to this? Oh! the blackness of my soul! Oh, eternity, eternity!"—" But Christ is able to save to the uttermost," said Mrs. Nelson. "Ah! he may be *able*, but he cannot be *willing* to save me." — "Are you willing that I should pray with you?" — "Oh, yes! pray if you can pray in such a place as this, where prayers are never heard except in impious invocations for curses, for death, for annihilation." — "Will you pray for yourself?" — "I will try; I will do any thing if I may have but one gleam of hope." Then Mrs. Nelson kneeled by her side, and prayed. The poor girl responded in sighs and prayers and groans; then clung to her hand, and kissed it; then thanked her again and again, and said she appeared *so much like a mother!* Then she settled down into a sort of drowse, from which she did not fully recover. Mrs. Nelson called at the door several times during the night, and found her praying: "Lord, have mercy! Lord, save me! Oh, pity me!" At last, when near her end, she clasped her hands together, either in agony or in triumph, and said, "*Mother!* Sister! Jesus!" and she died.

Oh that there were more missionary converts like Mrs. Nelson to thread the lanes and alleys of want and woe! Oh that Christian men would come down from their high stilts of profession, and enter into the real gospel work! Oh my brethren in the ministry! let us hear the cry of the despairing! Let us come down from the pulpit where we have been perspiring in windy declamations over imaginary evils! let us meet the enemy face to face! let us beard the lion in his den! A thousand wretched victims in this locality cry for help. From beneath the curb-stones, the very earth quakes with their groans. The spirits of our forefathers shudder at the sound. Their saintly shades quail at the sight. They rise from the ashes of the Old North Church, and weep tears of blood. They whisper from the chimes of the seven bells, and upbraid us with keen rebuke. The graves on Copp's Hill quake with fright at the increase of iniquity. The bones of the Mathers stir in their tomb like those of Elisha. Every day's hearse is loaded with victims, and every meridian bell strikes the knell of many a lost soul. Oh, **awake, awake!**

CHAPTER XXVI.

THREE VEHICLES. — A TRINITY OF WOE. — CLARISSA LELAND.

WE now speak of three vehicles which are a trinity of woe, — the dead-wagon, the "Black Maria," and the steamer "Henry Morrison." The dead-wagon is a plain, square, covered vehicle, used for a hearse, going round to desolate houses to obtain the corpses of those who have died during the night by contagious diseases or otherwise, who have no friends to pay for a Christian burial. It is driven at the city's expense, and carries its victims to the Potter's Field. Could it speak of the sufferings of its passengers, it would tell of horrors little dreamed of by the outside world.

The "Black Maria" is a carriage with locked and bolted door, used to convey prisoners to their destination. Like an angel of doom, it passes at midnight around to the various station-houses of the city, and gathers up the unfortunate culprits who have transgressed the laws of the Commonwealth, and bears them to the tombs for trial on the following morning.

The "Henry Morrison" is a steamer employed by the city government to transport paupers, criminals, and victims of the small-pox, to Deer Island. These three vehicles form a trinity of woe which is beyond sectarian dispute or cavil. Plato called the three Fates the daughters of necessity. Clotho held the distaff, and spun the thread of nativity; Lacheses marked the portion of each span of existence; and Atropas cut the thread of life, without regard to age, sex, or condition. So these three messengers of woe are the daughters of dire and terrible necessity. The sins and ills of life demand their existence. Like the Parcæ, they are the progeny of Nox and Erebus, and their associations are with deeds of darkness.

Sometimes, however, these vehicles are ordered before their time. A servant girl,* near Roxbury, broke out with the scarlet rash. The mistress, thinking it the small-pox, ordered a carriage immediately, and sent her to the North End to get a pass for Deer Island. To obtain that pass, she waited in the carriage two hours in the street, in the dead of winter, and then was placed on the "Henry Morrison." Had the disease been small-pox, then the exposure to the cold would have killed her; but it proved to be only a rash caused by overwork at washing. She was borne to the island, and placed among the victims of that terrible scourge. Next morning, the physician informed her that she had not the small-pox; she had only a rash; but, as she had been exposed to the small-pox, she would have it now. So she did have it in the old-fashioned way.

The steamer " Morrison " is the Charon of the nineteenth century: it is more than the Bridge of Sighs, because it seems instinct with feeling, and stirs and weeps and sighs with the woes of its mortal cargo.

Clarissa Leland was a pale, delicate, yet handsome featured girl of tender years. Her disposition was amiable, her intellect more than the average, but she was becoming lax in her morals. She had chosen company that her mother knew must prove her ruin. The mother expostulated and forbid, but in vain. At last the girl came home sick by her ill conduct, needing a mother's care. The mother, though poor, and obtaining her bread by the labor of her hands at days' work, left all, and administered to the child as a mother only can do. When she recovered, the mother expostulated with her again, and entreated her to choose proper society. The girl was still wayward, until at last the mother said, "Now, Clara, I have left my work to nurse you this time; I have done all that a mother could do; but, let me tell you, just as sure as you go with that company again, sick or well, your presence shall never darken my door. Mark that, and heed it, or your doom is sealed."

The girl laughed at her mother's threat: that mother had forgiven her a hundred times, and would do it, she thought, as many times more; so on she rushed, headlong into crime.

But sickness came again, and the child's heart was turned towards home. A carriage drove up to that mother's door. A frail figure, covered with a veil, scarcely able to walk, was helped out by the driver, and tottered slowly up the steps. The bell was answered, the door opened, and the distressed child once more stood before her mother. Would that mother receive her? Clara raised her veil. Both stood silent and speechless for a moment, as they gazed into each other's eyes. There stood the erring child, and there the inflexible mother. The child watched the eye of her mother: it was the seal of fate upon the dial of destiny; for in it rested life or death. Then in plaintive, subdued tones of childlike eloquence, she said, "Mother, may I come home? Dear mother, will you take me back again? may I come home this time?"

The mother, not knowing how sick the child was, looked coldly on her, then calmly yet decidedly said, "No, Clara: I shall be as good as my word. You cannot come in." And she closed the door in her face. "My God! cried the child, wringing her hands, and weeping bitterly, — "my God! I'm lost, I'm lost! If mother will not receive me, then God cannot forgive me! O my soul, my soul! I'm lost, I'm lost!"

Then, reeling backward towards the carriage, ready to fall upon the steps, the driver seized her, and helped her in, and bore her away to some unknown place at the North End. But who cares for a woman that has lost her virtue? Who wants her about their premises? Who will allow their children to speak to her? Who will shield her from the cold? Who will shelter her when dying? Ah the curse, the bitter, irrevocable curse, that rests upon a fallen woman! Thieves and robbers may find sympathy; but there is no sympathy for a woman of the town. No one would house Clarissa Leland. She was now of no service to her vile destroyers; so they shunned her as they would the plague. As she had no friends to help her, it was decided to send her on board the "Henry Morrison," to the Island. Now came the bitterest pangs of her life. The thoughts of being torn away from all her acquaintances, with none to speak a comforting word, none to smooth her dying pillow, and none to bring a cordial to her lips, and no mother to pray for her, broke her heart. As she was borne to the steamer, she declared that all hope and desire to live were gone; she was taking passage to a bourne from whence she should never return. When she saw the boat, smoking and steaming, and weeping with the sighs of its unfortunate passengers, she said, "That is the ferryman of death." But when the small-pox wagon and "Black Maria" drove up, and emptied themselves of their victims of disease and crime into the boat, the poor girl groaned, and yelled with an unearthly shriek, and cried, "Holy God! Have I come to this? Is this the company for a child of prayer? O my mother, my mother!" And she fell down in despair, and never spoke again.

Little did she know that mother's distress and anxiety for her. The mother had relented of her severity, and repented: she was now threading the streets of Boston in vain to find her. As the child went by an assumed name, the mother knew not what name to inquire for; so she searched in vain. Oh, how gladly would she have soothed with a mother's love and prayer the dying moments of her child! For this, she would have given every cent she had in the world ; but she was denied the blessed privilege of giving one consoling word, or offering one parting prayer. When she learned the tragic fate of the child, she repined and blamed herself so much, that, for a time, she became deranged. The poor wretches on board of the boat, though hardened in crime, could not refrain from weeping at Clarissa's terrible exclamations of despair. They wept and sighed and groaned, and fell upon her neck, and tore their hair, and prayed to God aloud. They pitied her deplorable fate ; for her lot was so much like their own. But their efforts were of no avail, they could bring no relief.

The bell rings, the plank is taken in, the moorings are loosened, the compressed steam escapes — now a puff! — the wheels turn, and the " Henry Morrison " slowly leaves the wharf with its wretched freight of human woe. Oh, what a load of agony does it bear ! Oh, what shrieks and sobs of despair ! Oh, what crushed and bleeding hearts ! Oh, how many knells of hope are struck by that sounding bell ! Little do the city officials on the upper deck, smoking their cigars, and having a good time on a visit of pleasure down the harbor, — little do they know of the volcano of woe that rages in the hold.

What do they know of sighs and groans and broken hearts? what of individual merit or demerit? The city is a colossal step-mother, with stern look and strong arm, locking up alike the unfortunate and the vicious. She herds them in one indiscriminate mass; then bids them keep silent, and be thankful for their lives.

Nevertheless, there are sympathies that follow these poor, sorrowful creatures. Friends that knew them in their better days think of them; relatives and playmates remember them; mothers' prayers follow them; the condensed steam that falls upon this deck seems weeping with many a mother's tears; and the pressure from these safety-valves heaves with many a mother's sigh. But there is no comfort for Clarissa Leland: she is beyond the reach of earthly comfort. This pealing bell sounds the knell of her destiny; this whistle's shriek is but the echo of her despair; and these paddle-wheels are but the wings of the death-angel that bear her from shores of time to the judgment-seat of God. Oh the depths of the agony of human woe! But enough of this: suffice it to say that the child died on board of the boat during the passage. Thus the soul of that child of hope and prayer; that child of fairest prospects, susceptible of the finest feelings, of sweet temper and tender heart, fit to make the home of man a paradise, — that erring soul, from this ferry-boat of death, was ushered into eternity, to stand before its God.

WARNING. — Young reader, I have a word with thee. Hast thou broken the first sabbath, or repeated the first oath, or taken the first draught, or pilfered the first dollar, or spent thy first hour in debauchery? Stop right short; stop just here. Sin is alluring, deceitful: its end is death.

> "Stop, before thou farther go:
> Thou'rt sporting on the brink of everlasting woe."

High standing and prosperous as thou mayst have been, thy position may be gone in a moment, — thy friends, thy wealth, thy character, thy prospects, all gone; and the "Black Maria" may be on thy track, and the dead-wagon following its rumbling wheels. Privately between you and me, as we sit here alone, with none but God to see us, I say, Stop!

CHAPTER XXVII.

PHOTOGRAPHIC ALBUM OF NIGHT-SCHOOL TEACH-ERS. — NICHOLAS NOBODY.

NOW for the pedagogue album. Let us photograph some of the would-be night-school teachers. Perfect order and church-going decorum cannot be endured by the boys of the street; their fidgety, restless frames demand excitement: hence it requires a peculiar class of teachers to manage them. There is Mr. *Precise,* a sleek, well-dressed looking gentleman, but a great stickler for order. He looks into the room, and sees several classes reading at a time; and some of the boys are cutting up pranks. He is horrified at the sight, and cries, "Let me have a room by myself: I will keep order, be assured, sir."

So he takes his room, and a company of boys are called to fill it. Little do they know what a trap they are falling into. "Now, boys," says Mr. Precise, "order is the first law of nature. The world on its axis, and the planets in their orbits, move by law. Do you hear me? There!

I see a boy looking towards the door, as if to go out. Attention, sir! no more of that. I am an old school-master; I have had worse boys than you, and I always made them mind. I had a big salary in my time, and now I am going to teach you for nothing. Do you hear that? Oh, what gratitude I shall win from your hearts!" Yet the boys didn't see it in that light. "This night," said Mr. Precise, "shall be a night of discipline and order; the next night, you will commence the rudiments of study; the third night, you will be formed into classes; and the fourth night, you will be ready to acquire knowledge. Now let the school recline one minute in this position,—that's well; now two minutes in that position,—very well; now hold up your faces, and look me right in the eye; let me see if you are honest boys." But this was too much for them to endure: one boy started for the door, and then another. "Stop, there, you rascals! come back here!" But, as they did not come back, Mr. Precise said, "Well, let them go!" One boy says, "I want to write and cipher; I came to learn something: I don't want to be foolin' here in this way." — "I'll learn you something that you have not acquired, sir, if you do not obey orders," said Mr. Precise, sarcastically. Thus Mr. Precise taught. But he taught only one night: the next night he had no scholars, his room was empty, while the other rooms were overflowing. As the boys came voluntarily, he could not coerce them; so his regimen would not work for want of pupils.

The Blusterer. — There is the windy blusterer, full of senseless words, ostentatious in showing his brief authority. " Boys!" said he, in tones of thunder that set all the classes staring, — " boys! you must remember that I am master of this room, and I shall keep order. Do you hear? See to it! less noise! order, order!" Now stamping his foot on the floor, " Order, boys! you must keep still, still as mice; you must not speak a word: be still, still!" Then the boys began to laugh. " Tut, tut! none of your laughing. I see you laughing; stop that!" Now he hits one a knock; and all the boys ha, ha, right out, laughing, desiring no better fun. Now his anger rises. He takes another by the ears; and the whole school begin to yell and hoot and laugh, until the policeman comes in, and restores order. Mr. Blusterer finds himself unfit to teach, and leaves the school in disgust, ever determined after this to vote the native-American ticket.

There is Mrs. *Magic*, a pale, delicate, bright-eyed woman: she stands like an Elizabeth Fry among prisoners. Short, and small in stature, with no physical force, mild in her eye, and calm in her speech; yet her words settle on their hearts like balls of lead, and her calm, confident look tells them that she expects to be obeyed. She looks, and she commands attention; she speaks, and is obeyed. She has a certain magnetic influence that wins, charms, and awes to submission, when more pretentious powers fail.

There is Mr. *Soft and Easy*. He has recently broken off his sins, and is desirous of teaching street-boys in order to atone for the past. He comes several miles on foot for that purpose, and with the best of motives; but, unfortunately, he is unfitted for the work. The boys at once feel the loose rein, and skip about like unbridled colts. While the old man is making figures on the black-board, they are pinning papers to his coat-tail. Now he requests them to solve that problem; some of them commence, whilst others look demurely over his shoulder, pretending to be attentive, yet, at the same time, are chalking grotesque figures on his back. In vain does the old man try to command order: he leaves with a sad heart, mortified at their ingratitude.

There is Miss *Bigotry*. She is a cross between a true-blue and a hard-shell. Nothing is right but her particular sect and creed. To smile is a sin, and to laugh is a crime; and not to bore everybody with the points of her creed, and button-hole every expressman and milkman and paper-carrier, and pour into their ears a string of sectarian quotations, would be a dereliction of duty. "Ah, me!" she cries, "that school is not properly conducted. Mercy sakes! Why don't they read the catechism to these boys, and talk to them of the '*Mystery of Babylon, the mother of harlots,* and of that *man of sin, the son of perdition?*' Those teachers are not pious enough. Why don't they get these boys on their knees, saying prayers and singing psalms?" — not taking into account the kind of boys she had to deal with. She asked one of them, "What church do you attend?"—"I attend the Catholic Church, ma'am! Don't you think that be a good church?"—"Yes, I suppose so," said Miss Bigotry in contempt and derision; "good as *any devil's church,* I guess." When the boys found that she called their church the Devil's Church, they could hardly be restrained from insulting her, both there and on the street. Thus ended her career as teacher of street-boys.

There stands Mr. *Hopeless.* He is now only a spectator. He was an all-confidence man: he said, "Treat the boys well, and they will use you well; be faithful to them, and they will be true to you." So he commenced, and got his pocket picked the first night. Then he left the school in disgust, being confirmed in the belief of total depravity. None but those who have taught those young heathens know how low they have fallen, and how tightly their old habits and associations cling to them.

There is Mr. *Enthusiast*. He is sure of success, confident that he can change the nature of the boys at once. He tells them frankly that he expects them to right about face, and march to rectitude forthwith. He crowds on all steam, taxes every nerve; but he soon explodes the boiler of his zeal in utter despair.

There sits Mr. *Perseverance*, calm, collected, as if about to undertake some herculean task.

" When Ajax strives some rock's vast weight to throw,
The line too labors, and the words move slow."

He has calculated the work to be done, and counted the cost. He has to re-educate these boys, and extract the roots of bitterness one by one. They are morally depraved, intellectually dissipated; they cannot brook restraint, or concentrate their minds on one beneficent idea. Their bones ache for action, and their minds for excitement; and they have but little ambition to improve.

But, overcoming all these obstacles, Mr. Perseverance at last succeeds by dint of hard labor, and rescues many souls from crime.

There is Mrs. Nelson, and Nellie Nelson, just enough recovered from sickness to pay the school a visit. Mrs. Nelson no sooner sees a class without a teacher than she volunteers her services, and enters into the work with all her heart. At once she attracts their attention, she pleases and is pleased; the work is delightful,— just the thing to occupy her strong mind and energetic will.

See there! the policeman has a boy by the collar, and is about to thrust him out of doors. "Hold!" said little Nellie Nelson, "hold, Mr. Policeman! Please don't turn him out; please, sir, let me have that boy: I will teach him."

"You teach him!" sneered the policeman: "I guess you will, you little dove! Forty little bodies just like you could have no more impression on him than the blowing of the wind. He is a jailbird; I have had him up to the station-house a dozen times; nobody cares for him, he's got no friends: he comes here only to get out of the cold: he don't come to learn." — "Never mind that," said Nellie, in gentle, persuasive tones, her brightblue eye sparkling with hope. "Give me a chance, sir; please let me try him." — "Well, I will; but you don't know what you are talking about, Nellie. There!"—giving him a jerk upon the seat, as he sat him down by her side,—"there! teach him to your heart's content. And you, Nick, if you insult that girl, I will have you sent down to the Island in less than twenty-four hours. Do you hear that?"—hitting him a knock. "Yes, sir," Nick said, rubbing his head; but Nick was too well pleased to stay in from the cold a little while longer, to complain of bruises; then the thought of having such a lovely little being for a teacher awakened his curiosity. Nellie began to question him very affectionately, and then, to soothe him, she placed her hand upon his head; but she started back in astonishment at his strange replies. The boy was so accustomed to be knocked on the head, that, when she raised her hand, he dodged back, and drew up his fists as if to ward off a blow. "Don't be afraid, I am not going to strike you," said Nellie: "What is your name?"—"I 'hain't got no name," said Nick, gruffly. "No name! well, what do they call you?"—"They calls me *Nick!* didn't ye hear him call me so?"—"Well, what else do they call you?"—"Sometimes they calls me *Nick Knockdown*, 'cause I gits banged about so much; and sometimes *Nick of the woods*, 'cause I sleeps in the woods when I gits broke."

"Have you no other name?"—"Yis; sometimes they calls me *Old Nick*, 'cause I gits into so many scrapes. When I was little, they called me *Nicholas Nobody*, 'cause nobody wouldn't own me, and nobody wouldn't have me, and nobody wouldn't care for me."—"Hadn't you a father?"—"No: not as I knows on."—"Hadn't you a mother?"—"I 'spose so; don't remember none."—"Why would nobody have you?"—"'Cause us fellers he's of no 'count. There be so many left 'round on the door-steps now-a-days, that nobody wants 'em."—"How old are you?"—"Dunno,—older than I oughter be, I guess."—"Have you no friends?"—"Yes: I has got one."—"Well, what did he do for you?"—"He put me in the lock-up."—"Put you in the lock-up? What was that for?"—"'Cause I stole somethin'."—"Ah! why did you steal?"—"'Cause I couldn't help it: I was hungry, I was."—"What did you get?"—"I got a piece of pie, and two pieces of cake."—"Is he a pious man?"—"Yes: I 'spose so: he took me up for stealin' pies."—"What other reason have you that he is a pious man?"—"'Cause he licks the boys so."—"Do pious men whip boys?"—"Yes, they does: they licks 'em like sixty."—"What do they whip them for?"—"Dunno; guess they wants to beat good things into 'em through the skin." — " Why did your friend whip the boys?" — "He whipped 'em 'cause they come round his door to play. He keeps a great big horse-whip on purpose, he does; and, when he hears 'em make a noise, he licks 'em awful."

" Do you think that is the way to be a Christian?" — " Don't know: good as any way, I guess." — " Can you read?" — " No." — " Do you know your letters?" — " I knows some on 'em: I knows the round O, and crooked S, and broken-backed K; and I knows T, what you rich folks has for to drink; and I knows I, what you looks out of; and C, what you do when you looks. I looked at C on a show-bill. It said, 'Go C,' and cost a quarter, so the boys said." — " Will you try to learn if I will help you?" — " No, tain't no use," he said, scratching his head, and appearing uneasy of restraint. " Why won't you try?" — " 'Cause I can't learn. Everybody says I can't know nothin', and can't be nobody, I be sich a numskull." — " Then what are you going to do for a living?" — " I ain't going to live: I bee's goin' to kill myself; there ain't no use in livin'." — " Oh! don't talk so. You shall have friends: there is one that cares for you; God loves you!" — " No, he don't. God don't love street-boys; nobody don't love us: we be banged about, and 'spised by everybody. When we ask for work, then the man puts on his spectacles, and looks at our old clothes; then he pulls off our caps, and looks into our heads; then he 'zamines us,— this is the way he does it" (suiting the action to the word, as if placing a pair of glasses on his nose, and standing up, and bending over towards her in a comical manner)—" this is the way he looks" (turning his head first on one side of her cheek, then on the other); "then the man says, 'No, I don't want no sich lousy chaps as you. Begone, ye ragamuffins! get out, I say,' and he drives us fellers off like as a dog. No, God don't love street-boys; nobody don't love us; we ain't fit for nothin'."—" But I love you, I do, Nick," patting him on the shoulder. "You love me. Ha, ha! I guess you du! then let's see how ye du it, heh? Let's see ye give me somethin'. Come, give me a cent, then, if ye love me, will ye?" extending his hand, and drawing near to her. "But love is worth more than a cent."—" Then give me somethin' more; give me a quarter; give me that 'ar gold ring on your finger."

"But love is worth more than silver or gold: it is better than all the gold in the world." —" Well, I suppose so," said Nick, scratching his head in a thoughtful mood; but what are ye goin' to give me, any way?" — "I am going to give you that which is better than money, which cannot be stolen from you, and which will make a man of you." — "Oh, pooh! don't be foolin' a feller; I'm tired, I want to go."

But Nellie would not let him go until she had got control of his will, and made impressions upon his heart. She awakened in him an ambition and a hope, that he little dreamed of: he felt that he could yet learn to read, and become a man. The concentration of his thoughts became a wonder both to himself and all that knew him. He would often go to Nellie's house to ask questions, and report progress, so long as her health would permit; and, when that failed her, nobody was more sad, and none felt its loss more, than Nicholas Nobody.

It was decided, that, upon the termination of the night-school, Nicholas should be received into the household of Mrs. Nelson, where, with the united efforts of Nellie and herself, the work of reformation might be still further advanced.

CHAPTER XXVIII.

HOW NICHOLAS NOBODY WAS RECLAIMED.

THE work of reforming Nicholas Nobody was not accomplished in a moment. His crabbed nature was not subdued at once. His ideas of property, right and wrong, truth and honesty, were not rectified without many a severe and trying struggle. He seemed to have an intelligence entirely his own, perfectly original, and was possessed of no little shrewdness and acuteness in many things. Mrs. Nelson found that she had caught a tartar when she introduced him into her parlor. Its profuse ornaments were too tempting for a boy of his peculiar ideas respecting the property-rights of *meum et tuum.* He gazed about the room with the sharp eye of a revenue-collector, scrutinizing goods contraband for confiscation.

"Where is my porte-monnaie that lay on the mantle-piece?" said Mrs. Nelson to Nicholas, becoming alarmed. "Dunno, mum: I hain't got it." Well, sir, how did you buy that gold breast-pin?" — "Bought it with money, in course." "What money?" — "Money what I seed layin' 'round." — "It was *my* money, you rogue you. Now, where is the purse?" — "Dunno." — "Don't know, Nicholas, when you stole it?" — "Dunno: no, I don't." — "What have you done with it?" — "Threw it away, mum. There weren't nuthin' in it." — "Where is the money, then?" — "Ain't got none." — "What have you done with it?" — "Spent it; took the fellers to the theatre." — "Well, Nicholas, do you think that is right?" — "Guess so. *Findin' is havin'*, you know, mum." — "Yes; but I didn't lose it." — "Can't help it: it's gone, mum." — "What else have you taken, Nicholas?" — "Ain't taken nuthin' much." — "*Nothing much!* tell me what you have taken," she said, becoming startled with fearful apprehensions. "Dunno: nuthin' as is worth nuthin', I guess." — "Let me examine your pockets," she said, in a tone of command. "There! here is a bronze statuette of Webster; and, I do declare, a medallion of Lincoln. What in the world was you going to do with them?" — "Dunno. I likes to have somethin' in my pockets to throw at the fellers." — "Well, if this isn't the height of impudence. You don't understand the *meum et tuum* in regard to the rights of property, do you?" —

"*Mum te um?* Why, who is she, mum?"— "No matter! I will search your other pockets: I believe it pays. As I live, here is Nellie's gold watch! and you call *this* nothing, do you? Oh, you impertinent thief! how could you be so wicked and ungrateful? I must at once turn you from the house."—"What's that for?" said Nick, with a look of surprise. "It won't do me no good to turn me off."—"It will teach you to appreciate a good home."—"I allus did spreciate um, mum."—"I should think you did, with a vengeance! Now, Nicholas, are you not sorry for stealing from your best friend?"— "S'pose so; I didn't mean nuthin'."—"You didn't mean to be caught, I suppose. O Nicholas! I deeply regret ever having taken an interest in you, you are so dishonest and ungrateful: you don't appreciate any kindness that is shown you. I fear you will come to no good end."— "I'll try to be gooder," said Nick, dropping his head, and looking at the figures on the carpet,— "I'll try to be gooder if you won't turn me off, and talk so."—"Ah, it's no use, Nicholas! you don't care for anybody or any thing: you will not try."—"Yis, I will try too: I do care for you mum," said he, the tears starting in his eyes. "You has been so good to me, an' let me come here, an' gin me things: but somehow, I bees sich a hard un, I allus be doin' wrong."

Mrs. Nelson seeing his penitential tears, and finding him tractable, discovered some signs of hope, and began to impress on his mind the duty of obedience, and the love and fear of God.

Nicholas appeared deeply affected, and seemed to realize in some measure his accountability to God, and his duty to himself and fellow-men. So she dismissed him, trusting that the lesson would prove beneficial.

Nicholas, on his way out through the kitchen, encountered Dinah. Now Dinah and Nick, from the first, had agreed to disagree, and many a *ruse de guerre* they resorted to; but Nick, by his shrewdness and adroitness, generally came off conqueror.

"La sus! hab you come here again, you Nicklesum Nobody? La sus! how sheepish you do look! Guess you have been doin' sumthin', and missus found ye out, heh?"—"Hush up, you chimbly-sweep! who be a-talkin' to you?" said Nick, starting up in anger.

"La sus! ye be getting right smart! How awful toppin' ye is! Hope missus will lick ye awful de next time."

"I'll lick *you*," said Nick, "if you don't shet up," seizing an armful of clothes which she was ironing, and throwing them over her head.

Dinah, shaking them off, said, as her dark face

appeared through the white clothes, like a black berry in a pan of milk, "See here, you limb of Satin! muxing up all dese fine clothes; you must quit dis ar work; you ain't for to do no sich mischief in *my part ob de house:* does ye hear? I'll swash you all ober with de dish-cloff, ye Nicklesum Nothin! Go way dar, 'bout yer bizzness, or, I do declar', I'll throw sumthin'." — "Yah, yah, yah!" sneered Nick, "ye can't catch me: ye can't see nothin' nor nobody. Who's afeard?" Dinah, getting into fever-heat, replies, "Ye be a poor, dirty wagabone! *You* cum a-here, insultin' a quality woman like *me*, heh? Guess ye better be gwying away, an' right smart too. You nebber hadn't no gemman father, *you* didn't." Nick, resenting the intended insult, said, "I bees as good as you bees, and a pile gooder. You don't know who your father bees no more nor I, 'cause you run wild-like. You be dirty more nor I, an' sand-paper won't scratch um' black off you nohow." Nick dodged his head to escape the dish-water, which Dinah seemed always to have at hand when any disrespectful allusion was made to her color; and crying, "Yah, yah, yah! *quality gal!* you be a smart un'," beat a hasty retreat.

In his exit, he stumbled against pussy, who, from his first appearance in the house, became terrified at him, and who at once put herself on the defensive, leaving upon him striking marks of her displeasure; but, generally, the cat was the more humane of the two.

With all Nick's peculiarities of temperament, his love of fun and mischief, his disposition to teaze and quarrel, his thirst for revenge, for real or imaginary wrongs, it was singular to witness his tenderness and watchfulness over Nellie. She seemed his guiding-star, leading him through many difficulties and dangers, and pointing him to the God of the fatherless. In all his tribulations, doubts, or perplexities, she was his sole confidant; and he received her decisions as from an angel of heaven. He would watch every opportunity to do her some little favor, and render her assistance in a thousand ways.

"Nicholas, come here!" said Nellie, on a beautiful May morning. "Do you love flowers? You know God made the flowers; and now I have found a handsome bouquet in my own little vase. I didn't put it there; and I know there are no fairies about, to do such things. Do you know who put them there?" Nicholas, rejoicing that she was pleased at his offering, forgot the weary tramp he took early that morning to secure them, and replied, "Everybody likes Mayflowers, an' I thought you might; so I put them there."—"You are very kind, Nicholas. How much joy and pleasure it gives us, if we can but look away from self, and endeavor to add to the comfort of another! Now you feel happier than if you had taken these flowers into your own room, don't you? I know you do, and I feel very grateful for them : for you know, Nicholas, I can't go out into the beautiful green fields, and run round, nor roam over hill and dale, now. And, Nick, the good book says, " It's more blessed to give than to receive ;" so, as you have commenced the month with such a good start, I earnestly hope you will continue through to the end. And now, Nick, I have something serious to say to you. You have some good qualities; you have a tender heart and willing disposition; but you are dishonest. This must prove your ruin. I fear the jail and the gallows stand looming up before you. There is only one hope; that is, in turning right about, and breaking off at once. Now, Nicholas, you knew it was wicked to steal my watch. You thought nobody saw you: but there was one eye upon you, — the all-seeing eye of God. His eye is ever upon you; he sees all your sins and crimes; and he will surely punish the guilty." Nick was abashed at her reference to the watch, and said, " I only took it for fun, to wear a day or two among the boys." — " But,"

Nellie replied, "you couldn't have taken the money for fun. O Nicholas! you are a bad boy. I fear you are lost; what can I do to save you?"

"Oh, don't think so hard of me, Nellie! don't *you* give me over, 'cause then I'll wish I were dead, and buried in the buryin'-ground." — "But I can't help you, when you are dishonest."

"Then, Nellie, I'll try to be honest: *I will try.* I won't touch *nuthin'* 'cept I ask leave : I *will* be gooder, if *you* will only trust me."

"Ah! you have said that before: how useless for me to try. What hope is there for you?" — "Oh, don't say so, Nellie! you'll 'scourage me. I feel kinder differenter, somehow; an' I wants to do right, I do," said he, bursting into tears; "an' I *will* do right, — *yes I will*, God knows I will, Nellie, — if you will forgive me, this time." — "But you can't be good in your own strength, Nicholas: you need God to help you."

"Yes, I *do* needs God to help me. How can I git God to help me? 'cause *I do* want to be good, *truly*, Nellie! an' I don't want you to think bad of me, I don't."

"Ah, Nicholas! if I thought you were really in earnest, how cheerfully I would labor for you!" — "But I *be* in earnest, Nellie: I *be* 'tirmined to do better. O Nellie! *try me*, an' see if I ain't in earnest. Oh, don't let Mrs. Nelson send me off! 'cause then I would be wickeder, an' lost for certain."

"Well, Nicholas, if you are resolved to do right, I will give you some encouragement from the Scriptures. You know you are a great sinner; you have broken God's holy law; but for you there is hope, there is a Saviour. If you will but put your trust in him, he will save you from your sins. 'Though your sins be as scarlet, they shall be as white as snow.'"

"Oh! how can I find this Saviour? how can I be forgiven? how can I be gooder, Nellie?"

"By telling Jesus all your sins, and asking him to take them away."—"Where will I go to tell him?"

"You needn't go anywhere: Jesus is here. I feel him in my heart. You have only to stop doing wrong, say that you are sorry, and pray that he might forgive you."

"Oh! I *can't pray*, Nellie. I be such a hard 'un, tain't no use: Jesus wouldn't hear *me*, nohow."—"Yes *he will*, Nicholas. He came into the world to save just such sinners as you."

"But *I* can't pray, Nellie: I don't know what to say. *You* pray: you be such a angel like, God will hear *you*."—"I will pray for you, Nicholas, if you will get down on your knees with me, and try to pray for yourself." The boy gladly consented: and Nellie, taking his hand, knelt down by his side, and poured out her heart to God in prayer. In her prayer, she mentioned his trials, exposures, and temptations in the street. A poor, fatherless, friendless boy, knocked and beaten by everybody, without one kind word to cheer him, or one smiling look of encouragement, having no adviser, and no Christian heart to point him to the Saviour.

"O God!" she cried. "Thou hast promised to be a father to the fatherless. Oh look in pity on this poor orphan boy! forgive his sins, teach him how to pray, save his soul from death." At this prayer, Nick's heart was touched, and he cried bitterly to think what a great sinner he had been, and how good God was to send him such a friend as Nellie; and, through his sobs, he promised her, that, from that time forth, he would be a better boy.

CHAPTER XXIX.

CREATURES OF THE COAL-DUMP. — NED AND DINAH IN A CONFAB.

"WAKE up, Eddie, and open the door! I has got some breakfast for ye, poor darlin' crathur," said the old Irishwoman, with pipe in her mouth, as she came to Ned's door, fearing, that, from the effects of his sickness, he would not be able to rise. Oh! ye has got up, has ye? ye be much bater, heh? Lord bless yer latle heart, yer be a lookin' bater intirely! Speak, darling! I thought ye was goin' to die, an' be wid yer poor sainted mother. Cheer up, my latle! here be some mate, an' some brade, an' a latle tae; now fall to, and ate like a hungry latle pig."

Ned was sick and sore, but would not give up in despair. He rose, determined to shake off his sorrow, and to remember this benevolent woman's kindness, by getting her coal enough to pay her for all her trouble. So he rallied all his energies, took his basket and hoe, and started for the dump.

At the same time, Mr. Nelson had sent Dinah to visit Ned; but, not finding him at home in Orange Lane, she followed on, and found him at last at the coal-dump. Here she saw him in strange company, — strange indeed for a boy of his pretensions. She instinctively recoiled from the scene before her.

Now, it must be confessed that the society on these refuse-banks is not the most virtuous, select, or *élite*. Neither is it, properly speaking, *Boston* society; for it is essentially foreign in its composition. Its brogue sounds of court life; but, unfortunately, it has more of the police vernacular in its ring than of kingly patronage. It is what may be termed "mixed" society. Mixed indeed, it is; and sometimes, by the clouds of dust arising from the ash-carts, when all hands are squabbling over the emptied contents, for the much-coveted prizes, the society is *inextricably mixed*. Every society has its moral standard, its ultimatum. Among this people, the *ne plus ultra* of their ambition is the democratic idea of individual sovereignty. This is often made manifest by the free use of nature's defenders in assaults and defences for the protection of life and property. There are no poets or artists here; but, what is better, there are subjects for both the poet and artist, as well as the philanthropist. All society has its relief picture: even beggars may boast of heroes. A blind Belisarius with his medal, on which was inscribed, "*Gloria Romanorum,*" for restoring to Justinian his empire, may have been a beggar. But there is no Belisarius here. Homer, the prince of poets, may have been among their number, of whom it is sung, —

"Seven cities claimed great Homer dead,
Through which the living Homer begged his bread."

But we may safely affirm, that no poet *par excellence* is found among the coal-pickers and beggars of Boston. Columbus may have begged food at the convent of La Rabida for himself and son Diego; but we may assert, without fear of contradiction, that there is no discoverer of a new world among the dirt-pawers on the new territory of the Back Bay.

Morally, these vagrants are among the lowest classes of mamifferous species. As carrion, in summer's day, teems with animated nature, so do these ash-heaps and refuse-banks teem with the lowest, debased, most abject specimens of depraved humanity that ever swept on the tide-wave of foreign emigration. Why boys and girls are allowed to congregate here, and become a prey to these hags and harpies, is a mystery.

As we said, Dinah recoiled from the sight. Now, Dinah was dressed in her best attire, —

VIEW OF THE COAL DUMP. NED AND DINAH IN A CONFAB.

"La, Sus! Niggers would n't do dat ar work no how! Dey lets de white folks do dat! ha! ha! ha! La, Sus! ye has to be *right smart*, ye has, to be a 'spectable nigger." Page 305.

silks, tassels, ribbons, flamingo, *et cetera;* and, when she saw the extreme degradation of these creatures, she felt a sense of her own importance. She thought "right smart" of herself; and, tossing up her head, she strutted about large as life. She said, "O Ned! I has found ye. La sus! here ye is, for sure; right down in de dirt. Tush! fudge! what company ye hab got into, heh? I guess dese be de Yankee mudsills, or some udder sills, heh? I do declar! if day ain't de lowest folks ob de human animals dat I ebber did see. Dese be de Yankee spec'lators, I guess, — spec'latin' in de coal mines, an' de cotton cloff, heh? La sus! this does cap de climax. Dey say de slabe be a dirty critter; but, whedder he be or no, he wouldn't do dis ere work, no how. No nigger be like dese folks; he wouldn't creep like a worm in de dirt and ashes; he wouldn't be a scatchin' arter leetle bits ob rags and coal: no, not he! He hab more 'spect for hisself than dat. Niggers won't do dirty work, nohow. Golly, day leab dat to de white folks. Day be too toppin: day lets de mudsills do de scrubbin' and de scrapin', and de pawin' on de dump, heh? Ya! ya! ya! Ned, what does yer mean, bein' wid such critters, a right smart lad like you? See dat old woman puttin' a basket ob coal on her head. La sus! she ain't got clothes 'nough on her back to make a crow's nest. What, Ned! am dis yer Norfern society? Well, I guess us niggers better come up Norf, and teach yer Yankees some lessons on 'priety and etchepet" (she meant etiquette). "Dar, Ned! you needn't laugh 'cause I can't pernounce yer big words. See that udder woman, scratchin' and pawin' in de dirt, just as if she lubbed it. Show me a slabe dat would do dat, heh? See dat great strong man, dat great lazy lubber! what he do here? Why ain't he to work? He could earn a heap ob money. He be right in de prime ob life; an' dar he be pickin' leetle bits ob coal. La sus! if Massa Lee had him, I guess he'd make him stir his stumps! See dem lookin' gals dere! how dey look! and how dey do talk! What stuff dat be for gals to say! Ned, does ye hear it? an' don't ye blush, and drap yer head for shame? See dem fight, and steal coal an' rags from one 'nodder. Now de cartman hab to shake de horsewhip at 'em to stop 'em. Now dey be fightin' for an old boot; now for a broomstick; now de policeman comes, and say he lock 'em up if day don't keep still. La sus! be dis your company, Ned? See dem ar bad boys: day be here all day, and learn nuthin' but bad dings, and wicked dings. Day ought to be to school: dis be no place for boys. Ye tell about Yankees bein' smart, able to take care ob demselves, an' all that. La, sus! if a nigger down Souf be idle an' lazy like dese folks, massa sell him to de fust buyer. Like de town paupers, he let 'em out to de lowest bidder. La, sus! ye has to be right smart to lib in Old Wirginny! Ye has to be some pumpkins to be a wallable slabe: ye has to be right smart to be a 'spectable nigger! Put such lazy folks as dese down Souf, an' day wouldn't fotch nuthin'; day wouldn't sell for 'nough to keep dem ober night. I guess when day paw over *Mrs. Nelson's* ashes day don't find nuthin' much. Ya! ya! ya! La sus! what a world dis am we lib in, heh? Ned, why don't you speak, and say sumthin'? Ye be lookin' as if ye be 'shamed; and I guess ye be. Ye be 'shamed of bein' found amongst such critters, heh?"

Now, the truth is, Ned could have no chance to speak; he could not put in a word edgewise: besides, it must be confessed that he quailed not a little under Dinah's lecture, and was not in proper mood for talking on that subject.

At last he said, "Dinah! O Dinah! what did you come here for, to this coal-dump? It is no place for you." — "Nor you nudder, I guess," said Dinah, contemptuously turning up her nose, and showing the white of her eye. "Say, what did you come here for?" said Ned. "La sus!

I almost forgot what I did cum fur, my thoughts am so 'fused wid dese sights. Well, dis be it: Massa Nelson hab sent for you, Ned; he want to see you." — "What does he want of me?" — "Dunno; s'pose he wants you to go to work again." — "Well, you may tell him that I am done working for him; so he may set that at rest." — "What's dat ye say, Ned? Ye speak as if ye got yer back up! What! won't work for Massa Nelson? Why, how big ye hab got, pickin' on de dump, heh? Ye be quite toppin; ye be a mighty big cock, struttin' about, an' crowin' ober de dirt-heap. Guess dese ere dirt-scrapers make ye proud, heh? Won't work for Massa Nelson? Den it more 'spectable to work here dan to work for a merchant, an' a gentleman, heh?"

"Gentleman! gentleman! did you say? don't call that man a gentleman: he is a villain, a rascal!"

"Tut, tut, Ned! look out, sir, look out for yer tongue! be carfull what ye say. If Massa Nelson hear dat, he hab you put in de lock-up. He has got money, an' he can send you off to de Island right quick, he can."

"Let him do it; I dare him to do it. I will repeat it to his face: he is a *mean, low villain!*"

"Oh dear! Lordy massy, Ned! ye be a *spill*

child; I seed that plain 'nough. Ye be cock ob de walk ober dese ar dunghills: it is all ober wid ye now. Oh dear! what a change hab cum ober ye! Ye used to be meek an' tender like, an' talk about yer sick mudder; but now — whew! — ye be like a rattlesnake! Bang what a gun! La sus! tell me what Massa Nelson hab done dat you speak so."

"Done! done! did you say? Why, didn't you *see it with your own eyes?* Why do you ask *me?*"

"La sus! he only gib you a lickin': dat's nuthin'. I used to git a lickin' eber day; I got so used to it, dat I lubbed it; I couldn't eat my supper widout a lickin': it started up my appetite, an' made me feel sorter, kinder good arter it."

"Well, it may do for a slave to speak lightly of whipping, but not for a *free-born American boy.* Besides, I have just learned something bad about Mr. Nelson: he was the means of my mother's death (his eyes filling with tears); yes, my sainted mother, — a woman as much better than he as he is better than Satan himself. Do you think I can bear that?"

"La sus! Ned, somebody has been a-foolin' ye. I tell ye, young lad, ye better look out how ye 'cuse Massa Nelson: he hab got money, an' he fetch you up in less than no time, boy! look out, sar, how you insult him."—"And how is it," said Ned, "that you have all at once fallen in love with such a man? What does it mean?"—"Well, Ned, I tell ye. Ye know ye got de licken, den I got a licken too. It didn't hurt me much; but it made me awful mad; and, if it hadn't been for Nellie, I would have left Mrs. Nelson in less dan no time. But Nellie was so kind, and taught me to read, and prayed for me so sweet, I couldn't leab Nellie, no how. Den, Nellie, arter dat, went to prayin' for her mudder. Jerusalem! how she prayed; an', don't ye think, Mrs. Nelson turned right squar about. She say her prayers now, an' go to de meetin', an' gib to de poor; an' she go into de night-school, an' takes a class, an' let Nellie teach de boys too. So you see a mighty change hab cum ober her. She used to hate de boys ob de street, and chase dem off wid de broomstick. And Massa Nelson seems better dan he used to was somehow: he stay in de house more, and lub to talk wid Nellie; an' he lub Mrs. Nelson now; an' we all gits along fuss rate. So you see what a good home you lose if you leab him. If ye knows which side of de bread de butter be on, ye will come."

"I can't come under the present circumstances," said Ned. "If Mrs. Nelson has become a Christian, she will see that justice is done me;

and I wait for that." — "Justice, did ye say? justice to ye, dat call Massa Nelson *sich hard names?* La sus! if ye be a-lookin for *justice,* I guess ye gits more than ye bargined for; dat ye does, heh? Ya, ya, ya!"

"Well," said Ned, "I am content to live among the lowly, and be poor, if I can keep honest, and have a good heart; but I will never be disgraced by being whipped: no, never! so help me God! Mother said, *if I do no wrong, something good will come to me;* and, God being my helper, her words shall be my motto till I die."

"Now, Ned, I has got somethin' to tell ye; dar be come to Mrs. Nelson's, since you left, a low, dirty wagabon' of a feller, dat don't know nothin' 'cept to blackguard 'spectable folks, and turn eber ding topsy-turvy like."

"Ah! who is he? what is his name?" earnestly inquired Ned. "*Name!* did ye say? He ain't got no name; he neber had no name; day couldn't find no name for sich a non-scrip' in de booktionary. I is awful feared dat Massa Nelson take a fancy to him though, 'cause missus fetched him from dat ar night-school; and she make a heap ob him. Now, Ned, ye better come, or ye lose ye chance." Ned promised to consider the matter: so they parted.

CHAPTER XXX.

NED SUSPECTED OF BOND ROBBERY, PERILOUS STATE.

"HERE'S the Heral', Jirnil, Trav'ler, 'Ranscrip'. Paper, sir?" cried Ned Nevins, as he passed the office of Solomon Levi, the Jew. "No, I vants no paper; but I vants to see you, Ned," said the Jew.

"Come in, my boy: let's have von leetle talk. Ye has left Mr. Nelson, heh? He be von bad man, heh?" — "No, sir!" said Ned, "he is not so very bad; but he beat me, and struck me: I shan't go back till he makes 'pology." — "Dat's right: stick to yer rights, and ye make von great man. Now, Ned, I hash got a plan tat vill make ye rich. Ye vill not be compelled to vork on te dump, nor sell papers, nor vork for Mr. Nelson any more for a livin'; ye may be rich and smart, and dress fine, and have a carriage, and take te gals out ridin'" (tickling Ned's ribs with a knowing smile). "Yah, yah! ye can ride wid de gals: and ye can go to 'musements, and live in von nice house, and have goot tings to eat, and be von fine young gentleman. Does ye see?" — "Yes, sir: I see what you mean," said Ned; "but I can't see where the money comes from?" — "Tut, tut! ye don't look: I tell ye tar ish von big heap of money in tis grand speculation. Money come just as free as water! Does ye hear, my boy!" — "Yes!" said Ned, "I hear; but I don't see it." — "Vell, ten I make ye see it mighty soon. But first I must know if ye can keep secret? Keep von big secret, heh? Von tousand-dollar secret? Can ye keep him, heh?" — "I cannot do wrong," said Ned. "Bah, bah! I didn't say any ting about wrong: I asked, Can ye keep von secret?" — "I can keep a secret if it ain't wrong," said Ned: "my mother said, if I do no wrong, something good will come to me."

"Nonsense! Ned, ye be foolin'. Ish it wrong to make moneys? Ye bes von leetle fool! Everybody loves moneys. Money makes te fine clothes, te fine carriages, and te fine houses; moneys makes peoples rich and smart; moneys bes ever ting." — "No, money ain't every thing," said Ned: "an honest heart is better that gold, and '*a good name is rather to be chosen than great riches.*' This much I learned in Sabbath school."

"Come, come! Ned, none of yer preachin'! Away vit yer Sabbath schools! Tay vont make ye rich! Tay bring ye no silver dollar, no gold dollar, no round ten-dollar eagle, no tousand-dollar greenback; tay make ye poor and despised. Come! take a leetle vine to drink; and ye tink different. Vine vill cheer up yer young heart."

"No, sir! I have pledged myself to touch not, taste not, and handle not." — "Vell, vat of tat? Pledges be nothin'; everybody breaks pledges. Ministers break 'em; husbands break 'em; wives break 'em; rich folks break 'em; merchants break 'em ven day can make a leetle more moneys; everybody breaks em', I say, ven it be for tare interest to do it. Now, try tis vine over a pledge, and see if it don't taste jist as goot and sweet. Yah, yah! it be sweeter, I guess, for te pledge. Stolen waters be sweet, ye know, heh? It make yer eyes sparkle, and yer thoughts bright; it make ye feel goot and smart and happy. Come, cheer up, and take a leetle: take von glass vid me. It cost you nothin'."

But the noble boy stood firm as a rock; therefore the Jew was perplexed. Finding him strong in his determination to stand by his mother's maxim, he said, "Here is von goot vatch, my lad; I gives him to you for von present. Now you can keep de secret, heh?"

But Ned refused in such a positive manner

that the Jew bade him go about his business for "von poor, good-for-nothin' fool."

That night Mr. Nelson's store was broken open, and robbed. Suspicion at once rested upon Ned Nevins and his associates. He had taken in some lodgers who were bad boys, and they and Ned had been seen loitering around the premises that day. It was known that Ned had worked in the store; he knew the situation of the safe, the shape of the key, the condition of affairs, and how to open the back shutters; he was angry, had a spite against Mr. Nelson, would not work for him: all this tended towards his crimination. The truth is, the Jew's financial embarrassments had make him desperate. He had met with astounding losses in gold speculations, and many goods in his clothing store had mysteriously disappeared; he was driven to a strait; must have relief in twenty-four hours, or go under. Now, the Jew was not a malicious and brutal man, like his tool and accomplice, Bill Bowlegs, but was simply acting on false premises. Confidence is the soul of trade: Levi had no confidence in God, man, or the principles of morality. That confidence must be based on the eternal principles of truth and righteousness as revealed in the gospel: the Jew had no gospel. Truth and justice are a man's commercial base of supplies: cut off his base, and he may forage for a time, but must eventually surrender.

Of the two men, the Jew was the more dangerous, because most jovial and attractive. He would cheat you with smiles. Bowlegs was harsh and repulsive, of a bull-dog nature; no one would fall in love with him: he was fit for deeds of blood. Levi was a man of the world, a fast-liver, generous in his way, and accommodating, but destitute of moral principles. His natural parts were good, but he was educated in the wrong school. When making a tool of Bowlegs to oppress poor needle-women, he little thought that the man who had starved and cheated them might one day try his hand on his old master. Bowlegs had purloined goods as adroitly from the Jew as he had money from the poor sewing-girl. Now the Jew was driven to extremities: money must be had. He had deposited a large amount of Government stocks with Mr. Nelson, as surety for debt. He wished to obtain them without an equivalent. He had tampered with the boy, but found him incorruptible, and unfit for the task. Bowlegs is brought into the ring, and does the work. He contrived to have the boys appear around the premises several times that afternoon, calling for goods Mr. Nelson was known not to have, so as to draw upon them public suspicion; yet they were ignorant of the part they were playing in the dreadful drama. The Jew immediately disposed of the stolen bonds to meet his liabilities, and also to get them on the wing before the robbery should be published. But fortunately for Mr. Nelson, and for the reputation of Ned, the numbers of the coupons had been recorded, so they were at once advertised as protested. This opened the eyes of the Jew to the danger of his situation. What could he do? In twenty-four hours they would come back on his hands: he had no other securities by which to redeem them, and no way of escape from impending doom! To be poor and penniless was heart-rending for a Jew, whose God was money; but to be implicated in a robbery, to be tried and condemned, and be incarcerated in a prison, was more than the terror-stricken man could endure. So, to relieve himself and his family and the courts, he committed suicide by poison.

Poor Bowlegs did not get out of the difficulty in so quiet a manner. He was too brutal to awaken sympathy: too many injured ones were ready to testify against him; and the general opinion prevailed, that he had not only robbed his master of goods, but had stolen the bonds from Mr. Nelson unbeknown to his master. Levi was commiserated as an injured man; but Bowlegs was tried and condemned on two indictments, and is now working out his sentence in the Charlestown State-Prison.

Thus two characters disappear from the scene of action. We may as well disclose the fate of two others in this connection. Patrick Murphy and his mother, old Mag Murphy, are quietly ensconced on Deer Island; one in the House of Industry, the other in the House of Reformation for juvenile offenders. Whether Pat will fulfil the intent of the institution by reforming is a mooted question. He now stands at the wheelbarrow, and his mother at the wash-tub and flat-irons. He fills up the void of his young life by emptying dirt on the flats: she absolves herself from crime by soap and water; and, with the flat-iron, she smooths down the wrinkles of an exceedingly crumpy character. Some of her "lady-boarders" are enjoying the hospitalities of the same institution. They are dressed in blue frocks with short sleeves, and white aprons, and, under the regimen of Capt. Payson, look plump and hearty. Pat's blue, brass-buttoned, long-tailed coat is carefully rolled up, with his roomy and airy unmentionables, in a fitting bundle, labelled, "No. 212, Patrick Murphy." They will show a better fit to his person when he shall have grown to their size, a few years hence. On the Sabbath, the boy Pat from the gallery in the chapel looks down on his mother Mag on the main floor; and they exchange mutual glances of filial and maternal affection. As the Sabbath service, however, is not according to their creed, they do not relish it. A bottle of whiskey would be more inspiring.

Ned also became unfortunate about this time: he lost his trunk, which indeed was a misfortune; but his taking in a set of unruly boys for lodgers awakened suspicion against his character, which was a worse evil. One of the boys was a candy-peddler at the theatre, one a bill-carrier, and one a bill-poster: all had free access to the theatre; and, returning very late at night, they awakened the suspicion of the police. If Ned were honest, why should he fellowship such company? It is true he took them out of pity, in hopes to benefit them: but, finding his mistake, why does he not discharge them? Yet this is not an easy thing for a friendless, helpless boy. The fact is, Ned has got into bad company: his temper is changing, and his chances for life are lessening every day. Something must be done for him, or he will go the way of many others, who were once as honest and strong-minded and persevering as himself.

Ned's trunk was stolen, with all the mementoes

of his mother, and could not be found. In vain did he search the stores of pawn-brokers, junk-dealers, and second-hand clothing stores: he could get no clue of them. Orange Lane itself was not increasing in morality: thirteen wretches, of various ages and sexes, were arrested at one time: some for drunkenness, some for lewdness, some for stealing chairs from the sidewalk while people were moving, some for stealing sheets from a corpse, and some for burglary.* Such were the surroundings of Edward Nevins, the lamb of gentleness, and the child of prayer! How long can his young heart stem the tide of iniquity that threatens every moment to overwhelm him? Ah! little does the unsympathising censurist know of the besetments and temptations that befal an unprotected child in this Babylon of iniquity. He must run the gauntlet of almost every crime. Hold, dear reader! before you condemn a boy like this, pause for a moment, and think of his disadvantages and surroundings. Be sparing in your blame, be bountiful in pity.

---

* Since writing this book, Orange Lane has been declared a nuisance by the city authorities; and its miserable dwellings have been torn down. Some of the unfortunate inmates, still clinging to the cellars, were crushed and killed by the falling of the walls. Boston, September, 1866.

CHAPTER XXXI.

MR. NELSON'S SECRET VOW. — UNFORTUNATE OCCURRENCE.

"PAPA! where do the angels dwell?" asked little Nellie Nelson, as she lay on her little bed one Sabbath morning, while her mother and Dinah had gone to church, and Mr. Nelson was left to take care of the house. "Papa! where do the angels dwell? Be they all in heaven, or are some of them here, and in the air, and on the leaves of the trees?"—"One of them is here, I guess," said Mr. Nelson; "one as bright as any of them; one about your size, my daughter, with bright blue eyes, a sweet countenance, and tender heart: here she is, all tucked up in her little trundle-bed. Oh, let me kiss you, Nellie! there, my dear, a thousand, thousand thanks for that! Oh, this is angelic! What makes you ask about the angels?"
—"Because, papa, I thought I saw and felt them around my bed."—"So I did just now: I thought I felt one too (giving her another kiss). Yes I did, my child; and I see one now, I guess (look-

ing into her eyes). Oh, what comfort such angels as you bring to a parent's heart! You make a little heaven all around you: the air is full of music where you are, and the light of your eyes speaks with angel voices, and the breezes echo them back to God. Cheer up, my darling, and talk about the birds and the flowers, and the pretty school-children: these are angels enough for you. Come, cheer up, and talk about something else." — "But, papa, believe me, the angels *are* here! I hear their voices! I hear them call me! Oh, how sweet they sing!"

"Pray what can angels be here for, my child? You are not going off with them, are you? You are not going to leave your father and mother, and all your pretty things, are you?" — "I don't know, papa; but I like the angels best, because they obey God, and keep his commandments."

"Then you don't love me; you don't love your father." — "Yes, papa, I love you, and pray for you; but then you are not good as the angels are."

"Not good! how do you know that I am not good?" — "Because you use strong drink, and sometimes you swear; and you whipped Ned, and you have been unkind to mamma!" — "But your mother has been unkind to me." — "Yes, she was once unkind; but God gave her a new heart, and made her a Christian; and now she is good, and going to heaven." — "Am I not going to heaven too?" — "Oh, no, papa! — 'no drunkard shall inherit the kingdom of God.'" — "You don't call me a drunkard." — "Yes, papa! if you get intoxicated, you are a drunkard." — "Oh, Nellie! you do wrong to call me such hard names. If you were not sick, I should be severe with you. You spoil my visit with you this morning. I thought when the house was quiet, and all were gone, and you and I were here alone, we should have a nice little time; and I could talk with Nellie about the good things that we eat, and the fine things we wear, and about riches, and pleasure, and all the nice things you are to have when you get well." — "But riches don't make us happy, papa! money won't save the soul." — "I was not talking about the soul: why do you get on that subject?" — "Because, papa, the soul is of the most importance; the soul is every thing: don't you believe it?" — "I believe we had better talk about something else," he said gruffly. "No, papa! Nellie is going to die." — "Don't say so, my child." — "Yes, papa! I am going to die, and you will have no little girl on earth. I shall be in heaven with Jesus and the angels. I know papa will be lonely and sad without Nellie: he will have nobody to bring home sweet things for; and papa will want to come and see Nellie in heaven. So I want to tell you how to come, papa: may I tell you?"—"Oh, my child! I can't be a Christian now, I am too wicked; ask of me any thing else, and I will do it."—"Then, papa, I want something to remember you by when I get home to heaven. Will you give it me?"—"If I can I will, with all my heart; pray tell me what is it?"—"I want you to sign a writing, papa."—"Ah! I see: you want me to take Ned home; but I cannot do that, for he is a bad boy."—"No, papa, not that: I want you to sign a pledge that I may remember in heaven."—"Oh, pugh! my child, you are joking: what pledge do you want?"—"I want you to sign the temperance pledge."—"Temperance pledge! what good will that do you?"—"It will do me much good, papa! for after that you will be a Christian, I think, and meet me in heaven."

"But I can be a Christian without signing the pledge."—"No, papa! I fear you will not. You must break off your besetting sin first." Now Mr. Nelson became thoughtful: the stings of a guilty conscience pierced his soul. He had more than once come to the brink of financial ruin, through strong drink and the machinations of the Jew. Strong drink had debased his soul, alienated his friends, grieved his wife, who was trying to be a Christian; strong drink was barring his soul from heaven. This he had felt for some time, but never more forcibly than now. The child seemed inspired of Heaven to speak the fitting word: he could not resist what appeared to be the voice of God. So he said, "I will pledge you, my child, to be more careful in the future."—"Ah, papa! that will not do: you must pledge me that you will not drink at all."— "Well, wait, and let me consider: I will think of it," he said, thoughtfully. "No, papa, I cannot wait: I want you to sign now, while your heart is tender, and while Nellie is with you." Then she climbed up into his lap, as she left her bed, and threw her arms around his neck, and kissed his cheek, and looked up into his eyes with the loving confidence of innocence, and cried, "Papa, you will sign the pledge now, won't you, papa? Oh, how glad I shall be! and how happy mamma will feel! You will sign now, won't you? Do sign, papa, just now! oh, sign it now! I know you will, won't you?"—"Yes, my child, I will," said the weeping father. Then, after much feeling and prayer, and many solicitations not recorded here, he wrote a pledge on the fly-leaf of the family record of the Bible, and signed it, asking God and Nellie to bear witness. Nellie, having succeeded in this, was now bent on another object.

After some time had elapsed, she broke the silence, by saying, "Papa, who do you suppose was Ned's father?"—"How do I know?" said Mr. Nelson, rising upon his feet, and pacing the room much excited. "Why do you ask me?"—"Because I thought a father that would forsake a child so young must be very cruel."—"He might have died, and been buried, for ought you know," said Mr. Nelson, wishing to change the subject. "But, if he were dead, why would not his mother have said so?"—"I don't know; I suppose she had her reasons: come, let us talk of something else."—"Did you ever see his mother?"—"Did not I tell you to drop the subject? What do you mean?"—"I mean to speak a word for poor Ned," she said, much agitated, with tears rolling down her cheeks. "You whipped him, and drove him off, and broke his little heart: I *must* speak, papa! I *can't help speaking*. I wish you had whipped *me* instead of that *poor boy!* Oh, how cruel you was, papa! you know you was." This little burst of feminine eloquence completely subdued the father, and he was again willing to listen for a time, until another accidental suggestion came pop into his face. "Papa!" she said, "hold down your head; let me look into your eyes. There! if they don't look like Ned's eyes." —"Don't talk so much about Ned, my child; you will drive me mad."—"Well, I guess you was mad, papa, when you gave him such a whipping. Oh! how could you be so cruel? How could you whip him? See! I have got a lock of his hair! It looks just like yours, papa! how could you whip a boy that looked so much like you?"

At this moment a knock was heard at the shutter, and the handkerchief stirred that Nellie had placed there in token of friendship to Ned. Ned had touched it, and changed its position; but he was now gone, for he was ashamed and afraid to enter. "What do you go so often to the window for, my child."—"Ah, papa, I must tell you. I had a trap there, papa! a bait to catch a lover with," said Nellie, laughingly. "There! that's right, my child; I love to see you laugh a little: now cheer up, and be happy. To catch a lover, did you say? pray what sort of a lover could such a little minnow as you catch?"—"Oh, it's a shiner papa! a regular gold-fish."—"A shiner, bah! it is a boot-shiner, I guess. Who is it that you are making signs to at the window, my love?"—"Oh, papa! it is the boy you so much despise and hate, poor Ned Nevins."—"There it is again! Ned Nevins must always be on your tongue: oh, how I hate the sound of that boy's name!"

Now another tap was heard at the shutter;

and the handkerchief was again moved from its place. This time, Ned had mustered all his courage, and was determined to await his doom; for despair had made him desperate. Now it was that Mr. Nelson went to the door, and saw a sight that would draw tears from any other eyes but his.

There stood Ned, all covered with dirt and blood and bruises, received from boys whom he had accused of stealing his trunk. He feared to apply for protection to the police; for he knew that the police were suspicious and jealous of him, and opposed to him, as he was still held at court on probation for good behavior. One other complaint in court would seal his fate forever. What could he do at this critical hour of trial? How could he break from those boys? how recover his trunk? and how be protected from the insults of their fiendish sports and malice aforethought? O ye who have never come in contact with this substratum of diabolism! — have never been the mark of a mob, — ye know nothing of vengeance and perdition. Thousands are their arts: let them but spot their victim, and, in some way or other, that victim is most sure to fall. They will falsely accuse him; set the police against him; get up a fight, a hoot, and a yell; change their hats and coats in a jiffy, so as to blind the police; then leave him to suffer the penalty of the law; while they, withal, escape. Oh the hell of their malignity! Oh the infamy of their hearts! My blood runs cold, my hair rises, and my veins shrink with horror, when I think of what I have witnessed in Boston, while striving to protect the innocent. The tears were in Ned's eyes as he stood at Mr. Nelson's window, and the blood was running from his wounds. When he saw Mr. Nelson coming instead of Nellie, he thought at first to run; but, recovering himself, he resolved boldly to stand his ground, and state his case. Perhaps, if Mr. Nelson cared nothing for him, Nellie might intercede in his behalf. "Ah, Ned! is this you?" said Mr. Nelson. "So you haven't gained much by refusing to work for me, heh? What's the matter, Ned? so you've been fighting, heh?" — "No, sir, I haven't been fighting; but I am awfully hurt, and I don't know what to do," said he, bursting into tears. "Ah! who has hurt you, Ned?" — "The bad boys, sir." — "Bad boys? why did you go with bad boys?" — "I didn't go with them: some of them came to lodge with me, and I found they were bad; but I couldn't get rid of them." — "So you have learned that I was your best friend, after all?" — "No, sir! if you had been a friend, you would not have whipped me: neither would you have *suffered my poor mother to starve!*" — "Your mother!

what do I know about your mother? I tell you, young lad, I have heard enough of your cant! I have heard of nothing but *Ned Nevins*, and his *mother*, in my family for months. I am heartily sick of it. Now, my boy, I will have you a little further off: your probation was to end with your first quarrel; now I will have you sent to the Island." — "Oh, don't, papa! don't! you will kill me!" said Nellie, as she climbed up into the chair, and looked out of the window, and saw Ned all covered with *blood!* The sight of the blood, and the shock of her father's angry words, threw her into a fit; and she fainted, and fell upon the floor, crying, "Oh, don't, papa! don't! you will kill me!" Poor girl! The car was near, as a precursor of death; she heard the sound of the engine as she once heard it in Orange Lane. The cars were full of passengers, rolling towards the river; and the sound made her nerves twitch and tremble as she was called to mount the train. On, on, rolled the locomotive, with all its ponderous load. On, on, went the vast multitude; and the city of their destination stood just before them over the river. On, on, she seemed whirling on! Her young spirit was hastening towards the undiscovered bourne whence no traveller returns.

CHAPTER XXXII.

NELLIE ALLOWS STRANGE VISITORS TO HER SICK-ROOM.

"RING, ring, ring! It be nuthin' but ring and run, ring and run, run to de door, all day long. Oh, dear! dar be nuthin' but peddlers and beggars comin' all de time. I wonder who comes dar now?" said Dinah Lee, running to the door, and finding a little ragged girl on the steps, with a face wan and pitiful, who said, "My mother wants to borrow your baby agin."

"Borrow my baby? Borrow my baby, did ye say? La sus! I hain't got no baby! I neber had no baby! I neber was married; and I ain't goin' to be, nohow. I shan't neber hab no baby; I shan't hab nuthin' to do wid any baby. Pray, who be you? and what does yer mudder want ob a baby?"

"She wants it to go a beggin' with." — "To go a beggin' wid? La sus! I guess she don't want Dinah's baby to go a beggin' wid: what does ye mean?" — "I mean the white woman's baby."—"La sus! de white woman hain't got no baby but Nellie; and I guess she don't let her go on dat ar business: I guess ye has got de wrong street, and de wrong house, heh?" The poor girl looked crest-fallen and bewildered. At this moment a furious old hag came up behind her, as if watching the child's mistake; and, with a terrible blow upon the head, knocked her prostrate, felled her to the pavement. "There! lie there, and die, ye latle loggerhead! Didn't ye remember what I sid? Is this Albany Street? is this the 'ouse I told ye?"—"Oh, dear! Oh, dear! you have killed me! I shall die!" said the girl, kicking and sprawling, and tumbling on the pavement: "I thought it was Albany Street; they told me so. I can't read: oh, dear! oh, dear!" Then the old woman picked her up, and they started off. "Ring, ring, ring! Dar 'tis agin: I wonder who comes now! La sus! is it you, boys? Well, ye can't see Nellie any more. Nellie be so sick, we fear she be goin' to die." Then Dinah burst into tears; and some of the boys began to cry also, as they reluctantly turned away from the door. "Call them back a minute," cried Mrs. Nelson, from the room where she was watching her sick daughter: "Nellie will grieve and worry, if she be not allowed to see them. Call them in: it will stop her worrying." So the boys took off their hats, and slipped in carefully, one by one, until they all stood in the room where Nellie lay. What a sight was before them! such as they had never seen before! There were the beautiful curtains, the gilded picture-frames and looking-glasses, and chandelier; the splendid furniture, soft carpet, rosewood sideboard, marble table, cushioned chairs and sofas and ottomans, while the boys stood abashed, and ashamed of their seedy appearance. Some of them had seedy heads and uncombed locks, and were out at the knees and toes and elbows. They smiled, and ogled each other, and tittered in their sleeves, at their awkward position, then gazed upon the couch before them, where lay their little benefactress, never to visit the school-room again. Nellie gazed upon them for a moment with a benignant look, as if she comprehended, little as she was, the perils of their forlorn condition.

There was the orphan, helpless, and almost friendless, standing on crutches, tottering, and hobbling on the brink of want and despair. There was another orphan, boarding with his uncle. No father's care protects him, no mother's prayers soothe him to sleep, or echo in his dreams. He sees his little cousins receive the warm kiss from their mother, then wonders why he could not have a mother to kiss and love him. Wonders why he was born; why he is always in the way; why his fortune is made so hard. Poor boy! who would not pity him? There is the son of the scrub woman. His mother is out early and late, almost constantly, and things are much neglected at home: children run riot, but a mother's care and prayers and love repair much of the disorder when she returns. The boy runs of errands, and carries market-baskets, so as to help pay the rent. Oh, how acceptable would be a donation of a little tea and sugar to him, as a token of good behavior in the night-school, that he might carry it home, and cheer his poor mother's heart! How she would prize it! not for its value alone, but for the token it brings that her boy has won favor. There is a boy whose mother is bedridden, and he is almost her only support. See how ragged he is! Nearly all his earnings go to his mother How acceptable to him would be a suit of clothes! What a lift it would give him from despair! What encouragement to press on! There is the gentle, lamb-like child, whose father is a drunkard. When the father works, he earns fifteen dollars a week; and then all have enough to eat. When he drinks, he spends what he has earned, and wife and children starve. Oh the anguish of that wife when she sees the whole week's wages swept away by one spree, and Saturday night come without a dollar for rent, or a loaf for the Sabbath! The child seems to say, —

> " My father's a drunkard, but I'm not to blame ;
> ⋅ . . . . . oh pity me with your tears ! "

There is the boy who has taken his first step in crime. Oh how he repents of it, as he gazes upon the bed of the dying! Oh for a friend to encourage him in his firm resolve never to transgress again! Alas, for him! friends for such boys are exceedingly scarce: he must battle with temptation alone, and fall, we fear, at last. There are some already steeped in crime, but who have escaped detection. Nellie rose up in her bed, like a little angel of mercy, and thus addressed them. " Dear boys, I must tell you I am going to die. Nellie is not afraid to die ; she is going to heaven, going to be with Jesus and the angels. You will not see me any more : you may inquire for Nellie, but she will not answer. I am little, I cannot say much ; and I am weak and sick ; but I want to say something which you will remember. Some of you have been bad boys : you have said bad words, and done bad things. Some of you have stoned your teachers in the streets. You thought it cunning then, for you knew no better; but now you have learned better. Some of you have injured me and my mother: you pulled my hair in the school-room, and called me names, and insulted me. Now I want to show you how I can overlook it all, and forgive you, even as Christ forgave me my sins." At this, several of the boys wept to think how cruel and thoughtless they had been, and wept at Nellie's forgiving words. Some of them tittered and wept at the same time. Nellie fell back upon her pillow somewhat exhausted; then called Dinah for some water, and then continued. "I am little, I said, and weak and sick: I cannot do much for you; but I can pray for you, and love you. All the day long do I pray for you, and pray for all the poor boys of the streets. I ask God to be a father to you, and raise up friends for you, who will pity you, and love and forgive you when you do wrong, and help you to do right, and give you work and wages, and food and fire, and homes and instruction. I wish I had a home and a book to give to you all. I wish I were rich, and had money. Oh, how I should love to go about, and give it to the poor, and make them so happy! Oh how I wish I could make you happy! I love you, and I pray for you, and I dream about you. I dreamed that I saw Nicholas sick in his room: he had no father nor mother to help him. Then I and Dinah went to his room, as we did to Ned's; and I got some good things for him, and helped him: and oh, how thankful Nick was! He got down on his knees, and said his prayers, and thanked me, and thanked God who had sent me. Then how happy I was that I had made him happy! I dreamed that I saw you boys turned away from the doors of the rich, because you were ragged, and had no father. Then my Saviour said, 'Suffer them to come unto me, for I am meek and lowly.' Oh, how I loved that Saviour when I found he would receive the poor and needy, and them that had no helper! Now, boys, I am going to that Saviour: will you meet me there?" The poor boys were so overcome they knew not what to say; and Nellie became too much fatigued to proceed further. "There," said the mother, "that will do for this time: I fear this is too much for you, Nellie." "Oh, no, mamma! I should like to talk all day, I should; but then my head turns round, and my bed turns round, and I feel strange and dizzy." — "There! I thought so. You must stop now: so bid them good-by, and we will let them go." — "Now, boys," said Nellie, "I would like to talk with you longer, and like to take you by the hand, and bid you good-by; but I am too sick: you must excuse me. Mr. Benedict and others have left some articles here, and directed my mother to distribute them among the worthy and needy. Here is a suit made for Ned Nevins: he says he cannot receive it now, as he can get his own living, and buy his own clothes. I give it to the boy who has improved so well, and learned so fast, 'Nicholas,' or 'Nick of the Woods,' he says he is called. Now, Nick, take it, and remember Nellie." The tears started in Nick's eyes, as he shyly and simperingly came forward, and received it from the hand of Mrs. Nelson, for Nellie was too weak to handle the articles.

"Here is one for Tim the Tumbler. Now, Tim, you have frolicked long enough: it is time for you to be a man, and throw off your boyish sports." Tim appeared a little ashamed, as he came forward, and remembered what a fool he had made of himself in tumbling about like a foot-ball, instead of improving his mind.

"Here is one for Tom the Trickster. You are the boy that thought it cunning to pull my hair, and insult me and my mother: may God forgive you as I forgive you!" Tom trembled, and turned pale, at hearing his name called; for he was ashamed of his own name. "Here are some shoes, and some tea and sugar, for Johnny McCurdy the newsboy. Now let the other boys come," she said, "whose names my mother shall call : I am too weak to say more." So the boys came up, and received their portion of garments and groceries, as best suited their condition; and, passing by the bed of Nellie, they took a farewell look of the holy apparition that had lighted up their dark pathway, and cheered them with the light of comfort and hope. Nellie waved her hand as they passed, and smiled at every face, until, weary and exhausted, she sunk heavily upon her pillow, her cheeks flushed with fever, her eye vacant, her breath short: she became lost to outward objects, as the ever-rumbling car came nearer and nearer to the station, and the morning whistle of the engine seemed ringing in her ears. Now she rallies for a moment, and opens her eyes with a wild stare, and cries, "Mamma! ain't we almost there?" then, sinking into oblivion again, as her nerves twitch and tingle, she seems rumbling away on the uneven way, borne by the merciless engine whose tender is laden with diseases and blasted hopes. On, on, over the valleys and round the curves, the fiery messenger wheels along, receiving new accessions continually, and new impetus from the close-connected fever-tender which is always feeding the flames, yet always full: on, on, she is borne towards the spirit world.

CHAPTER XXXIII.

NED'S LAST INTERVIEW WITH NELLIE.

"RING, ring, ring! who comes dar, so early dis morning as dis, I wonder? said Dinah Lee, going to the door. "La sus! it be you boys, heh? Well, ye can nebber see Nellie any more: she be too sick to see anybody."—" We didn't 'spect to see her," said Nick, holding a bunch of flowers in his hand, and dropping a tear as he spoke,—" we didn't 'spect to see her: we only wanted to send her these flowers. We boys went without our suppers last night so as to buy them for her." "La sus! ye needn't do dat! Nellie hab flowers 'nough ob her own: ye better sabe yer money for yer selbes."

" Then what *could* we give her?" asked Nick. " *You* gib *her!* La sus! ye needn't gib her nothin'. She don't want nothin' from *you!* she hab eber ding she want herselb. Nellie be rich, she be."—" Oh, dear!" said Nick, "I be feared she won't take 'em: then all us boys will cry so, and feel so bad! Oh, dear! Nellie has made a man of me: I didn't know as I could be anybody till I seed her. Oh, how good she spoke to me! and told me to be a good boy; and I *has* tried to be a good boy: yes I has!" Then he burst into tears, and all the boys cried with him.

"Well," said Dinah, "I will see ib Nellie take 'em; perhaps she may." Then when Dinah came back, and told them that Nellie would receive the flowers, the boys smiled, and clapped their hands, and scampered away with every demonstration of joy. Considering that they were the offering of poor street-boys, who had given their all, even all their living, no earthly gift could be more acceptable to Nellie: they were wreaths of victory, flowers brought to the conqueror. Alas for the world! the sweetest flowers, the most delicate and short-lived, the sweetest and fairest of the children of men, die early. Their marks are seen in short graves in churchyards, in small figures on tomb-stones, in the vacant chair and cradle, and in stricken and bereaved hearts. Nellie fell back, and gazed upon the fading flowers in which she saw her own decline and doom. She gazed in dreamy reveries, till at length a voice of conversation from the room below broke the spell of her meditations. It was the voice of Ned talking to Susie Pinkham and Nellie Stedman, daughters of the seamstress and washwoman, who had come to inquire after Nellie's health. Ned was afraid to appear at Mr. Nelson's when Mr. Nelson was at home: yet, through the favor of Nellie and Mrs. Nelson, he ventured at times to approach the house. When Nellie heard his voice, she said, "Oh! Eddie! can't I see Eddie? Please, mamma, call Eddie." Then she said, "O Eddie, have you come? Nellie is dying: Nellie has got most home, Eddie. Why did you stay away so long? I have been very sick, Eddie! Oh, how sick Nellie has been! You didn't come to see me when I was so sick. I know you had to work hard; but you might have come to see me: I thought you would; I didn't think you would stay away so long. O Eddie! you don't know how much I think about you, and love you, and pray for you, and dream about you. Last night, I dreamed that I saw your mother in heaven. She smiled as she saw me, and asked me how Eddie was getting along. I told her Eddie was a good boy; but he had a hard time of it, poor boy! bad boys troubled him very much, and I was sorry to say my father had been unkind to him. She asked, 'Does he keep from doing wrong?' I said, Yes, he wouldn't do wrong for the world. Then she kissed me, and thanked me for bringing such good news. Then she showed me the beauties of the place; and when I saw the banks of the river all covered with flowers, and the tree of life, and the golden streets, and the saints and the angels, I wanted Eddie to come, and share the kingdom with me: then we would strike hands together, and roam over the fields of life. Eddie, won't you meet me there? Speak, Eddie! I want to hear some sweet words from your lips."

Ned took Nellie by the hand, and kissed her forehead, and parted her locks, and said, "Ah, Nellie! I would have come to see you often, you know I would, but for your father." — "O Eddie! you shouldn't mind that: he don't mean to harm you; there is simply a misunderstanding between you." — "More than that!" cried Ned: "he seems determined to banish me from the city." — "Oh, no!" rejoined Nellie, "my father is not the man to do such a thing: you don't know him, Eddie." — "Yes, I do, Nellie! Ah! this is a hard world; I almost want to leave it, and go with you, Nellie, and be with my mother. I never should have borne up under my trials but for you. You came to my bedside in Orange Lane, when I had been whipped, and was sick: I could not have recovered but for the comforting words you gave me. I should not have been the good and honest boy I've tried to be, but that I knew

I must respect myself, for there was one that loved me. O Nellie! you can't tell how your words have cheered my poor heart. In every trouble I seemed to see you looking out of the window, and waving that little white handkerchief, and saying to me, 'Don't give up, Eddie. Try again; better luck will come by and by: *if you do no wrong, something good will come to you*;' and so I took courage. If the world had many such angels as you, Nellie, then we poor street-boys would not be so bad, and the wicked would be scarce."—"Don't talk so, Eddie, I have done nothing; I wish I could do something for you: I would give every boy a book and a home if I could. And you, Eddie, I would give a mint of gold,—yes I would. I wanted to give you some presents, but you would not receive them: why wouldn't you take them, Eddie?"

"Because, Nellie, I wanted to be self-reliant and independent, and take care of myself, as my mother told me to do. No present could cheer me like a kind word and a loving heart."—"But I am going, and you will have nothing to remember me by."—"Yes, I shall, Nellie. I shall have this rescued soul and body of mine: they shall stand a living monument to your memory."—"O Eddie! you praise me too much; you try to flatter me."—"No, Nellie, this is no flattery: my mother would thank you a thousand times if she were here." — "Well, Eddie, what shall I tell your mother if I see her in heaven?" — "Tell her that you have been the angel which God has sent, through her prayers, to rescue her darling boy." — "Don't say so, Eddie: I am but a child, — a poor, sick child: I have done nothing. Oh, I fear you think too well of me, Eddie." — "No, Nellie, I don't think *too well* of you, but I think *too much* of you. Alas, for me! I can think of nothing but you. I think of you all the time. You hide my Saviour from my sight; but I cannot help it, Nellie! When I pray, you are in my prayer; when I dream, you are in my dreams; when I look at pictures, I see Nellie's image; when I open my prayer-book, I find Nellie's name; when I look at the the stars, I see Nellie's eyes; when I listen to any loving child, I hear Nellie's voice. And when I think that this may be our last meeting, that I may never see your face again" — here his words choked, the tears started, he turned away to wipe his face, so as not to hurt Nellie's feelings; but his compressed emotions would not be restrained: he was obliged to change the subject, or leave the room. "O Nellie!" he said, "it is hard parting; but I must not grieve: my loss is your gain. This visit is worth a lifetime to me. Oh, how I thank your mother for allowing me to come!"

"But I want to give you something to remember me by," said Nellie: "can't I, Eddie?" — "I don't know, Nellie! if you choose to give me a lock of your hair, I should like it." — "Yes, Eddie: you shall have the prettiest silken lock I have upon my head. You shall have the little curl which hangs over my forehead. Go, Dinah, and bring me the shears: I will cut it off." — "Oh, don't!" said the mother, " don't, Nellie! your hair will be ruined : you won't look pretty at all with one curl gone." — " But, mamma, you may have the other curl; then they will both be gone." — "Ah, Nellie, that would not do; you would be shorn of your prettiest ornaments. Can't you give Ned something else?" — "No, mamma: there is nothing which he would like as well."

"But, Nellie! you may yet live; then how you would look without your curls!" — "Oh, mamma! if I live, they will grow out again ; but I cannot live, mamma: I must die." — "Then, Nellie, give him a lock on the back-side of the head." — "But, mamma, he would not love that so well as this. This grew over my two eyes that have wept for him, and bathed it with their tears." — "Then, Nellie, if you must give it to him, wait till after you are gone, and I will present it to him." — " Oh, no, mamma: I want to give it to him myself, with my own hands, so that he will know how much I love him. I wish I had a better lock to give him: I wish it were all solid gold, and such gold as heaven is paved with. I wish my tears had been crystals of silver, and each had been the weight of a talent; then he should have them all." — " No gold or silver could be so precious to me as the lock itself," said Ned. " But," said the mother, " I wanted to see you look pretty in the coffin, — that is, if you must die, — to see you with all your little curls and ribbons and laces and flowers when your little friends come to the funeral." — " But I *shall* look pretty, mamma, if I am good: Jesus makes *all good* children pretty when they die. So, mamma, you take this curl for yourself; then cut off this one for me, and give it to Ned, won't you, mamma ? " — " Yes, my child, if you must have it done; but it is hard for a mother to do it, Nellie."

Then with reluctant fingers the mother cut off the two locks, and combed back the remaining hair from the alabaster forehead, which now stood out so prominent, that it seemed even more beautiful than before. " Now, mamma," said Nellie, " I want to give Susie Pinkham and

Nellie Stedman something before I die: may I, mamma?" — "Oh, yes, my child! what shall it be?" said the mother. "I want to give them my two new dresses." — "Perhaps you may get well, and want them yourself, Nellie?" — "Oh, no, mamma! I shall not get well: but, if I should, then you could buy me more. Here, Susie, is a white dress, emblem of purity, — one which your poor mother washed and starched for me. Take it, and remember me; and be kind to your poor, hard-working mother who has done so much for me." The tears started as Susie came forward to receive it from Mrs. Nelson's hand. "Now, Nellie, here is a silk dress for you, — one which your mother cut and made. I never wore it: take it, and remember me; and, when you wear it, think of that Nellie who will lie in the cold grave."

"Boo, hoo, hoo!" cried Dinah, as she fell down back of the bed upon the floor. "Boo, hoo, hoo! La sus! Nellie be goin' to die; Nellie be put in de cold ground, and all cobered ober, and Dinah hab no more Nellie to pray for her. Oh, dear! Oh, dear! Nellie gib away all her nice dings; she don't dink ob Dinah. Nellie no remember Dinah; no she don't! Boo, hoo, hoo! Oh, dear! o-o-o d-e-a-r!" — "Get up there: don't be so silly, Dinah!" said Mrs. Nelson.

"Nellie will have something to give you. Get up, and behave yourself." — "Yes," said Nellie, with her voice now failing, yet struggling to say more, — "yes, yes, mamma, Nellie will remember Dinah. Here, give Dinah this accordion, and ask her to play, —

"Glory, glory, hallelujah!
Jesus leads us on."

Then she sank back, and became almost insensible.

Pleased with the gift, Dinah took the instrument, half in smiles and half in tears, with a low courtesy, and a "thank a mam." With the musical talent peculiar to her race, she commenced to play; but she could not catch the tune until she had hummed over in her mind the original, —

"John Brown's body lies a mouldering in the grave,
But his soul is marching on;"

then she played a little: but her heart was too full to proceed, and she gave it up.

Nellie's mind wandered at the first sound of the music, and she seemed conversing with invisible spirits. When the music stopped all was silent, a breathless stillness prevailed: it was as the silence of the grave. Each breath was suppressed, the clock went "click, click:" the death-tick was heard in the wall; the flowers seemed to droop and fade; and each heart beat with suppressed sound. At last Nellie, as she lay upon her mother's arm, opened her eyes, and said, "What is that I see there, mamma?" — "Where, my child?" — "There, mamma, — there, at the foot of the bed, see! There, it moves now: it stirs, mamma!" — "O my child!" said the mother, weeping in pity. "Why, Nellie! don't you know? That is Ned! Don't you know Ned, your own dear Eddie?" — "Oh! it is, heh?" gasped the child in convulsive effort. "I wish, I wish" — But her voice failed her, the dry husky lips would not allow utterance; and, as the rattle and gurglings were heard in the throat, the rumbling car seemed nearer than before. She was hurrying away, over head-land and stream and bridge and shore, to the last station, where the baggage is examined, and the passport presented with the "white stone; and in the stone a new name written, which no man knoweth, saving he that receiveth it" preparatory to crossing the river.

CHAPTER XXXIV.

MR. BENEDICT'S ADDRESS. — SCHOOL-BOYS' VIEW OF BOSTON.

"HERE'S the 'Heral, Jirnil, Trav'ler, 'Ranscrip'. Paper, sir?" cried a dozen boys at the corner of Park and Tremont Streets, waiting for Mr. Benedict to arrive. Now, Mr. Benedict was a modest and retiring man, scarcely ever seen on public occasions, and almost unknown to the boys; for his charities had been distributed to them by other hands than his own. He, however, had promised for once to take a view of Boston, with some of them, from the State Capitol.

"Boys," said he, "do you want to be rich?" — "Yes, sir! yes, sir! yes, sirree! we does!" they said, as they came scampering around him. "Then, if you want to be rich, you must be truthful and honest," said he. "Now, let me give you the history of a few Boston boys for your encouragement. There is a man walking on the Common, who, when a boy, collected grease and ashes in carts on the street. He now has command of a line of steamers. His income last year was thirty thousand dollars. He was converted in a sabbath school, and became a teacher, then superintendent; and now is among the foremost in all benevolent enterprises.

"There is the house of one, who, in early years, drew a hand-cart in the street; he now has become president of a railroad: there is one who sold papers; he is now partner of a firm on Franklin Street: there is one who peddled small wares from a hand-cart; he is now president of a bank: there is a man living on Beacon Street, who once peddled fish in the street; his income last year was fifty thousand dollars (he gives thousands of dollars every year for religious and educational purposes): there is a man in Tremont Street who once drove a breadcart; his income last year was ten or twenty thousand; he, also, gives largely for spreading the gospel. These were all street-boys, or boys that got their living, and had their first start in business, on the street. True, they did not remain long on the street; neither will you if you are faithful and aspiring. Is there not hope, then, for you? There is a man in South Boston who owns a factory: he was a poor penniless boy when he joined the church; he is now able to build a church. There are on Beacon Street the houses of two of the richest men in Boston: their several incomes last year were more than a hundred thousand dollars. They were at first errand-boys in dry-goods stores; finally they became clerks, then partners, then owners, and now are millionaires. All these men, I believe, profess the religion of Jesus Christ. I might speak also of the Appletons, the Brookses, and the Lawrences. They were once poor boys, who began at the lowest round of the ladder, and who finally became the merchant princes of Boston. Their munificent charities are as widely known as Boston itself. Is there not hope for you? Do you want to hear any thing more about Boston?"

"Yes, sir! yes, sir! yes, sirree!"—"Well, I will tell you more. Boston was named in honor of Rev. John Cotton, one of its earliest preachers, who came from the town of Boston, Lincolnshire, England. Its Indian name was *Shawmut*, which means *living fountains*. It was formerly called *Tri-Mountain*, or the three-hilled city: it is now called the *City of Notions*. Why so called, I know not, except on account of its peculiar notions with regard to inventions, thrift, learning, wealth, criticism, religion, politics, and pride. Its pride is peculiar: one writer has said, 'There is such a thing as pride of wealth, pride of rank, pride of talent; and, distinct from all these, there is *Boston pride.*' Meet one of her citizens anywhere the world over, by land or sea, consul or minister, tourist or journalist; and he straightens up in his pride to tell you, 'I am from Boston, sir, — Boston, Massachusetts, North America.' Boston has the reputation of being always on the *qui vive:* her people, like those of Athens of old, are looking after some new thing. It is a city much admired, loved, and hated. Those who love it make it the model city, — almost the New Jerusalem. Those who hate it hate it with a perfect hatred. By one party, it is abhorred as a great meddler and mischief-maker in national affairs; turning the world upside down by its pseudo philanthropy and fanaticism: by the other, it is considered on account of its puritanic principles, its vigor of thought, its keen perception of events, its free schools, free press, free speech, free libraries, munificent charities, and benevolent institutions, — by them it is reckoned the *beau-ideal* of Christian civilization. It has a book and a home for everybody in need, — a home for the aged, a home for the orphan, a home for boys of the street, a home for the inebriate, a home for the fallen, a home for the soldier; besides its public institutions for the poor, the blind, the insane, and the vicious. Any person may have a book from the public library, without question or doubt as to its return, except his word of honor. Thieves, — there are but few of them that would steal a book from the public library, or pluck a flower from the public garden; such is the honor and self-respect that free institutions inspire. In the face of such public trusts and confidence, and munificent endowments, a man is ashamed to be dishonest or mean.

"In learning, Boston is called the 'Athens of America.' In commerce, it is the second city of the Union. In inventions, it is called '*Bosstown*,' or the town of boss-workmen. In politics, it is said to be the '*Hub of the Universe.*' Boston is said to govern New England, and New-England ideas to rule America. Perhaps it is called the '*Hub*' on account of its golden dome on Capitol Hill, looking like a hub. Here the assembled wisdom of the State centres once a year as spokes centre in a hub. When these men move, that is, when the spokes turn round, they bear on their shoulders the periphery of the outside world.

ASCENT. — "Let us ascend this dome, which is three hundred feet above tide-water, and take a view of Boston and its suburbs. In front is a statue of Webster, by Hiram Powers; and one also of Horace Mann, by Miss Emma Stebbins; and within is one of Washington, by Chantrey. Now we enter the vestibule, a large circular hall with pillars and cornices, hung with relics from the revolution and rebellion. Pendent from these pillars are flags stained with the blood of almost every battle-field of the war. Here are the colors of the Massachusetts Sixth, that first passed through Baltimore, April. 19, 1861. There are shreds and tatters of flags, with the golden names of Port Hudson, Fort Wagner, Newbern, Petersburg, and Gettysburg. Now we ascend the spiral stairs, and get into the hub.

"*Northward.* — Look to the north: there is Charlestown, with its Navy Yard, State Prison, and the tall granite monument on Bunker Hill. Just beyond lie Lexington and Concord, of Revolutionary fame; and there, as Webster says, 'They will remain forever.'"

"*Eastward.* — Looking towards the east, we see the beautifully dotted harbor of Boston, interspersed with many islands. There is George's Island, on which stands Fort Warren, the key to the harbor. It commands the open sea, and stands defiant with deep-mouthed columbiads, ready to repel all intruders. This fort has been the receptacle of many traitors during the war, among whom were Mason and Slidel, ministers plenipotentiary from the would-be Confederacy. There is

Castle Island, now bearing Fort Independence. One mile north of Castle Island is Governor's Island, on which stands Fort Winthrop. This island was demised to Gov. Winthrop in 1632, twelve years after the landing of the Pilgrims. There is Long Island, with its lighthouse; and in the rear are Rainsford's Island, and the quarantine-grounds. Near by is Thompson's Island, on which is situated the Farm School for boys rescued from poverty and temptation, and educated to habits of industry. There is Deer Island, on which stand the Almshouse, and House of Industry and Reformation. (This is where Pat Murphy, and his mother, old Mag Murphy, were imprisoned: the name of it awakened some sensation among the boys.)

Mr. Benedict continued: " Further up the harbor, lying at anchor, is the Massachusetts Nautical School Ship, for boys who have been sentenced for juvenile offences. Many of them, by the science acquired here, become expert navigators. To the left is Noddle's Island, now called East Boston; to the right are Dorchester Heights, or South Boston, where Washington placed his guns to expel the British fleet from the harbor. Beyond these many islands is the peninsula of Nahant, one of the most delightful watering places in the world. Nothing is more terrific than an ocean-storm as witnessed from these heights. The mad waves, rising against these immutable rocks, rave and foam, and dash, like the tide of rebellion against the pillars of liberty.

"*Prophecy.* — The time is coming when this city will include in its ample range the cities of Roxbury, Charlestown, and Chelsea, and all the islands and headlands of this spacious harbor, each of them adorned with trees, gardens, flowers and statuary, where taste may display her genius, and art revel in affluence; when Boston, becoming the Western Venice, with her hundred islands united by bridges and ferries, sitting in gorgeous splendor amidst the waters, unrivalled in beauty, unequalled in influence, with every citizen feeling the dignity of his manhood: then, as now, to the very ends of the earth, shall Boston be heard from her triple hills, speaking, as she ever has 'spoken, for republicanism and Christianity, humanity and God.

"*British Steamer.* — Look down the harbor: there is one of the Cunard line of steamers, — a gigantic palace on the waters. Now she stops, or slackens her speed. See that smoke: hark, a gun! A pilot goes on board; she dips her flag to Fort Warren; they exchange compliments, and she passes on, bridging the old world to the new by ties of fraternal and commercial interests. Oh, long may the united flags of Albion and Columbia wave over the hearts of the free and the homes of the brave! May the lion and the eagle cultivate fraternal feeling, and contract ties of indissoluble alliance, until they shall dictate constitutional liberty to the belligerent civilizations of the whole earth.

"No, niver!" said Michael O'Brien: "that kin niver ba. The British lion will tremble when us Fenians gits hold on him: we will scratch his eyes out, that we will. Hurrah for the auld Emerald Isle! Say, Mister," continued Mike, "When do you think us Catholics shall rule America?"

"Don't interrupt me," said Mr. Benedict, as he continued, and said, —

"*Westward.* — Turning to the west, we see the city of Cambridge, the seat of Harvard College, the oldest and best endowed institution in America. There Rev. John Harvard immortalized his name by planting the seeds of New England's learning and prosperity. Harvard thinks for Boston, and Boston thinks for the world."

"Just beyond is Mount Auburn, City of the Dead; beautiful necropolis! laid out in exquisite taste, and adorned with mementoes for the loved, the lost, the gifted, the great, and the untimely dead, whose bud was blasted before the leaf of promise could develop the seeds of hope, and scatter fragrance of thought on the desert of life. Beyond Mount Auburn is Watertown, seat of the United-States arsenal, — a place of lively interest during the war. The grounds contain forty acres.

"*Southward.* — Turn we to the south : there is Roxbury, the home of Elliot, the apostle to the Indians, and translator of the Scriptures. A little beyond is Forest-Hills Cemetery, with its shady walks and avenues and sylvan retreats, its purling streams and glassy lake, on which the graceful swan slowly glides as a messenger of sorrow, but whose fabled notes are now hushed in presence of the silent dead. Still further on is Mount-Hope Cemetery, and the Potter's Field." (At the mention of the Potter's Field, Ned Nevins trembled and sighed, for there his mother was buried.) Now Mr. Benedict changed the subject, and talked of —

"*Inventions.* — Look at Boston's inventions. A Franklin starts a printing-press, the first in America; and he, by the wires upon his kite, converses with the lightning of heaven. Morse the elder travels States, and makes geographies. Morse the younger, with his speaking wires, spans continents, telegraphs across oceans, and communicates with the speed of thought around the world.

" Dr. Charles T. Jackson and Dr. Morton discover the application of chloroform in surgical operations, annihilating pain, and inspiring the patient with pleasant dreams. Dr. Channing, jun., discovers or invents the fire-alarm telegraph.

"Erastus Bigelow eclipses Europe by his power-looms. The first railroad-track was laid from Boston by Boston men. Ruggles's printing-press and Dickinson's rotary press are Boston inventions. Whipple and Black are noted photographers. Blanchard invented a machine for duplicating busts and lasts.

"Copley and Stewart, Alexander and Harding, were great portrait painters. Thomas Ball has in mould an equestrian statue of Washington, said to be the best extant. King and Billings are artists of merit.

"Prescott and Bancroft wrote their world-renowned histories in Boston. The poets Longfellow, Holmes, J. Russell Lowell, though living in the suburbs, are claimed by Boston. Also Judge Story the commentator, and his son the sculptor, distinguished even in Italy, the home of art; and Judge Parsons, Judge Shaw, Daniel Webster, Edward Everett, R. C. Winthrop, Rufus Choate, old Samuel Adams, John Adams, John Quincy Adams, John Hancock, Dr. Joseph Warren of Bunker-Hill fame, and the Otises and Quincys.

"Miss Dorothy Dix, the world-renowned philanthropist, a ministering angel among prisons, hospitals, and insane retreats, is a Boston lady. Boston, in private and public charities, is unsurpassed by any city in the world. It expended seventy-five thousand dollars last year in a free hospital to relieve the sick and maimed of every class and nation.

"Boston also boasts of the greatest organ and the finest musical talent in America. One thing Boston does not boast of: she has no titled lords; every man is his own duke and sovereign. Titled aristocracy and hereditary nobility cannot live on Puritan soil. She enjoys the enviable position of being hated by all European oppressors.

"New England is a thorn in the flesh of oligarchy, an eye-sore to tyranny; and Boston is the head and front of New England. Boston has been much abused by the lovers of caste and of treason; but she deserves it all, and can live on the pages of history when her assailants are forgotten.

"*Enterprise.* — Look at Boston's enterprise, both at home and abroad. Look at the schools and colleges and railroads, which she has established in the Far West, and look at her mechanical and benevolent enterprises at home. Boston says to yonder mountain, 'Be thou removed;'

and it is removed into the depths of the sea. By steam the mountain is removed, with all its 'shaggy locks;' and by steam it is borne into the Back Bay.

"Three-fourths of Boston have been reclaimed from the grasp of ocean. Where once the sea roared, now stands the 'sycamine,' plucked from its roots, and planted in the depths of the sea. Where fishermen threw out their lines, now stand dwellings, churches, and galleries of art. Where the mammoth hulk of the Indiaman once ploughed the foaming main, and dropped in swelling tides her ponderous anchor, are now located spacious streets and warehouses.

"As Boston has enlarged her borders by aggressions on the sea; so have her peculiar ideas forced themselves on every State and nation on the globe. Her ideas seem charged by fate, and they conquer by the divinity which inspires them.

"Her Agassiz, seeking to fill the fountains of knowledge, is now feeling for the sources of the Amazon; and, to add to the wealth of the world, he is penetrating the hidden stores of the Andes.

"For the galleries of science and natural history, he is gathering sinews and vertebra from the '*back-bone of the world.*' By a Boston citizen is he supported, and for Boston pride does he toil. Boston ships carry Boston principles over every sea to every shore.

"What boy does not feel proud to walk her streets? What pride and manliness and holy ambition does she not inspire? Her area covers but a few square miles; but her wisdom and her fame fill the spacious earth. What heart does not throb with hope, at sight of her free schools, free presses, free lecture-rooms, free library, and her ever open and free ballot-box, to black and white, where the poor man's vote is just as potent as that of the merchant-prince? What boy does not raise himself in his shoes, and stand erect in self-gratulations, when he can say, 'These are mine! I am a Boston boy!' With such privileges as Boston presents, who can afford to be mean or ignorant or vile?

"Oh, my boys, may every one of you prosper in life, and may you all be an honor to Boston! I am now old and infirm: I shall probably never see your faces again. Let the counsel of one who came a poor boy to this city sink deep in your hearts. Be truthful, be honest, be virtuous. Do good to your fellow-men, and God will do well by you. Fear God, and keep his commandments, and you shall prosper and be happy. Farewell! May we meet in another, and a better world!"

CHAPTER XXXV.

SEALED VISION. — THE PHILANTHROPIST'S REWARD.

VISION of Sophia, daughter of Hezekiah. It came to pass on the seventh month, and the seventh day of the month, as I, Sophia the afflicted, lay upon my bed of shavings, in Orange Lane, falling into a trance, I saw the vision of the Almighty, having mine eyes open. The veil from the invisible was rent, hidden mysteries were revealed; I saw things that are to be hereafter; I learned knowledge from the Most High. Hear, O heavens! give ear, O earth! to the cries of the needle-woman, and the prayers of the widow and the fatherless. Their prayers reach the ears of the God of Sabaoth; lo! the day of their redemption draweth nigh. Peace be to the ashes of the philanthropist! Let me die the death of the righteous, and let my last end be like his! Witness, ye saints! behold, ye philanthropists! and see how a good man dies.

It came to pass as the venerable Mr. Benedict was called to his reward, I, Sophia, the distressed but not forsaken, saw in a vision the glory of his departure. He died crowned with honors, in good old age, as a sheaf of corn fully ripe, and ready for harvest.

I saw the curtain drawn from the spirit world, and the glories of the heavens revealed. The chariots of God descended, and the angels came to the chamber where the good man met his fate. Scores and hundreds of little children, like cherubs having wings, gathered round him, and settled over his dying bed. They were once children of his care, children of the street; but now they were among the glorified, rescued, and redeemed. Their faces were radiant with smiles, and their eyes bright as burnished diamonds. The texture of their garments was too fine for mortal sight, and none but they to whom it was revealed could behold them. They had floral crowns upon their heads, and golden harps in their hands; and they sang, "Blessed are the dead that die in the Lord, from henceforth and forever; and their works do follow them." And the chamber was radiant with light, and the glory of God made it brighter than the palace of a king. And the walls echoed with celestial minstrelsy, the tapestry was hung with pearls, and the furniture seemed of solid gold.

A form appeared unto Mr. Benedict, — a form like unto the Son of man. He had scars upon

DEATH OF MR. BENEDICT.
The Philanthropist's reward. Page 366.

his hands, upon his feet, and upon his side; his temples were scarred, and a crown of thorns was upon his brow. He said, "Come, ye blessed of my Father, inherit the kingdom prepared for you from the foundation of the world. For I was an hungered, and ye gave me meat; I was naked, and ye clothed me; I was a stranger, and ye took me in." Now, Mr. Benedict was a modest man, — one of those who do good by stealth, and blush to find it known. Though he scattered his goods of charity like water among the needy, yet he felt that he had done nothing, and merited nothing, and could not endure one word of praise. Therefore he blushed at the words of the Son of man, and said, "When saw I thee an hungered, and fed thee? or naked, and clothed thee? or a stranger, and took thee in?" Then He answered, and said, "Verily I say unto you, inasmuch as ye have done it unto the least of my brethren, ye have done it unto me." Then the angelic choir sang, "Worthy art thou to receive honor and power and glory and immortality! Come up hither! Come up hither!"

Now the scene changes. I saw the heavens open, and a great white throne, before which all men, both small and great, must appear in judgment. And I heard a loud voice, saying, "Awake! ye sons of men, and come to judgment, and ye shall be judged according to the deeds done in the body." Then appeared a vast multitude, that no man could number, from all nations, kindreds, and tongues. And I heard a voice, saying, " Whose name shall be first in the Lamb's Book of Life ? "

Then appeared one of earth's greatest *monarchs*, having just vacated his throne. He said, " I have changed the face of the earth, established thrones, created monarchies, given security to government, brought order out of chaos, become famous. I have won a name that stands highest among mortals." — " Yes ! " said the recording angel, " thou hast conquered empires, but thou couldst not govern thyself; thou hast ruled kingdoms, but not thine own spirit; thou hast governed men, but not thine own lust; thou hast lived in extravagance, wasted the goods of thy subjects, oppressed the poor, been a glutton and a wine-bibber; away with thee! thou art not first on the roll of immortality."

Then came the mighty *warrior*, fresh from the fields of victory, with the echo of a nation's applause still ringing in his ears. He said, " I have drawn my sword in a righteous cause; I have put down rebellion, relieved the oppressed, broken every yoke, bid the captive go free; I have wrested victory out of revolt, established order, government, and law." — " But thou hast not broken the yoke from thine own neck," said the angel: "thou art thyself a slave to sin, a profane rebel, a traitor against God. Thy name is not first."

Then came the *orator*. "What hast thou done?"—"I have electrified and swayed vast audiences; I have conquered and subdued the hearts of men; I have guided the acts of the multitude, and turned their thoughts as rivers of water are turned; I have played upon the passions of communities, as one plays upon an instrument; I have run through every octave of feeling, and aroused the listening auditory to the rapture of ecstasy; I have changed the thoughts of a nation from vice to virtue, and led them up to God; I have won the applause of the good and the great, and have coined words and sentences that bear the ring of immorality."—"But thou hast courted the applause of men, rather than the favor of God; thy name is not first." Then came the *poet*. "What hast thou done?"—"I have given melody to rhyme; my numbers have echoed in a nation's song; I have touched my harp, and a world has stood silent and entranced to catch its sound; I have sung of love, and the world has melted into tears; I have sung of war, and nations have rushed to arms; I have sung of liberty, and shackles have fallen from the slave; my mission has been to awaken noble sentiment, inspire courage, defend the truth, and stir the kindlings of pity for the distressed and down-trodden."

The *artist:* "What hast thou done?"—"I have transferred the living feature to canvas, made it live and look and breathe for ages after the breath had left the body; I have revived memories, suggested associations, elevated the purposes, ennobled the hearts, transformed the real into the ideal; I have made the bronze to speak, the stone to weep, and the bust to breathe; I have formed the architrave, erected the pillar, carved the cornice, moulded the frieze, and shaped the entablature; I have placed the monumental shaft to the memory of heroic deeds, and have perpetuated the honors of the heroic dead."

The *inventor:* "What hast thou done?"—"I have yoked art to science, and drawn the car of enterprise round the world; I have harnessed the iron horse, and sent it screeching into the wilderness; I have started the printing-press, and poured forth its sheets of literature as the leaves of the forest; I have chained the lightnings, invented the telegraph, and spanned continents with the net-work of communication; I have invented the telescope, and weighed the planets in their orbits, and measured the stars in their courses; I have counted the ages of sidereal rays, and reckoned millennials of light."

Then came the *moral worthies*,—first the *agitator* and *reformer:* "What hast thou done."—"I have stood up almost alone against sin and oppression; I have pleaded for the down-trodden and afflicted, I have spoken what others would not dare to say; I have battled against principalities and powers, and wickedness in high places."—"Well done, good and faithful servant! thou shalt have thy reward; but even thine eye is not single: thou hast an eye to be seen of man."

Then came the *minister* of the gospel: "What hast thou done?"—"I have spent the strength of my years in preaching the word; I have ministered to the sick and dying; I have bound up the broken-hearted, proclaimed liberty to the captive, and the opening of prisons to them that are bound."—"Well done! but thou hast had thy earthly reward; thou hast lived by the altar, and popular applause has followed thy preaching."

Then came the *martyr:* "What hast thou done?"—"I have not only preached the truth as it is in Jesus, but I have sealed it with my blood. Before a vast multitude, I stood up for the cause, and let the flames consume me."—"Well done! but thou mightest have done this to win a name: fame is alluring; thy motives might not have been the purest; therefore thy case must be examined."

Then came the *man* of *beneficence*, the donator of public charities: " What hast thou done ? " — "I have supported institutions for learning, organized schools, endowed colleges, erected orphan-houses, built asylums, given to public charities, and supplied the wants of the missionary." — " Ah ! " said the angel, " thou givest only thy surplus; thou endowest institutions for a name; and, when thy gold can be of no more use to thee on a dying bed, thou buildest a monument to thyself in shape of charitable institutions: thy charities are not the most disinterested."

Then came the venerable *Mr. Benedict.* When on earth he was dressed in black, but now he wore a white robe. He had builded no monuments to himself in the shape of charitable institutions, but he had scattered his goods on the streets; like water spilled upon the ground, they had fallen not to be gathered up again. Some had fallen on unworthy objects, and some had even been discarded. But this was not the giver's fault. Poor boys and girls of the street looked up to heaven, and thanked God for Mr. Benedict's favors, seeing no other agent but God.

"What hast thou done?" said the angel. "I done?" said Mr. Benedict, modestly blushing. "What have I done? Why, I have done nothing, nothing at all. I had a little money, which the Lord lent me. I knew that it belonged to Him, so I thought I would give it to his children. The Lord's children, I trust, are the honest, industrious poor: so I gave it to them. I have no merit in this; I gave because I loved to do it. It was no sacrifice, but a pleasure. Please say nothing about it; please let my name be a secret."—"Well done!" said the angel; "thy name stands *first!* for thou dost not let thy left hand know what thy right hand doeth; thou hast scattered thy bread upon the waters, not expecting to find it again. Thy motives are the most pure and disinterested; thy charities are the most heartfelt; thou shalt have the highest seat on the throne of love." Then Mr. Benedict blushed, and gazed in astonishment, and looked aside, and sought where to hide himself.

Then came the great army of children which he had fed and clothed; and, laying their floral crowns at his feet, they sang, "Worthy to receive gratitude and honor from those whom thou hast redeemed from suffering and want. Joy be to thy heart! and crowns of honor be upon thy head! Come up hither! Welcome! thrice welcome to the seats of the blessed!"

Then came the decrepit and the infirm, which he had helped on the earth. Their crutches were now thrown away. They sang, "Hail! thou noblest of almoners! Thou hast given when no eye could see thee, and no earthly power could reward thee! Thou hast visited the widow and the fatherless in their affliction, and thou hast kept thyself unspotted from the selfishness of the world! Welcome home! The benedictions of the hosts of heaven be upon thee!"

Then came a long procession of widows, those who had come out of great tribulations, but who now wore white robes, made white in the blood of the Lamb. They sang, "Because thou deliverest the poor that cried, and the fatherless, and him that had no helper, let the blessings of them that were ready to perish be upon thee! for thou wast eyes to the blind, and feet to the lame; thou causedst the widow's heart to sing for joy!"

And the multitude of orphans greeted him as they passed: they had floral crowns of amaranth upon their heads, and harps of gold in their hands; and on cherubic wing they gathered round their ancient benefactor, and sang.

CHAPTER XXXVI.

DEATH OF NELLIE.—ITS EFFECT ON THE NEWS-BOYS.

"DON'T talk so loud, boys! hush yer noise!" said Johnny McCurdy to Nick of the Woods and the other boys, as they clung to the high wall around Mr. Nelson's back-yard. "Don't, don't speak so loud! you must whisper! if we speak loud, Mrs. Nelson will scold us, and drive us off."— "Then keep still yerself!" said Nick, "yer alus preachin', but ye don't mind what ye preach yerself."— "Hush, there!" whispered Tom the Trickster, "Look! see there! I seed a priest goin' in; I guess Nellie be a dyin'."— "'Tain't a priest, ye fool you!" said Tim the Tumbler. "Don't ye know a priest? That ar man be a minister."— "Well, I thought it was some kind of a churchman," said Tom; "there comes out the doctor, see! how he shakes his head, and looks sad! Now he gits into the carriage, and drives away. I bet ye he has lost his case this time. I guess Nellie be a goner!"— Oh, don't!" said Nick, "don't say goner; that be low; 'don't speak so circumspectful of Nellie (he meant disrespectful); don't be foolin'! 'cause poor Nellie be a dyin'; yis she be, and we shan't see the like of Nellie agin."

Thus the conversation continued, each rebuking the other for breach of etiquette, and each holding on to the wall, and peeping through the iron paling, to get a glimpse of any thing that reminded them of Nellie. When Nellie discovered that they were there, she ordered Dinah to wave a white pocket-handkerchief at the window, in token of recognition; whereat all the boys, with joyful exclamations, cried, "Good! good! bless poor Nellie! she be still a livin'." — "What are these boys here for?" said Mr. Nelson, as he came home, distressed about his daughter. "Ah, sir! we be waitin' to hear 'bout poor Nellie; we be feared she be dead, and we wouldn't know nuthin' 'bout it, sir!" — "Well, I can't have you here, boys!" said Mr. Nelson: "I can't have your noise about the premises; you will disturb my dying child." Then they hastened down, and scampered away; but every few minutes, some of them returned, climbing up the wall, and peeping over, and, when they caught any sign of news, they bore it back to their companions. Such is the respect and gratitude that even untutored minds express towards one that pitied and loved them. Oh, how many souls might be saved, crimes prevented, characters reformed, and hopes recovered in the world, if there were a few more Nellie Nelsons!

Silence reigns in David Nelson's chamber, — almost breathless silence. Nothing animate moves; no sound is heard save the "click, click" of the clock on the marble mantle-piece, and in still lower sounds the "tick, tick" of the lever-watch in Mr. Nelson's pocket. The fire in the grate whispers in subdued murmurs; each breath is hushed; even the canary bird refuses to sing, for Nellie is dying. The reverend minister has performed his last rite of consolation, the physicians have just felt the pulse for the last time, and with ominous looks have departed. Nellie is bolstered up in bed, leaning upon her mother's arm. The newsboys' bouquet of flowers stands in the vase, fading and withering like Nellie herself. She gazes on them in dreamy revery, then closes her eyes, lost in thought. Dinah stands by the bedside, weeping and sobbing wofully. Mr. Nelson stands back of his wife's chair, looking on in anxious suspense. Could not a child of such prospects be spared to enjoy the fortune of an heiress? Could not death be bribed by the vast treasures which Mr.

Nelson had acquired? Was money of no account? What more was needed to make a child happy? The richest of foreign and domestic luxuries, every article that palate could suggest, or fancy conceive, were at her command. What brilliant equipage! Furniture of sandal-wood, rosewood, and ebony; porcelains filled with rare perfumes; floors covered with costliest carpets; halls frescoed, and drawing-rooms adorned with the most exquisite *chefs-d'œuvre* of art; paintings of the old masters, coins, gems, precious stones, shells, alabaster statuettes, curtains of silk and brocade, struggling blushingly to veil the golden features of the sun, whose ambitious beams seemed impertinent in striving to penetrate the room, to get a peep at the dying girl. But all the gold of California, all the diamonds of Brazil, and all the gems of ocean, could not loose the grasp, or bribe the fell purpose, of the unrelenting destroyer. The father bends over his child; he kisses her pale cheek, and weeps; he bends down to Nellie's ear, and cries, "O Nellie, my dear child, I cannot see you die!" But Nellie shrinks back alarmed, as if the touch of a viper had met her. Perhaps she recoiled on account of pain. Perhaps she did not know what she was doing. At any rate, Mr. Nelson took it to himself, and thought she shuddered and shunned him on account of his treatment of Ned. Ah! how that repulse touched his conscience, and pierced him to the quick. It was as the lightning's stroke to the heart.

"Don't shrink back, and shun me," said the father: "I will treat Ned well; yes, I will, my child. Forgive me this time, Nellie; I will do just as you tell me to. Speak, Nellie, and say you will forgive me!" But the sick, dying child made no reply. How embarrassing was David Nelson's position! One false step may make a man limp awkwardly, and hobble for a lifetime. That step he had taken; no subterfuge could conceal it: yet he could not explain it to Nellie. Some acts on the character are like the stroke of the hammer upon a glass vase: they are irremediable. Some follies are worse than sin, because they are irreparable. Some sins are worse than a crime, because they are unatonable. If a man in anger destroys an eye, that eye can never be restored. If a child playing with a hatchet amputates a limb, that limb can never grow again. There are some follies and sins that can never be effaced. Though apparently forgiven, the ghosts of their committal ever rise upon our pathway, and haunt us through life. David Nelson, with all his wealth, was a very unhappy man. The sins of his youth followed him, and the ghostly shadows of the heart which he had wronged tormented him. Poor man! his soul stood in abject desolation, even in the midst of luxury and wealth. What was all this pomp and show of wealth compared with one hour's peace of mind and holy communion with God? The heaviest blow that he had ever received was now coming in the loss of his child: we fear he had not grace for the occasion. "Are we almost there, mamma?" said the child, her eyes brightening up as from a dream. "Where, Nellie? almost where? Tell mother, what do you mean?"— "The cars, mamma! Oh, the cars! how they rumble! I be so tired! I, I"— then her voice choked, her eyes became vacant, her thoughts wandered; she fell into stupor again. Ah, gentle traveller! thou art indeed almost there: the invisible wheels are bearing thee onward; thou wilt soon arrive at the depot of immortality in the invisible world. Again, at another lucid interval, she cried, "Oh, beautiful, beautiful! how beautiful it looks!"— "What, my child? what is it?"— "Oh, this car, mamma! how beautiful! It looks all covered with gold! 'tis borne on angels' wings. I be riding in the chariot of God, mamma! Oh, I wish all the world might come! Papa, won't you come? Say, papa, won't you go to heaven with me?" Then she said, "I wish all the poor boys could come;" and then she strove to raise her dying hand, and wave her handkerchief, as if beckoning to the newsboys; and smiled, and clapped her little hands; then fell back, and became for a time insensible. Like an expiring taper, her mind at intervals darted up with preter-natural brilliancy, then settled down almost to expiration itself.

Silence reigns once more in David Nelson's chamber, — almost breathless silence: the clock sighs, "click, click," counting the moments to eternity; the fire in the grate murmurs softly; and the watchful canary-bird looks on in silence. The loved and petted bird forgets its song, and neglects its food, to see its young mistress die. Its bright eye is turned towards that bed as intently as if it were the guardian angel that holds vigils over the struggling spirit. Its song is hushed, its head droops in sadness at the sight. Nellie's soul, like a bird encaged, beats against the ribs that bind it to mortality, and labors to be disinthralled. That golden bird, like the angel that sees the travail of the soul in the last beating of the pulse, in the last heaving sigh, in the last throbbing of the heart, when the mortal bars break, and the spirit is borne on angels wings to God, is her constant watcher.

The soul of that child is like the tiny insect floating in its tide-driven bark upon the watery deep, striving to burst away from its casket-hulk, and spread its wings in upper air, strugling to be free. Now Nellie is picking at the bed-clothes with her fingers, as if striving to remove a weight from her breast; now a sigh heaves from her bosom; now an unintelligible murmur; now she cries, "*I'm so, tired!* mamma! Nellie be so sick. Oh, this rumbling! *ain't we almost there?*" Poor child! the struggle is almost over: its moments are numbered. Now she starts up with the hallucination and fever of excitement that appear alarming. But the excitement is that of rapture: the angel indeed has come, and given her victory. "O mamma! I see the angels, I do," she said, suddenly rising from the pillow and pointing upward; her cheek glowing, and with eyes flashing unwonted brightness. "I see Willie and Jennie and Jesus! I see the saints on the other shore: they are coming down the flowery banks to meet me. All the saints have crowns upon their heads, and harps in their hands, and they sing songs of joy: they do, mamma, — songs of the redeemed. They say to me, 'Nellie, come up hither: come up hither.' Oh, how I want to go, mamma! I long to go: yes, I must go, and be with Jesus and the angels. I see the angels all about me: the room is full of angels. Ah, I'm going to be an angel too; yes, I be, mamma! Oh, how the angels sing! I want to sing with them, mamma: I do." — "Oh, no, my child, you are to sick to sing, it will hurt you," said the mother, weeping aloud, with emotions of fear and hope, at the wonderful phenomenon.

"Then *you* must sing, mamma! and *Dinah* sing, and *papa* sing. Sing, —

"'There are angels hovering round
To carry the tidings home,' —

mamma! won't you? And that one,

"'Come sing to me of heaven when I'm about to die;
. . . .
There'll be no more sorrow there.'

Do sing, mamma! won't you?"

But all hearts were too full to sing: no music could be heard save sobs and sighs. But the dying girl heeded them not: her heart was too enraptured with joy to think of tears. She commenced herself to sing, —

"I want to be an angel;"

but her strength failed her, she settled back upon her pillow. Then, placing her little hands together in prayer, as if praying for more unction from on high, just a little more strength, — then, sweeter than the dying swan's fabled notes by classic fountains flowing, sweeter than Orpheus' harp or Æolian lyre, sweeter than the lute of Jerusalem's fair maids on Chebar's banks, moaning in captive bowers their lovers' fate, sweet as as angel's song, that gentle voice arose, bearing in its strain the last hope of a mother's love, and all on earth that a father and a mother held dear. She sang in soft gentle accents, from lips that ne'er might speak again, —

> "I want to be an angel, and with the angels stand,
> A crown upon my forehead, a harp within my hand;
> And right before my Sav — my — my" —

but the voice ceased, the car had stopped, the passenger was called, and the strain was finished in the spirit-world. On, on, rolls the never-ceasing train, by many a father's door. On, on! bearing thousands upon thousands of weary passengers, young and old, the beautiful, the loved, the gifted, the favored of earth: but Nellie, the meek, the gentle, the amiable Nellie, is not on board; she has stopped at the last station, and taken passage over the river.

CHAPTER XXXVII.

NED IN A FRACAS WITH THE PAWNBROKER.

"I hain't done it, I hain't done it, Mrs. Nelson; I've done no such a thing," said Ned Nevins, as he rushed in, and fell upon the parlor floor, at Mrs. Nelson's feet. He was followed by Patrick Kelly, the policeman, and Jeremy Jacobs, the pawnbroker. Ned was a pitiable sight to behold: he looked like a fright, with hair erect, eyes wild and crazed, nostrils bleeding, clothes torn and covered with dirt by falling and scuffling: for he had been drugged and crazed by that hunchback of a pawnbroker, who was now seeking to arrest him.

Poor, unfortunate boy! If the innocent ever deserved protection and pity, that boy demands our commiseration and aid. Ah, the cruelty of poisoning a defenceless boy! of destroying his reason; of blasting his hopes: angels weep at the sight! But enough of this: perhaps we are becoming too sentimental.

I said Jerry was a pawnbroker. Well, he was, though he did not exhibit the sign of the three golden balls. But he was more: he was a jack at all trades. He kept a beer-shop, and a second-hand store, and a repair-shop, all in a very small way; therefore, his beer must have been *small-beer*, or Ned would never have drank it. Jerry's sign was the red Indian, with his arm extended holding cigars, or was holding them before the hand was broken off. The sign was a cast-off, second-hand one, placed there more for a guide to boys in the night than for a cigar sign. What Jerry sold was of small account: this was only a blind for more extensive operations. If the poor Indian, with his piercing eye, could tell us what he saw, he could make us blush at some of the deeds of modern civilization. But signs don't speak; and, if they do, they don't always tell the truth.

Jerry's low, wooden, dingy dwelling had two entrances — one in front at the beer-shop, and one at the side alley. In front, he kept beer and candies and cigars; the candies being well specked over by flies and dust, and the cigars appearing as ancient as if they had been exposed for sale in Noah's ark, that is, if smoking was indulged in by Shem, Ham, and Japheth. He had also a few second-hand articles, altogether about a wheel-barrow load. Everybody thought Jerry was poor, because he kept a small shop, and had few customers; therefore he did not excite the envy of the trade. Back of the beer-shop, he had a little workshop, where he pretended to file saws, and supply keys: the latter thing he did to *boys in great abundance.* Under the shop-floor he had a place of deposit, entered through a trap-door, where he kept a furnace almost continually burning, so as to melt bits of lead and brass, and other stolen metals, to avoid detection. In his narrow chambers he could stow away quite a number of boys, when daylight prevented their escape.

The reader asks, "Why didn't the police break up such an establishment?" We may say, Why didn't they, or why don't they, do a great many things? The truth is, policemen are like other men, and perhaps no better. We gentlemen dressed in *black* confess that we all have "gone astray like lost sheep." Perhaps some in our profession have gone further than lost sheep. Now, I know not why we should expect more of gentlemen dressed in *blue* than those dressed in *black*, especially when we take into account the relative position of the parties. When we in black retire from the pulpit, with headache and heartache, we have a world of sympathy bestowed upon us, such as the policeman does not enjoy. All the mammas and grandmas, and daughters and grand-daughters cry, "See how pale our pastor looks! What hardened sinners we are to vex his righteous soul so much! See how he coughs! Poor man! he won't live long." But when the policeman comes down from the witness-stand, having declared the "whole truth and nothing but the truth," he receives no such *balm of comfort from his erring parishioners.* In short, if it takes a thief to catch a thief, we must not expect more sanctity in a rogue-catcher than in other men.

Now, Kelly the policeman loved to take a drop or two of the "crather," and took it whenever he got a chance. Kelly was occasionally tired; why not step into Jerry's a moment, and rest? even soldiers need rest. Jerry had an easy-chair for Kelly's weary frame: what a comfort for a tired man! He had also a "wee bit of the crather" ever ready, "without money and without price," free as salvation's streams. Was not that a haven of rest? "*Friendship that pays something is worth something*" was Kelly's motto. We gentlemen in *black* understand this; why not those in *blue?* When we in black have the Thanksgiving turkeys brought in, and see our parishioners pay up their pew-rents generously, we don't feel like calling them such *big sinners!* such *awful* sinners! such *outrageous* sinners! as we do when preaching to them on *fast-day with nothing to eat.* I tell you, gentle reader, bread and butter make *some* difference even in *preaching.* Why not in *practice?* We in black describe the sinner; they in blue catch him. Ours is easy work; theirs is a most unthankful task. If meats and drinks somewhat temper *our* zeal, why not *theirs?* especially when whiskey is taxed two dollars per gallon! " Friendship that pays is worth something." Kelly, however, came near being reported at head-quarters for being disguised in liquor at court, during his other encounter with Ned Nevins; but was let off on account of his family, so he still walks his beat before Jeremy Jacobs's door.

Now, Jeremy Jacobs was an interesting character in his way, quite a lion among the boys, especially among junk-stealers. The boys swore by Jerry, they drank health to Jerry, they sang songs to Jerry, and they talked to their girls about Jerry. Jerry was a short man and humpbacked, so that his head was about on a level with theirs; and he put himself on a level with them in more ways than one. He sang songs with them, drank with them, played pickpocket with them, praised their adroitness, suffered them to beat him in the game, and to beat him *over the head* occasionally, so as to encourage them. When the boys had beaten Jerry over the head, they had plenty of fun, a "bully of a time." When some of them were "hard up," Jerry actually favored them with a little money. Such was the character of Jeremy Jacobs: he was just the man for the business; no phrenologist could point out a fitter man for the place. When excited, he stuttered a little, but that only added interest to his character.

Ned Nevins suspected that Jerry had got his trunk; so he loitered round the premises occasionally, Jerry thought, as a spy. How could Jerry get rid of him? One sinner in Jacobs's code of ethics, might destroy much good. Therefore the street must be cleared of Ned Nevins. Jerry sent a boy who had a key to Ned's room, with some tools from his shop, with orders to place them under Ned's bed. This was done, and Ned slept there one night without discovering them. Next day, when Ned appeared at Jerry's, he was offered some beer, of course in a friendly manner, but, unfortunately for Ned, the beer was drugged; hence the fracas. Ned became excited, just what Jacobs wanted; high words and blustering accusations followed; so the beer was working admirably. Now threat succeeded throat, and blow to blow, till at last, when Ned saw the policeman Kelly coming, he suspected the plot, and, crazed as he was, and reeling with intoxication, he broke from the grasp of Jacobs, and ran with all his might and main, and fell almost senseless and exhausted at Mrs. Nelson's feet.

Kelly, glad of the opportunity to do his friend a favor, put chase to Ned, while Jacobs came puffing and wheezing after, trying to stammer out, "Stop thief! stop thief! hang the rogue! there he is, going in there!" as Kelly sprung to the door so as to prevent Dinah from closing it in his face.

"I hain't done it! I hain't done it, Mrs. Nelson! I've done no such a thing: you may cut out my tongue, put out my eyes, bury me alive, if I have taken a thing, if I have stolen a cent from anybody. No, no, Mrs. Nelson; you know I hain't; you know Ned wouldn't steal! No, I wouldn't steal for the world! If I do wrong, nothing good will come to me. God will forsake me. O Mrs. Nelson! I have been poisoned! I feel my head turning round like a top; that man has given me something to kill me! Oh! I am dying! I am dying!"—"It is f-f-f-false!" stuttered Jacobs, "that b-b-b-boy is a r-r-r-rogue! Mr. K-k-k-Kelly will tell you so, Mrs. N-n-n-Nelson."—"Ah!" cried Ned, "that is the man who has got my trunk and my mother's ring and prayer-book. O the villain! what does he want of a prayer-book? O Mrs. Nelson! don't let me be taken away from you! Let me die here! Let me die beside of Nellie's bed! Let me die at your feet! O Nellie, Nellie! does she see me? Can she weep in heaven? Ah! Mrs. Nelson, you are the only friend that can save me! don't let me be carried to the prison! don't let me go to court! no one will have any confidence in me, if I am taken again! I shall certainly be sentenced, disgraced, ruined! Oh, I fear Mr. Nelson is at the bottom of this! Ah, he hates me! he has a spite against me! He seems glad that I have lost my trunk, with all the relics of my mother: he wishes me banished from the city, — banished from his sight! God of the fatherless have mercy upon me! pity me, ye angels! O Mrs. Nelson, turn me not away! You are my last hope! my only hope! If you forsake me, Eddie Nevins is lost! ruined! forever ruined! Nellie's lock of hair which I wear in my bosom would blush and stir with grief. Her picture would weep for shame. Her bones would stir in her coffin. But you *won't* turn me away! I *know* you won't! I see you weep! Ah! you feel for me, though you do not speak! Eddie has one friend! you won't see this policeman take him away! No! I know you won't!"

"La sus!" said Dinah, standing in the door, half frightened to death, "La sus, "de patrollsman shan't hab Ned! No, I know day shan't! Ye better go off, ye wicked critters! go off! and let poor Ned alone!" And Mrs. Nelson, staring in astonishment, inquired, "What does this mean? What is this policeman here for?"

"Ah!" said Ned, "he is here to ruin me! he takes up what boys he wants to, and sends them off just to please this pawnbroker. More boys are ruined in this way than are saved by all the ministers and churches in the city! I knew this policeman before: he is more cruel than the grave! Boston has no match for him! I prayed to him when my mother was sick and dying. He would not hear me! I rather pray to a bear. There is no pity in his eye, no feeling in his heart! he has no heart! a rock is softer! Oh, drive these men from your door! You will do God service, and humanity service! They are a disgrace to cannibals! Hyenas are more respectable! Oh, deliver me from their hands! Oh, save me! save me! O heavens! vengeance! murder! murder!" Then falling, and throwing his hand to his head, he said, in lower and more subdued tones, "O my head! my head! it will split, it will split! Oh, how it whirls round! oh my head! my head! O! O! O!"

As Ned uttered these words, and fell almost lifeless upon the floor, Kelly himself was somewhat moved to pity; yes, even an Irish policeman had some little feeling: but then there stood Jacobs, and Jacobs was an old friend. "Friendship that pays is worth something;" therefore the wants of old friends must be attended to.

"Excuse me, madam," said Kelly, very obsequiously, "excuse me; I hope I am not intruding, madam!" Now he took off his cap, and bowed gracefully, and continued with bland, affable smiles, "This 'ere gintleman has lost some tools from his shop; he thinks they ba in this 'ere boy's house." — "*They ain't in my house!*" cried Ned, gasping and almost lifeless on the floor: "he lies if he says so!" Then Kelly smiled, and said, in mild, persuasive tones, "Excuse me, madam! if you will be kind enough to get me his key, I will examine the room; then, if they ba not there, it will ba all right; yes, all right, madam!"

"He shan't have my key; they stole my trunk!" muttered Ned, in gasping throes of defiance; but Ned was too far gone to speak further, or to resist their efforts. So Mrs. Nelson gave Kelly the key, and requested Dinah to accompany the men, to prevent collusion, while she remained with the senseless boy to cogitate on her own reflections.

CHAPTER XXXVIII.

NED'S RECONCILIATION TO DAVID NELSON. — HIS ADOPTION.

"AH! what does this mean? what is the matter? is this Ned?" asked David Nelson, as he came home, and saw Ned lying on the floor, and Mrs. Nelson wiping his his face, and placing a pillow beneath his head. "Drunk! hey? Well, I thought as much: I thought he would come to some bad end; been in a fight, hey? perhaps he'll want me to get him out of the scrape; but I shan't do it: I'll let him go to the Island. Say, Mrs. Nelson, what is the matter?"

"Matter enough," said Mrs. Nelson, "the boy is poisoned."

"Poisoned! oh, fiddlesticks! then he is poisoned with whiskey," said Mr. Nelson. "I tell you that boy is drunk: he looks just like it. Say, what was that policeman here for?"

"He was on a bad errand, sir!" replied Mrs. Nelson; "he was after Ned. He declares that Ned has stolen some burglars' tools; but I would not allow him to be taken until his room was searched for the tools."

"Well, you may rest assured they will find the tools," said Mr. Nelson. "Depend upon it, Ned is guilty; he has got drunk to avoid being taken away from you."

"I hain't done it, Mrs. Nelson! I hain't done no such a thing," muttered Ned in deep guttural tones, with groans and sobs, unconscious of what was going on around him.

"Oh, I can't think he is guilty!" replied Mrs. Nelson: "the precepts of his mother are not so easily lost as this."

"There it is," said Mr. Nelson: "these women are always preaching up charity and love; they would spoil the best of boys by their misplaced sympathy; they would humor them to death. When you have had as many boys to deal with as I have had, then you may get your eyes open."

"I feel it is better to err on mercy's side," said Mrs. Nelson, "though once I was cruel myself."

"I hain't done it: I am poisoned! murdered! Oh, dear! I fear that Mr. Nelson is at the bottom of this," said Ned, as he rolled upon the floor, yet coming a little to his senses. "Don't let me go! don't let me be taken away, Mrs. Nelson! let me die here, let me die with you!"

"There it is again," said Mr. Nelson; "the boy is accusing me : what have I done?"

"Ay, sir!" said Mrs. Nelson, "I fear you did it all : to start with, you was the guilty party ; but enough of that."

Now, in come Kelly and Jacobs in exuberant spirits of high satisfaction, as they threw down the tools upon the floor by the side of the prostrate boy. Dinah still remained at Ned's room to gather testimony, and see if the old Irish lady with a pipe knew any thing about the tools. When the rattling irons fell with hideous jar by the side of Ned's head, then the terrified boy, started by fright and indignation, leaped and raved like a wild tiger; and, seizing one of the irons, he cried to Jacobs, "Oh, you old thief and burglar! you detestable old knave and villain! you've poisoned and almost murdered me ; you stole my trunk ; you placed these tools there yourself, that is, if they were found there, for I never saw them. *Here, take that, you old scamp! take it, if I die for it!*" as like lightning he hurled it at Jacobs' head ; but Jacobs dropped his head to dodge the missile, crying, " St-st-st-stop the r-r-r-rogue, st-st-st-stop the r-r-r-rogue, and allowed the iron to pass his head and strike a large looking-glass, which it broke into a thousand pieces.

"Th-th-th-there! th-th-th-there! Mrs. N-n-n-Nelson! you s-s-s-see wh-wh-wh-what sort of a b-b-b-boy he is."

And Kelly, seeing that it was a proper case for arrest, came forward with cord and twist sticks to bind Ned's wrist's, and to put on the handcuffs.

"Hold, hold!" said Mr. Nelson; "never mind the glass, let us have fair play in the matter. The boy seems conscious of innocence, or he would not be so bold: something is wrong, I fear."

"O Mr. Nelson!" said Ned, in gladness and surprise, as he fell upon his knees before him; O Mr. Nelson! have you come? do I see your face? Oh, sir! I am as innocent as a lamb. I have been drugged, crazed, murdered by this fiend of a pawnbroker. Believe me, sir! I never saw these irons before; I know nothing about them. What do I want of burglars' tools? I have no locks to break, no shutters to pry open. Do not let me be taken away! don't let me go to court! Let me be a servant for you. I will be any thing, and do any thing, if you will but receive me, and forgive me. I will wait upon you by day, I will watch for you by night; I will build your fires, black your boots, sweep your streets, carry your burdens; I will do any thing but be dishonest or mean. I will live upon half a meal; I will wear these fingers to the bone, and these hands to the elbows, and my feet to the quick, and blister my back with burdens, until I convince you that I am innocent of these charges, and that I am an honest boy."

"He's not an honest b-b-b-boy!" cried Jacobs: "he st-st-st-stole these t-t-t-tools."

Ned continued, "I am not only honest, but I hope respectable. O Mr. Nelson! you don't know what a good boy I would be for you. I would not work for you before because you did not respect me: you would not allow me to come to your house; you whipped me, and treated me like a beggar; and you thought me too free with Nellie. Now that Nellie is gone, oh! sweetly would I fill Nellie's place in your affections; how tenderly fill up the mighty void in your afflicted heart! How kindly would I wait upon you! oh, how I would win your love! how I would work my way into your heart! Ah! you do love me now; I know you do: and you pity me. Hard has been my lot, Mr. Nelson! It is hard to have no father, no mother, no home; to be kicked about like a dog, without a friend to protect you in the great wilderness of this wicked city. How you would feel to be so neglected? and how would you weep if you had a boy so exposed! Then pity me. It is hard to be the mark of every body's suspicion, because ye have no father; hard to have the police ever on your track, watching every step; hard to be drugged, and falsely accused."

"Come, come!" said Kelly, "we have heared enough of that: let him talk to the pint. He shall have a fair trial."

"O Mr. Nelson! it is hard to be falsely accused; hard to be shut up in jail without a crime; hard to have no one to take your part. What if I were your boy, — would you not pity me? Why not pity me now? You do pity me; I know you do. Your eyes look tenderly on me; your heart beats gently, though you have seemed so stern. Severe has been your look, but gentle your heart. Oh! I know you must feel for me; you want to see me do well. My grandfather was a preacher; my father I know nothing about, I hope he was a true man; my mother was a noble-hearted woman. She said if I had respect for myself, and did no wrong, something good would come to me; and I have obeyed her precepts."

"Yis, I guess he has," said Jacobs: "he has kept her pr-pr-pr-precepts in st-st-st-stealin' these t-t-t-tools."

"Hush your mouth!" said Mr. Nelson, "let the boy speak."

Ned continued, "The reason I did not love you before, Mr. Nelson, was because you did not respect me. I was willing to work, willing to do the hardest work; I love work, none loves work better; but I want a man to feel that his home is not too good for me to sit down in, that he is of the same flesh and blood as myself. Yet when you scorned me, and whipped me, and drove me from your door, I was true to your interest. When Solomon Levi the Jew sought to ruin you, I exposed his plot to you, and helped you regain your money. When the boys told me there would be that night a fire in the neighborhood of your store, I came and warned you. When your own dwelling came near being consumed, I prevented it. You gave me no reward, no thanks, but spurned me from your presence. I asked for none; the consciousness of doing right was reward enough. O Mr. Nelson! I am an honest boy: I never took a cent from you, or anybody else. Please, sir, take me on trial! take me into your family; try me, and see if I am not an honest boy; and Heaven will reward you."

"No, he will not," said Kelly; "but I will do it. I will take you on trial; I will give you a fair trial to-morrow morning at nine o'clock; meanwhile I will keep you in the station-house and the tombs."

At the sound of the "station-house and the

tombs," the child became perfectly infuriated. He thought of his past experience in the tombs: he shuddered and raved and chafed like a wild beast at bay.

"Oh, save me, Mr. Nelson! save me from these dreadful men!" he said, as he fell upon his knees, and grasped Mr. Nelson's hand. "Save me, I cannot go to jail; I cannot be locked up in a dungeon; I cannot be at the mercy of these terrible men! don't let me go, Mr. Nelson! pluck out my eyes, take away my life, rather than let me leave you; I rather die a thousand times, than be disgraced; let me die, but do not let me leave you."

"Ah, Ned! if you do go, you shall have a fair trial: I will see that you have fair play," said Mr. Nelson soothingly.

"Fair play! fair play, did you say? Fair play among felons? fair play in the hands of these men? fair play with Jacobs for a witness? fair play with this policeman? as well throw a lamb to hyenas as to place a friendless orphan among such men! Fair play in jail? fair play in court, with not a witness for you? No, sir! let me never be taken from your door! let my trial be here, and now!"

"But I am your friend," said Mr. Nelson, as the tears started in his eyes, "though you may doubt my friendship."

"A friend to me, and allow such men at your door! a friend, that thrusts me into their hands! a friend, that drives me from your house! a friend, that sends me to jail! a friend that will not shelter me! Out on such frendship! let me trust the Evil One quicker."

"But I shall be a better friend if I find you innocent," said Mr. Nelson.

"Innocent! do you doubt my innocence? Can you doubt it? Do you believe me guilty? Is it not a sin to doubt? Is not suspicion akin to knavery? Have I been guilty before? When you have trusted me with hundreds, did you lose a cent? When Solomon Levi tried to bribe me, did he succeed? When I was first accused in court, did you not pity me because I was innocent? If I have refused to take money, even hundreds, do you think I would steal these old irons, these burglar's tools? No, Mr. Nelson, you know better: you don't believe I would; you can't believe it. Then thrust these men from your door."

"No, he can't do that!" said Kelly; "he must not resist an officer (straightening up in his official dignity), "there is a big fine 'ginst the man that resists an officer."

"Officer!" said Ned, "you an officer? you to execute the law? you to teach virtue? you to protect the innocent? God of justice deliver me from such an officer! O Mr. Nelson! you say you are a friend to me: show it by banishing these men from my presence! Let them not gloat on my sorrows! let them not sport at my woes! They are monsters! child-murderers! hell moves to meet them! My eyes roll wild at sight of them! My blood freezes, my pulse stops, my nerves tingle, at their approach! My heart shudders with the horrors of death at the very thought of them! My ears ring with the wails which they have caused! My brain reels at the gulf's brink where they have brought me! Oh, the depths! the depths! Oh, I am sinking! sinking! Oh, my head! my head! save me! save me, Mr. Nelson!" he said, as his head fell on Mr. Nelson's knee, and he clung to it like a drowning man to a floating spar.

"Come, come!" said Jacobs, "let him t-t-t-talk about the t-t-t-tools!"

Ned clung to the knee, and sobbed and cried, and hugged it as if it were an angel, such as Jacob wrestled with,—an angel that held the destiny of his life. Finally, with heart more subdued, and in gentler tones, he raised his face, and, looking into Mr. Nelson's eyes, and climbing into his lap, and printing a kiss upon his cheek, he said, with that innocence and childish confidence which characterize the prayerful, "O Mr. Nelson, you do love me a little; you say you are my friend; then let these men be gone. I want to speak with you; a poor orphan child wants a word with you. I have something to confess to you. Oh, I want to tell you how I love you! I love you for appearing, as I hope you do, to save me. I love you for hearing my complaint; for listening so long and so feelingly. I love you because your nature seems so much like mine. You would not do wrong; neither would I. Give me your hand; let me smooth your locks; let me hug your cheek. Oh, how like a father you seem to me! There! thank you for that! thank you for Nellie's sake! you have a tender heart, you do pity an orphan; you love me a little; you say you are a friend; now order these men away. Do but this, for this once, and I will forgive all your cruelty and coldness towards me."

"La sus! Ned, you needn't be so afeared," said Dinah Lee, as she came rushing into the room. "La sus! I has got a witness what will help ye: she's comin'; she be here in a minute!" Then in came the old lady with the pipe, who said, "Don't ye's be hurtin' that 'ere innocent cheeld! he ba a darlin' latle crather; he wouldn't stale a cint for the world; no, he wouldn't. I seed that ere pawnbroker's boys go into Ned's room with some irons; and I hears the irons fall on the floor over my head, I did; yis, I did. I has seed the boys go there before: they has got keys to Ned's rooms, they has. Oh, ye's miserable crathers! Bad luck to ye's! ye'll be the ruin of that ere cheeld!"

"Good heavens! is that so?" said Mr. Nelson, in astonishment. "Is there a conspiracy against the boy? Has Ned so narrowly escaped? If he had been caught before reaching my door, nothing would have saved him. Are boys taken in this way? Is this the way the streets are cleared, and justice is administered? O ye worse than scoundrels! Out of my house!"

"She t-t-t-tells a f-f-f-falsehood," said Jacobs.

"Leave, instantly, or I will have you both arrested," said Nelson.

"But you must not resist an officer," said Kelly.

"Officer! officer! resist an officer?" said Nelson, indignantly: "resist the Devil, and he will flee from you! begone! or I will have your silver star and blue suit stripped from you in less than twenty-four hours."

"Oh, I thank you, Mr. Nelson! you are, indeed, my friend," said Ned, as he fell upon his knees before him.

"No thanks, my lad," said Mr. Nelson, much excited: "rise, and stand upon your feet; here, give me your hand; you have been a lamb among wolves, yet bold to assert your innocence; henceforth, my hand shall protect you."

"Oh, I thank you!" said Ned; "how can I reward you for this great favor?"

"By being as truthful and honest in the future as in the past," said Mr. Nelson.

"But that will not satisfy you, and reward you for all your trouble," said Ned.

"Yes, it will, my boy, more than satisfy me, to have an honest boy in my house."

"In your house? what, Mr. Nelson! you are not going to take me home?"

"Yes, Ned, you shall never more want for a home; my house shall be your home forever; you shall take the place of Nellie, and become my son and heir," giving him a kiss and a tender embrace, crying, "O my noble boy! may I be as true to you as you have been to yourself. Oh, how I pity you, and love you, you little hero, and faithful saint of your mother! May God smile upon you and bless you! ten thousand blessings on your head, my child!"

"Oh, I thank you, Mr. Nelson! you have been more than a father to me."

"No thanks! no thanks, my son; all I have is yours! enough of this."

"La sus! Ned," said Dinah, "I didn't know dat ye was goin' to be Massa Nelson's son and arr! La sus! if ye keeps on, and ye does nuthin' wrong, I guess somethin' good will come to ye."

CHAPTER XXXIX.

PARTING WITH THE REMAINING CHARACTERS. — CONCLUSION.

WE now part with our remaining characters. David Nelson has retired from business, and moved into the country, taking with him the remains of little Nellie, and burying her by the sunny hillside and brookside on his new estate. Ned has gone to school, and become assiduous in his studies, hoping, if he proves true to Mr. Nelson, and " does no wrong, something good will come to him."

Not the least of the influences brought to bear on Mr. Nelson for reconciliation was a threatening note from Mrs. Nevins's attorney, concerning a certain bond signed by Mr. Nelson in Fairfield County, Connecticut, not twenty years ago. The bond was attested by a justice of the peace, and had but two conditions; viz., " maternal seclusion " and " filial integrity." Mr. Nelson, to avoid publicity, accepted the demand, and made the best of it.

Mrs. Nelson, true to her Christian sympathies, still labors for the poor and the boys of the street. Ned is her idol, the chief object of her love, made doubly dear by his associations with the angelic little Nellie.

Dinah thinks Ned a little proud now and then, and cries out, "La sus, Ned! yer feelin' *right smart* ob yerselb, ye be, hey!" But, nevertheless, Ned bears his honors meekly.

As to the other boys of the night-school, Tom the Trickster and Tim the Tumbler have found comfortable homes on farms in the country. Johnny McCurdy and a dozen or two of others still cry their papers in the streets. A score or two of boys have become cash-boys and office-boys; and one or more of them may be found in almost every large establishment where boys are employed.

"There! take that!" said a boy on board of the "Sabine," as I visited that school-ship for Uncle Sam's boys in New-London Harbor, "There! take that from Boston!" (giving his foe a leveller with his fist). "Boston is not to be sneezed at; none of your taunt about New England being left out in the cold; New England, with her cotton mills and sewing-machines and reaping-machines and books and newspapers and Parrot guns, *could civilize all creation, ye fool ye!*"

That boy was Nicholas Nobody. Only three years had elapsed since he left the night-school; yet he had become captain of a section, was promoted to the highest honors of the ship, and expected to graduate at Uncle Sam's expense in the Naval Academy.

If the night-school can bear but one such jewel in the crown of its rejoicing, the reward is sufficient.

We notice the two remaining characters. Patrick Kelly is now stripped of his silver star and suit of blue, and reduced to the rank of a private citizen. He thinks hard of it that his motives were not better understood, and his services not better appreciated. He feels that it is by malfeasance and political chicanery that he has been superseded, and he will never vote for the present incumbent of the appointing power. "Friendship that pays is worth something," but not worth so much when one has lost the spoils of office.

Jeremy Jacobs has curtailed his business since the new policemen have been appointed to patrol his street. He bewails the state of the times, and thinks business is not "as it used to was." He now furnishes no easy-chair for Patrick Kelly, and gives him no "wee bit of the crather." He goes upon the principle that "friendship that don't pay isn't worth any thing;" so he keeps his whiskey for more profitable purposes.

Now comes the most melancholy part of my story. I visited Deer Island, and found twenty of the night-school boys in the House of Reformation. I went to the Massachusetts Nautical School-ship, and saw ten more. There are also ten or a dozen at the Reform School at Westboro', making forty out of four hundred already under lock and key, and supported at public expense. Some of them had not a fair trial on the streets before being taken, while others were too far gone for voluntary reform. When I consider the much that is to be done, and the little that has been accomplished, my heart sickens at the thought. Though a hundred of the boys may have been improved or reformed, I can but think of the other three hundred who have been but little benefited; and, though the four hundred should all have turned out well, yet I must bewail the thousand that still remain in the streets.

When will the people of Boston be fully awake to their responsibilities? Oh, what a state of moral obliquity prevails! How many boys live by deceit, treachery, and guile! How many are already too debased to distinguish truth from falsehood! Some of them cannot speak an honest truth if they would. They have sucked deceit from their mothers' breasts; they lie, because it has become their nature; they steal, because their fingers itch for the theft; they burn your dwelling, that they may rejoice to see a fire. We sleep amidst organized gangs of incendiaries. Nothing but the fear of detection keeps down the torch; nothing but a strong police force gives us any manner of security. Where the blame lies is not for me to say; whether in the governments of the old country, or the church of the old country, or the laxness of our city authorities, or the inefficiency of the pulpit, or in all these combined, I know not; but one thing I *do know*, there is a mighty responsibility resting *somewhere!* May God hasten the day when it shall be laid at the right door!

If the ocean has depths unfathomable, so has Boston's bottomless sea of depravity. For over seven years have I been fathoming its turbid waters and brooding over its dolorous waves, until they have whirled my brain, unstrung my nerves, ruined my health, and made this crumbling frame but a wreck of my former self. My lungs have given way, sleep forsakes me; oh! what would I not give for one sweet hour of sleep? What for one single calm night of repose? I walk my room, and gaze at the stars, and see them, one by one, decline. I see changes in sky, changes on earth; I feel changes in the air; but there is no change for this restless mind, these unstrung nerves, this whirling brain; no change but the last great change that comes to all. During the lone watchings of December's night, I see stars appear, and storms gather and disappear again, and the moon rise and set; but no rest or sleep or change comes to this poor exhausted brain of mine. My restless frame has forgot the name of rest. The sorrows and delinquencies of this corrupt city have taken hold of me with the grasp of a plague. They cling to me like the garment of contagion. The very ink with which I write this blotted line seems drawn from the black carbon of my heart's blood, beating in muffled strokes and funereal marches to the tomb. The dark, aqueous atmosphere gathering round with its midnight damps, and falling from the eaves as droppings from the pen of doom, seems as the shadow of the angel of darkness itself, imaging my own horror and gloom. Such are the feelings of an over-taxed brain and over-worked nerves. But I have no one to blame but myself for this state of health. I should have assumed less responsibilities, and done less work. The benevolent people of Boston stood ready to relieve me; but I was too fearful to make my wants and burdens known. The assistance, however, has come; but, alas! it has come too late to restore my health. What is done is done, and cannot be undone.

But there is a relief to this picture: there is a satisfaction in doing good; there is gratitude experienced from the relieved that cheers the aching heart; there is comfort in friends that smooths the pillow of care; and there is consolation in the promises of God. There has been also a well of comfort, a fountain of revery and recreation, in writing this little book. In this I could choose my own society, and recall such characters as best suited my fancy. When care has oppressed me, and driven sleep from my eyes; when rest and quiet would not come at my wooing, then I have resorted to my pen. Conversing with the shadows that have surrounded me, and peopling them with the sombre fancies of my own imaginings, I have wandered darkly through the saddening chapters of street-life in Boston. During the still hours of night, the streets have been alive to me, though there was but the distant tread of the policemen heard upon the deserted pavements. When rays of comfort have broken in upon my soul, then I have penned the virtues of Nellie Nelson and the trials and triumphs of Ned Nevins. Much is real; but how much is unreal I cannot say: for the ideal, the imaginative, has become real to me; all the colorings seem a fact as real as the original characters themselves.

My task is done; the book is written. Nellie Nelson is no more; and Ned Nevins, rising from his low estate, wanders from my embrace. No more will he cheer my vigils by his imaginative presence, no more call out the undiscovered fountains of my sympathetic tears by his sufferings and misfortunes. Farewell, noble boy! yet I cannot say farewell while thy shadow lingers, and thy image is before me.

The world sleeps; it is past midnight; Ned fills my thoughts; clouds come and go; stars change; bells strike the hours as they pass, and I am left alone with Ned. Now one lone star peeps through the mist, and looks down upon us: it looks like the diminutive bright eye of little Nellie in heaven. It shines like a taper, gleaming with dim light on this naughty world. She seems to say, "Cheer up, sir; your toils are not all lost: if you have rescued but one soul from doom, you have done a great work." O Nellie! what joys must be thine to see that Ned has prospered, and is true and faithful. But enough of this. Now, Ned, we must part: the hour of our severance is at hand. Better than a harp hast thou been to me; thy voice has been as music to my soul; thou hast drawn out my sympathy and my love. I ought not to be selfish, and desire thee to tarry longer; yet I part with thee reluctantly.

Farewell, noble child! "if thou doest no wrong, something good will come to thee." Yet, one kiss more, as thy footsteps linger; one more look into those childish, confiding eyes; one more sound from those magic lips; one more gentle embrace. Adieu, my child! a long adieu! The clouds are breaking, the day is dawning, the light of morning kisses the waters of the harbor; this is no time for fancies; the light that is breaking in upon the waters is as the dawn of eternity, wherein there is no fiction, but all is stern reality.

Go, then, fair child! on the beams of the morning, go! tarry not! go on the breezes that waft the clouds behind the western hills; go towards the setting queen of night, now paling before her mightier peer; go towards that star that has peeped into our window so long, now blushing at being discovered by the all-seeing eye of day. Go in the shadows towards the Hesperian hills; and, as thou goest, let me watch thy receding footsteps over mount and vale, and by the brook and glen; let me listen to the last note of thy departure as I would to the dying echoes of sweetest minstrelsy struck by fairy fingers or a friendly hand. Now in mellow cadence thy harp-strings echo on the breeze, like Æolian symphonies when the winds are low, such as sound over the tomb of the loved and lost in dulcet whispers, "Farewell!"

Now I see Ned, beyond the precincts of the city, with eye aspiring and feet advancing, climbing the hills of learning, mounting the steeps of fame. Now, as the winds rise, I hear him sound upon the breeze with trumpet voice, his ever-to-be-remembered watchword and motto, — that legacy left him, and the generations that follow, — the successful motto that has carried him through every trial, and temptation; the legacy of a dying mother; words first on his lips at morning, and last in his heart at evening; a spell against enchantment, a charm against the charmer; hope to the desponding, comfort to the forsaken, shield to the accused; applicable to all men in all conditions of life; heaven-inspired, gospel-sanctioned rule of action, guide of life, — hark! I hear it sound upon the breeze, "*If I do no wrong, something good will come to me.*"

FINIS.

FINANCIAL VIEW OF THE BOSTON UNION MISSION SOCIETY, 1866.

THIS Society was organized Feb. 27, 1859, by the friends of Rev. Henry Morgan, for the purpose of carrying the gospel to the poor, clothing children for Sabbath School, educating boys of the street, and getting homes and employment for the needy. It embraces a Church, Sabbath School, Night School, and Benevolent Circle. Mr. Morgan was then preaching in the Boston Music Hall. He soon after accepted from the city authorities the free use of the Franklin Building, on Washington Street, near Dover Street, which he has occupied to this day.

The City Fathers have found the grant a cheap police investment, for the prevention of crime. Piety that pays is worth something. To reform a vicious and idle man, whose family is dependent on charity, saves the public the time and the wages of the man, — saves fifteen dollars a week. Such salvation pays. To educate two or three hundred boys evenings, and reform them while they are earning their own living on the streets, saves the State one hundred dollars per day, or fifty thousand dollars a year. Such salvation pays. Volunteer teachers, with moral suasion, battling against sin and ignorance, are more likely to succeed than hired officials, with whip and lash, in public institutions. Besides, reforms to be genuine must be voluntary, and in the face of temptation. Boys must learn to resist while the bait is before them. There is no virtue in fasting where there is nothing to eat. Plants in hot-houses won't stand the storm. The School Ship, last year, with one hundred and sixty boys, cost twenty-eight thousand dollars. The Westboro' Reform School cost fifty thousand dollars. Street reforms are cheaper and better than either. Churches are cheaper than jails. Congregating boys in public institutions vitiates them; evil predominates. By huddling fire-brands together, you increase the flame. Christianity individualizes; despotism centralizes. Away with despotism: it is costly.

RELIGIOUS MEETINGS.

Religious meetings have been held nearly every night for over seven years. Six services are held on Sunday. These meetings are profitable in various ways. They are self-supporting; they pay the pastor his salary; they furnish laborers for the Benevolent Circle, and teachers for the Night School; they are a shield to the young; they prevent crime; protect life and property; they moralize and regenerate society; they are profitable here, to say nothing of the "hereafter." They are the cheapest and purest of all recreations. "Sing unto the Lord, oh ye his saints!" None but the pure in heart can enjoy them; therefore their tendency is to elevate the life and soul. At these meetings, over a thousand persons have professed a change of heart.

The theatres of Boston cost forty thousand dollars a month. Places more questionable cost ten times as much. Sinful pleasures are costly. Piety pays.

CHURCH.

The Church is Congregational in government, Baptist as respects immersion, and Methodist in doctrine and modes of worship. It is called the "First Independent Methodist Church of Boston."

Receipts of the past year.   *Expenditures.*

Receipts		Expenditures	
Money raised by Society	$1,120	Paid Pastor	$1,000
Out-side Subscriptions	1,725	Sexton, organist, gas, fuel, &c.	860
Clothing received	1,615	Charities in goods and money	1,970
	4,460	Night School expenses	554
			4,384
Balance in Treasury			6¢

AUDITORS OF ACCOUNTS.

Dr. I. J. WETHERBEE, 46, Dover Street.
Dr. JOSEPH H. WARREN, 903, Washington Street.

CONTRIBUTORS TO THE MISSION, OF TWENTY DOLLARS AND OVER.

CLOTHING AND DRY-GOODS.

George H. Lane & Co.	$200.00
Whitten, Burditt, & Young	175.00
Isaac Fenno & Co.	150.00
J. C. Howe	100.00
Samuel Johnson	100.00
Knowles & Leland	70.00
Cushman & Brooks	70.00
Dresser, Stevens, & Co.	70.00
Simons, Brothers	65.00
G. W. Simmons & Co.	50.00
F. Skinner & Co.	50.00
Haughton, Sawyer, & Co.	25.00
Converse & Gray	25.00
Hovey & Co.	25.00
Chandler & Co.	25.00
Gardiner & Pratt	25.00
George S. Winslow & Co.	25.00
Curtis, Webster, & Co.	25.00
Jordan, Marsh, & Co.	25.00
March Brothers, Pierce, & Co.	25.00
George Burbank & Co.	20.00

BOOTS AND SHOES.

Potter, White, & Bayley	$85.00
Fogg, Houghton, & Coolidge	70.00
Boyd & Brigham	70.00

Alexander Strong & Co............................$70.00
William Claflin................................... 50.00
Field, Thayer, & Whitcomb......................... 36.00
Potter, Hitchcock, & Co........................... 30.00
H. L. Daggett..................................... 25.00
Cole, Wood, & Co.................................. 20.00

Hats and Caps.

Walko & Barnum $50.00
William H. Slocum................................. 50.00
Steele, Eaton, & Co............................... 50.00
Kent, Foster, & Peck.............................. 45.00
George Osgood..................................... 40.00
Carpenter & Pimpton............................... 20.00
Moore, Smith, & Potter............................ 20.00
Klous & Co.. 20.00
A. N. Cook & Co................................... 20.00
Shute & Sons...................................... 20.00
Bent & Bush....................................... 20.00

Millinery and Fancy Goods.

J. W. Plimpton & Co...............................$50.00
W. Heckle... 50.00
Sleeper, Fiske, & Co.............................. 50.00
Lane & Tuttle..................................... 50.00
Prescott & Co..................................... 50.00
Ordway Brothers................................... 40.00
Given Holmes...................................... 40.00
Miles, Mandell, & Burr............................ 35.00
John Harrington................................... 30.00
R. H. Stearns & Co................................ 30.00
N. D. Whitney & Co................................ 30.00
George M. Atwood.................................. 20.00

CONTRIBUTORS TO THE MISSION.

Fancy Miscellany.

J. I. Brown & Son. Troches	$50.00
Kelly & Edmunds	47.00
D. P. Ives & Co.	40.00
J. Burnett. Extracts	40.00
M. Salom	40.00
S. W. Creech	40.00
Heyer Brothers	30.00
Henshaw & Co.	30.00
F. A Hawley & Co.	30.00
E. A. & W. Winchester	30.00
C. Copeland. Confectionery	30.00
George W. Vinton, & D. Fobes & Co. Confectionery	20.00
C. Wakefield. Carpets	30.00
Goldthwait, Snow, & Knight	30.00
Forbes Richardson & Co.	50.00

Books.

Ticknor & Fields	$25.00
Lee & Shepard	25.00
A. K. Loring	25.00
Crosby & Ainsworth	25.00
Oliver Ditson & Co.	25.00
L. Prang & Co.	25.00
J. E. Tilton & Co. and Brewer & Tileston	20.00
M. H. Sargent. Mass. S. S. S	20.00

Jewellers.

Shreve, Stanwood, & Co.	$45.00
C. A. W. Crosby	42.00
Haddock, Lincoln, & Foss	35.00
Josiah Gooding	35.00
Bigelow Brothers & Kennard	35.00
Crosby & Morse	35.00
Palmer & Batchelders	20.00

CONTRIBUTORS TO THE MISSION.

Cash.

James L. Little	$50.00
Peter C. Brooks	50.00
A. Wigglesworth	50.00
Mrs. Bowditch	50.00
Mrs. A. Hemmenway	50.00
E. R. Mudge, Sawyer & Co.	50.00
J. M. Beebe	50.00
Gardner Brewer & Co.	50.00
Foster & Taylor	45.00
Naylor & Co	45.00
N. Thayer	25.00
James Parker	25.00
Elisha Atkins	25.00
Charles Amory	25.00
Parker & Mills	25.00
Robert Waterston	25.00
William Munroe	25.00
William H. Boardman	25.00
J. E. Daniels	25.00
Israel Nash	25.00
T. H. Tyler	20.00
Glidden & Williams	20.00
Misses Newman	20.00
Mrs. B. T. Green	20.00
Richard Fletcher	20.00
James Savage	20.00
Miss Julia Bryant	20.00
Miss Pratt	20.00

Dr. Schenck, of Philadelphia, whose Pulmonic Syrup has been the means of relieving Mr. Morgan from a lung difficulty, gives two hundred dollars in medicine for the poor of the Mission.

The city pastors and others, who have preached or lectured for the Mission, are Rev. Drs. Kirk, Blagden, Gannett, Neale, Hague, Parker, Stone, Webb; Rev. Messrs. Manning, Dexter, Haven, Hepworth; Gov. Andrew, Hon. Josiah Quincy, E. S. Toby, Judge Russell, Joseph Story, Marshall Scudder, J. H. Stephenson, Aldermen Nash and Paul, Ex-Mayor Wightman, Wendell Phillips, and J. D. Philbrick, Superintendent of Public Schools.

NOTICES OF THE BOSTON PRESS.

NED NEVINS THE NEWS BOY, or *Street Life in Boston*, is the title of a book written by REV. HENRY MORGAN, which is selling very rapidly, most of the first edition being sold wholly in Boston, and within a few days of its publication. It reveals much of the life of the "dangerous classes," as they are termed in England, or the poor and vicious, as they are generally spoken of in this country. Mr. Morgan is at the head of the mission enterprise established in Franklin Building, near Dover Street, and has devoted himself to the work of reclaiming and benefiting the lower classes of our population with great earnestness and much practical wisdom, and, there is reason to believe, is accomplishing great good. This book of his is deeply interesting, as it presents in vivid colors the daily life of the juvenile outcasts of the city, and their mental and moral characteristics, as well as the causes which lead them into vice and crime. It is a book that all may read with profit, and especially those who take an interest in reformatory movements.

Mr. Morgan is receiving many calls to deliver his lectures on "Life in Boston," and "Fast Young Men." — BOSTON JOURNAL.

The volume before us, NED NEVINS, or *Street Life in Boston*, by REV. HENRY MORGAN, gives a most life-like notion of the juvenile outcasts of the city, of the good and evil which are in them, and of the means and instrumentalities by which the good may be made to triumph over the evil. Mr. Morgan, in his paintings of life, belongs to the pre-Raphaelite school, and is anxious to reproduce his subjects with vivid distinctness. His boys seem to be taken out of the street, and put bodily into his book. Dress, language, deportment, *morale*, all are given. The author is an enthusiast for his self-imposed task of Christian reformer. He envies not the largest-salaried preacher of the richest Boston congregation, but evidently wonders why they do not envy him. To carry Christian consolation, Christian hope, and, above all, Christian help, into the homes of poverty and disease, seems to him the greatest privilege of a Christian minister. To be the first statesman, lawyer, soldier, man of letters, or man of science in the country, is to occupy, in his estimation, a less exalted position than falls to the fortunate lot of him who clothes the naked, teaches the ignorant, helps the erring, and reforms the depraved. — BOSTON TRANSCRIPT.

NED NEVINS is a most excellent book. It is the story of a newsboy who lived in Boston, and who had all the various vicissitudes of his class, until he met with better fortune, and found a comfortable home. It is such a story as young people should read, for it shows them the temptations to which the poor newsboys are exposed on every side. It will lead them to sympathize with the unfortunate, and guard them against certain temptations which sooner or later will beset all young people. It is a good book for the family or the Sunday School. Its teachings are all pure, its tendencies philanthropic, and its lessons religious. Every boy in Boston should read it.

Mr. Morgan has been doing great good among the newsboys, and other neglected persons in Boston. His church is an independent society, Congregational in polity, Methodist in doctrine, and Baptist in the ordinances. It embraces a church, Sunday School, night school, intelligence office, and benevolent circle; and the pastor deserves the sympathy of Christian people. We hope his book will sell well, and his work prosper. — *Rev. Dr. Eddy*, CHRISTIAN ERA, *Sept.* 27, 1866.

REV. HENRY MORGAN, well known in this city for his earnest labors among the poor, the vicious, and the unfortunate, has written a little volume with the title of NED NEVINS THE NEWS BOY, in which, in the form of a story, he gives striking facts and incidents drawn from his own experience and observation. The story is an affecting one, and nearly all the characters are taken from real life; and many of us, if we open our eyes, our hearts, and our hands to the world immediately around us, might say, with the author, " From the street have I learned lessons of humanity, and among the lowly have I found disciples of Jesus." — CONGREGATIONALIST.

Mr. Morgan has written this book with much earnestness and sincerity; and it will do much to call attention to the boys in our streets, and to incite interest and action in their behalf. — UNIVERSALIST.

Rev. Henry Morgan, of this city, is receiving many calls to deliver his lectures on " Life in Boston," and " Fast Young Men." He is the author of a new book entitled, NED NEVINS THE NEWS BOY, or *Street Life in Boston*, which is having quite a " run," the first edition having been exhausted in a few days after publication. This story is made up of true incidents and characters, gathered by Mr. Morgan, who is much associated with the newsboys, and well acquainted with their habits.

The success of " Life Sketches and Music Hall Discourses," induced the author to write this interesting volume. — ZION'S HERALD.

This handsome volume contains a story that is founded on fact, and therefore conveys a more impressive lesson than if it were wholly fictitious and romantic. We cannot too cordially commend the purpose of the author in this effective little tale, or in his entire work. We hope that NED NEVINS may be put by some kind, rich man, like another Amos Lawrence, into the hands of every boy in Boston. It would work untold good. — BANNER OF LIGHT.

SUCCESS OF NED NEVINS THE NEWS BOY. — Rev. Henry Morgan's book on STREET LIFE IN BOSTON, or *Ned Nevins the News Boy*, published by Lee & Shepard, is meeting with popular favor. The first edition was sold within a few days of its publication, almost wholly in Boston. A second edition will be immediately issued. Mr. Morgan is well acquainted with his subject, having labored as a missionary among the poor of this city for nearly eight years. He wields the pen with the same force and eloquence that he speaks: his characters are true to life, and cannot fail to win the sympathy of the reader. None can read the story of Ned Nevins the News Boy, his sufferings, temptations, escapes, and triumphs, without admiration and respect for this neglected class of street-boys. None can read of Ned's mother in Orange Lane, literally dying with needle in hand, without feelings of pity for the poor. The characters of Solomon Levi, of Nick, and of Nellie, scenes of high life and low life, the pathetic and the comic, the philosophic and the tragic, are portrayed in graphic contrast, while the enterprise and benevolence of Boston receive their proper tribute. We predict for this book a large sale. — BOSTON POST.

Nearly all the characters in this story are taken from real life. Mr. Morgan's eight years of missionary experience in Boston, among the poor, have furnished him with the facts of which he writes. Of these facts he has made good use, and produced a story of much worth, one in which we see a great deal of life as it is, and as it is likely to remain for some time; though, under the wise and benevolent labors of Mr. Morgan, and other good and able men, improvement must steadily take place. — EVENING TRAVELLER.

This narrative is of one of the waifs whom Mr. Morgan interested in his services. The boys will be interested in the story, which is told in a familiar and graphic manner. — COMMONWEALTH.

This volume gives the history of NED NEVINS, a representative of thousands of boys in Boston and other large cities; it describes his way of life, his associates, his temptations, his misfortunes, and his benefactors, in graphic and entertaining style. — COMMERCIAL BULLETIN.

In the form of an attractive story, the author has strung together, with skill, a great many facts in the real life of the poor and vicious in this city. There is much of pathetic and even dramatic interest in the volume. It will be welcome; and we hope it may move many a heart to second the philanthropical work of the home missionary. — THE VOICE (WORKINGMAN'S ORGAN).

A few days ago we heard a boy, under twelve years of age, exclaim, "That is a glorious book!" We asked what book? "Why," said he, "'The Newsboy.'" He had just been reading Rev. Henry Morgan's pictorial narrative of Ned Nevins, published by Lee & Shepard. We turned to the work at once, and were soon in sympathy with the boy's state of feeling. It is a picture of Life in Boston, truthful to reality. Among the fresh issues from the press there is no better gift-book for a boy, adapted to educate the heart and the conscience, to guard against temptation, and, in the doing of good as well as the resistance of evil, to nourish a manly, heroic, Christian spirit. — REV. DR. HAGUE (HERBERT) in *Watchman and Reflector*.

We are glad of the book. It will tell "the oldest inhabitant" something about the Yankee Metropolis that will be new to him, and we hope will warm many a heart to the calls of humanity. — BOSTON RECORDER.

He has succeeded in showing street life in Boston in its true colors. — FLAG OF OUR UNION.

NED NEVINS is one illustrious example that crowns the wisdom of such effort in the redemption of outcast youth. — AM. MISCELLANY.

Remarkably regenerative in its tendencies, and sharp and pointed in style. — WIDE WORLD.

In his portraiture of the Boston News Boy, he gives us some very graphic delineations of life among the lowly. — THE NATION.

It is written in a very taking, familiar style. — PLOUGHMAN.

The street-boy of Boston is depicted in a clear and forcible manner. — NEW-ENGLAND FARMER.

www.ingramcontent.com/pod-product-compliance
Lightning Source LLC
Chambersburg PA
CBHW051722300426
44115CB00007B/431